D0256844

THE YELLOW JERSEY CLUB

www.**transworldbooks**.co.uk

Also by Edward Pickering

One Way Road (*with Robbie McEwen*)
The Race Against Time

THE YELLOW JERSEY CLUB

Inside the Minds of the
Tour de France Winners

Edward Pickering

BANTAM PRESS

LONDON • TORONTO • SYDNEY • AUCKLAND • JOHANNESBURG

TRANSWORLD PUBLISHERS
61–63 Uxbridge Road, London W5 5SA
www.transworldbooks.co.uk

Transworld is part of the Penguin Random House group of companies
whose addresses can be found at global.penguinrandomhouse.com

Penguin
Random House
UK

First published in Great Britain in 2015 by Bantam Press
an imprint of Transworld Publishers

A CIP catalogue record for this book
is available from the British Library.

ISBNs 9780593073964 (cased)

Typeset in 11.5/14.5pt Minion by Falcon Oast Graphic Art Ltd.
Printed and bound by Clays Ltd, Bungay, Suffolk

Penguin Random House is committed to a sustainable future for
our business, our readers and our planet. This book is made from
Forest Stewardship Council® certified paper.

MIX
Paper from
responsible sources
FSC® C018179

3 5 7 9 10 8 6 4 2

For Ellie

Contents

THE YELLOW JERSEY CLUB

Prologue

This morning I presented a superb yellow jersey to the valiant Eugène Christophe. You already know that the race direction has decided that the man at the head of the general classification will wear a jersey in the colours of L'Auto. *The battle to win the yellow jersey will be a gripping one!*

Henri Desgrange, *L'Auto*, Monday, 21 July 1919

When the route of the one hundreth anniversary Tour de France was announced in late 2002, at the Palais des Congrès in Paris, the race organizers pulled together every living winner of the race to mark the occasion. From Ferdinand Kübler to Lance Armstrong (minus 1967 winner Roger Pingeon, absent for personal reasons), 21 Tour champions stood in a row on the stage to receive the applause of the fans, media and dignitaries.

It was there that the first seeds of the idea for this book were sown. Those 21 men represented one of the most exclusive sporting clubs in the world: the yellow jersey club. I was covering the event for *Cycle Sport* magazine, and the main focus of my commission was the route of the 2003 race, but the appearance of the living winners of the race was far more interesting to me.

As I looked from left to right along the line of men – who

ranged from downright frail to young and vital, from short to tall, from fat to skinny – I wondered what marked them out from the rest of the professional peloton, or from ordinary members of the public. I wondered what, if anything, they had in common. Two or three of them – Bernard Hinault, Greg LeMond and Stephen Roche – had been childhood icons for me. Others, like Roger Walkowiak and Lucien Aimar, I knew next to nothing about. Still more, like Bjarne Riis and Lance Armstrong (the only man on stage without a tie and the only one to vigorously chew gum through the entire ceremony), I was suspicious of, the rumours of the root of their sporting prowess having reached me via senior colleagues in the cycling press pack.

It struck me later that the yellow jersey club reminded me of watching the winner's presentation at the US Masters golf tournament where, in a masonic-looking ceremony in a masonic-looking clubroom, the previous champion awards the new champion with a green jacket. A rare sporting achievement, marked by the presentation of a garment of clothing which is imbued with symbolic meaning and history. It's fitting that the gaudy, brash, showy Tour de France has a bright-yellow jersey, a brassy contrast to the reticent and conservative milieu of a tradition-bound golf tournament, with its dark-green garment.

Initially, I'd wanted to go and interview all the living winners. The club has swelled in size since 2002, obviously, and there are now 26 living winners. Of the 21 men on the stage of the Palais des Congrès that day, two – Marco Pantani and Laurent Fignon – have subsequently died, and Lance Armstrong has been unceremoniously booted out of the club, while eight more riders have joined. But initial contact with Ferdinand Kübler's wife indicated that the 1950 Tour champion, who is now 95, was too frail to be interviewed.

If I couldn't interview all the living winners, perhaps I could pick and choose the most interesting riders for the book. But going back to the Second World War, out of 37 official winners of the race, 37 are fascinating characters – it was impossible to choose any over the others.

I finally decided to impose a chronological limit on my list of Tour winners. I would go back 40 years to 1975 and start there. That cut-off has the historical significance in that it was the first Tour of the post-Merckx era, which makes it a logical place to begin. Over the last four decades there have been 20 winners, plus Lance Armstrong (who I'll get on to in a moment), which makes 21 subjects, exactly the same number of people as there are stages in the modern Tour de France, which is symmetrical if not meaningful. I started with Bernard Thévenet, the 1975 winner, and went right through to the 2014 champion Vincenzo Nibali.

The one concession I have made to realpolitik is in the inclusion of Lance Armstrong. He's no longer officially considered a Tour winner, his seven victories between 1999 and 2005 having been stripped for doping offences. As one of only three individuals in cycling history (along with Maurice Garin and Floyd Landis, the initial 1904 and 2006 winners) to have been thrown out of the yellow jersey club, he perhaps shouldn't be here, but the difference I see between him and Landis, for example, is that Landis's Tour win in 2006 was given to the runner-up, Óscar Pereiro. The 1999 to 2005 Tours, on the other hand, officially have no winners, the extent of the doping problem obviously extending further than just the top step of the podium, and those years have to be accounted for somehow. It should also be added that Garin was never officially in the yellow jersey club – the leader's jersey wasn't introduced to the Tour until 1919.

As time goes on, the membership of the yellow jersey club will continue to expand, but the certainty is that whoever is allowed in, they will be, in their own way, interesting and complex individuals. The race has always attracted extreme characters and unusual personalities, and the yellow jersey club includes some of the best examples.

1

Bernard Thévenet

1975, 1977

My childhood world was always bigger than my village. As soon as I knew how to ride I grasped the idea of a greater world.

Paul Fournel, *Vélo*

Le Guidon is nowhere in particular. A cluster of houses and farm buildings around the fork in the road where the D20 splits off the D985 about eight kilometres south of Charolles, in the Saône-et-Loire department in central France. The nearest town is Paray-le-Monial. The nearest town you've actually heard of is Mâcon, sixty-five kilometres east. Le Guidon is so small that it doesn't even count as a commune, which is the smallest administrative subdivision in France – it's a *lieu-dit*, literally a 'place', a 'locality'. It's not even the only Le Guidon in France – Michelin lists 12 altogether – which emphasizes its placelessness, a generic hamlet in the vast expanse of *La France Profonde*.

This is where Bernard Thévenet, the Tour de France winner in 1975 and 1977, grew up, which makes it an apt accident of nominative determinism: *guidon* is also the French word for a bicycle handlebar.

Life is not easy in Le Guidon. This is not the commuter belt, nor a pleasant location for a second home – if you live here, it's because you work on the land, as Thévenet's parents Henri and Alice did. Henri and Alice Thévenet were tenant farmers who rented a 45-hectare farm from the landowner, and they worked, 14 hours a day, seven days a week, and practically 365 days a year. They were grooming their son to follow in their footsteps, but Bernard wanted out.

The gene pool for racing cyclists is comparatively broad and deep in the twenty-first century but, in the 1960s and 1970s, cycling was perceived to be a working-class sport, especially in France. The author Robin Magowan wrote in his book *Kings of the Road*, 'Professional roadmen generally come from the urban working classes, or more commonly, their rural equivalent, the small freeholders and landless peasants. This is the same school of suffering from which boxers traditionally hailed.'

Maybe there's something to be learned from the fact that these days, city boys, lawyers and media types like to dirty their white collars by taking up cycling. There's something about the grainy, gritty, black-and-white iconography of the history of the sport that appeals to people who've long since lost any real connection with the working classes or with the land. We fancy that a few hours' suffering on a bike will enable us to experience what it is to work in a factory, or on a farm, to empathize with Magowan's landless peasants.

Thévenet knew better. He tells me, 'Cycling is hard, but it's not as hard as working on a farm. It's a pleasant effort in comparison.' His parents had him working in the fields from when he was eight. 'After that, cycling is not so difficult,' he says.

The Tour de France passed through Le Guidon in 1961 (it did so again in the centenary Tour in 2003), and that's when 13-year-old Bernard Thévenet decided that he wanted to be a racing cyclist. He'd already been showing an interest – before car ownership got more widespread, the rural working classes did their shopping from a mail-order catalogue called *Manufrance*. *Manufrance* specialized in guns, hunting equipment, fishing rods and bicycles, but they sold just about everything, and by the time Thévenet was 11 he'd spent hours looking at the Hirondelle racing bikes in his parents' catalogue. His first hero was Louison Bobet, who'd won three Tours during the 1950s. He owned a clunker of a utility bike to get him to and from school, five kilometres away, and on his way back home he'd race the other children up the climb through the nearby village of Maringues.

But when the Tour came by, it was an epiphany. 'The priest held mass an hour earlier than usual because he knew nobody would turn up otherwise,' Thévenet recalls. 'The race came through around midday and the weather was beautiful. They came up a false flat for about 400 metres before Le Guidon, and I could see them coming the whole way. The sun was flashing off their toeclips and their bikes.' Thévenet was transfixed. 'I said to myself, I will do everything I can to be one of them.'

In a sense Thévenet was lucky with the timing of his career. His two Tour wins came in the eye of the hurricane between the Eddy Merckx and Bernard Hinault eras – five of the six Tours leading up to Thévenet's first win in 1975 had been won by Merckx, while four of the next five after his second win in 1977 were taken by Hinault. His wins had less of an air of destiny about them – Merckx and Hinault seemed to be born Tour winners; Thévenet had to graft for his. Thévenet might have been seen as a young pretender to Merckx, but in 1975 both riders were taking part in their sixth Tour de France – there was no doubt who'd been the more precocious talent. Thévenet worked his way towards winning the yellow jersey with the patience and pragmatism of a farmer who ploughs, sows, waters and tends his or her crops over months before harvesting.

However, Merckx might have done Thévenet a favour by being so dominant.

Thévenet's Tour debut, which came in his first year as a professional, 1970, was impressive, especially as he was drafted into the race with barely three days' notice, at the age of 22. 'I did a race in Brittany, and got back to my parents' house on the Monday. I didn't ride, because I got back late,' Thévenet says. 'I didn't ride on Tuesday because I couldn't be bothered, then went to a friend's house to go for a ride on Wednesday afternoon.'

The message got through that the Peugeot team's *service course* had called Thévenet at home and needed him to call back urgently. Thévenet was going to get the training ride done, then call later, but his riding partner suggested he call his team first. Gaston Plaud, the Peugeot *directeur sportif* informed him that Ferdinand Bracke and Gerben Karstens had both fallen ill, and Thévenet was to take one of the spare places. His main qualification for the spot was, he says, less the probability that he'd do well than the proximity of his home to the Tour's start in Limoges, which was on the Saturday.

Thévenet wasn't keen, but a friend in nearby Digoin, Victor Ferrari, a former Tour rider himself, told him to go. 'He told me, "There are 500 riders who want a place in the Tour. You have to take it." '

He suffered horribly for two weeks, then found himself recuperating comparatively well. The Tour de France might be sold as an exciting battle of attacks, feints and gladiatorial confrontation, but the reality can be more prosaic. It's trench warfare, rather than a fencing match. More than anything, it is a competition as much of who weakens the least as of who is the strongest, and Thévenet turned out to be a natural stayer. He came fifth on Mont Ventoux on stage 14, then won at the Pyrenean ski resort of La Mongie four days later. Overall, he was nowhere: 35th, an hour and a quarter behind Merckx, but a strong final week and mountain stage win might still normally have put a young French rider under undue pressure to carry the hopes of the nation. After all, the best French rider in the 1970 Tour was seventh-placed 34-year-old Raymond Poulidor. Poulidor was a perennial also-ran whose Tour career was dealt a bum hand combining world-beating physical talent, terrible luck and bad tactical choices, earning him the nickname 'the Eternal Second' along with the lifelong adoration of the French public. He was getting on a bit, so there was a vacancy for a great French hope. But Merckx was seen as so invincible that nobody expected Thévenet to beat him or even prove to be a serious rival any time soon.

While Merckx being so dominant did protect Thévenet from undue pressure, it was still unfortunate for him that he spent the first part of his career up against the best rider of all time. And it was equally bad luck to also come up against the only man who could beat Merckx when he was at his best, Luis Ocaña. Thévenet came fourth in the 1971 Tour, won by Merckx but only after Ocaña, who'd been the strongest rider in the race, crashed out. Thévenet improved to second in 1973, when Merckx won the Tours of Spain and Italy and sat out the Tour, which was finally won by Ocaña. But in neither race had he looked like a winner. He came second to Ocaña in much the same way that Walter Mondale came second to Ronald Reagan in the 1984 presidential election. 'I tried to get involved with Merckx and Ocaña, but in comparison we were small boys beside them. They were capable of doing things that others could not.'

Ocaña beat Thévenet by over 15 minutes in 1973, the French rider having crashed at a bad time and lost five minutes early on, so Thévenet's focus was more on defending second place than winning. 'During that Tour Ocaña was untouchable. But

I'd got into a big fight with José Manuel Fuente for second place – we were watching each other a lot and that let Ocaña take more time. But I don't think even Merckx would have beaten Ocaña.'

Ocaña blew hot and cold, however. It wasn't always necessary to find ways to beat him – he'd eventually defeat himself. Merckx, on the other hand, still looked invincible.

'It's not that I was really afraid of Merckx,' says Thévenet. 'But it was impossible to find how to beat him because he climbed well, he could time-trial, and he could outpace all the climbers on the flat. It was more a fear of not finding a solution. There were very few solutions to this problem.'

Merckx won the Tour again in 1974. Still Thévenet waited. Then came 1975.

The Col d'Allos is a sinuous one-lane road in the Mercantour national park in the south-east of France. It doesn't have the same chilly atmosphere at the top as the more famous Alpine passes further north – it's only 80 kilometres as the crow flies from the Mediterranean coast. The Tour used to cross it often, before the Riviera got too crowded to accommodate the race on a regular basis, and it's one of three parallel mountain passes, along with the Col de la Bonette and the Col de la Cayolle, which separate the Alpes-Maritimes from the Alpes-de-Haute-Provence. The summit slopes are covered with a thin layer of yellowy, acidic grass – barren and wide open, but not bleak. The Col d'Allos is where the cycling world caught its last glimpse of Merckx as the unbeatable Tour champion.

Here's what the situation was as the 1975 Tour approached the summit: Merckx, alone and moving clear, in yellow, a few hundred metres ahead of a handful of riders, including Thévenet, who lay second overall. Thévenet was suffering from a minor crisis – an attack of the *fringale*, or hunger knock. He couldn't follow Merckx's attack, and worse was to come, in the form of the descent.

Maurice de Muer, Thévenet's manager at the Peugeot team, once said that Thévenet 'rode like a postman'. Going down hills fast wasn't his strong point.

'I was a very, very bad descender. I suffered physically and mentally on the downhills,' Thévenet says. 'I slowed at every corner. Merckx knew this very well and he always went full pelt downhill.'

By the time they got to the bottom of the final climb, six and a half kilometres to Pra Loup, Thévenet's deficit was over a minute. Extrapolating forward, and going on your knowledge of what had gone before with Merckx's career, you'd have had to say that Merckx looked like he was going to win the race.

But closer observers had suspected otherwise. Following the Pyrenean summit finish at Pla d'Adet, the stage winner Joop Zoetemelk suggested that the rider who'd impressed him most that day had been runner-up Bernard Thévenet, who'd punctured 400 metres from the end, preventing him from contesting the victory. The pair had finished almost a minute clear of Merckx. 'With the Puy de Dôme and Alps, he could put even more time into Merckx. He is my favourite for overall victory,' said Zoetemelk. Daniel Mangeas, who retired in 2014 after 40 years as the Tour's official speaker, also thought at the time that it was always a matter of when, and not if, Thévenet won the Tour: 'As soon as he won a stage in 1970 at La Mongie I thought he'd win the Tour one day. Even in 1974 there were signs that Merckx was starting to dip in his level, when Poulidor had him in trouble on one stage.'

Merckx did build up a lead of 2-20 on the flat stages in the first week in 1975 – he finished in the top 10 in 10 of the first 13 stages, including two time-trial wins. But Thévenet had spent the Pyrenean and Massif Central stages chiselling time out of

Merckx's lead. The momentum in the mountain stages had been with the Frenchman. Merckx had also fallen victim to a bizarre attack by a spectator who punched the Belgian in the kidneys, accidentally or otherwise, on the Puy de Dôme climb (he still finished third, behind Lucien Van Impe and Thévenet).

In hindsight, Merckx's career at the top of the Col d'Allos resembled that point in the Road Runner cartoons, where Wile E. Coyote has run off the cliff, and is still sprinting, hanging in mid-air with nothing but fresh air underneath him, before the inevitable punchline. The fall to earth happened slowly at first, but then gathered pace and accelerated towards terminal velocity as a quintet of former and future Tour winners rode away from the rest of the race. They leapfrogged and jumped around each other like knights on a chessboard: Felice Gimondi caught Merckx, who was faltering, while behind, a rejuvenated Thévenet passed and dropped Van Impe and Joop Zoetemelk.

Pierre Chany wrote in *L'Équipe* the next day that Merckx's deceleration had been a dramatic one, and that he was now riding at the speed of 'a country postman'. With two kilometres to go, the man who descended like a postman rode right past the man who was now climbing like one. The straights between the hairpins on Pra Loup switch back between north and south, so there was no shelter from the harsh Mediterranean sun which was beating down on the Tour, melting the tar on the road. Merckx, in an appropriate metaphor for the predicament he was in, squelched up through the sticky bitumen on the left-hand side of the road while Thévenet had found a strip of good Tarmac on the right. He'd correctly foreseen that Merckx wouldn't have been able to cross through the worst of the melted tar, in the middle of the road, to get on to his wheel. He needn't have worried – Merckx was in no condition to follow him anyway.

There's a famous photograph from the Pra Loup stage, taken just at the point where Thévenet is passing Merckx. The Frenchman is out of his saddle, his eyes fixed on the road ahead. The image of Thévenet is sharp, so you have to know a bit about cycling to infer his momentum – if you look at the position of the chain on the front chainring, you'll see that it's on the bigger ring, which indicates a higher gear. Pushing a big gear on the fifth mountain of the day isn't easy. On the right-hand side of the picture, Merckx is still half a length ahead of Thévenet, but there's something in his demeanour which indicates that he's beaten. Merckx never looked great on a bike, but generally the speed at which he could ride it more than compensated for that. His body and head are at almost identical angles to Thévenet's, but if you look closely enough, Merckx looks like he's sagging. The contrast in facial expressions is even more striking: Thévenet almost looks like he's smiling, while a furrowed frown is corrugating Merckx's brow. In the next two kilometres, Thévenet piled just under two minutes into Merckx, turning his 58-second deficit into a 58-second advantage.

On one level, the Tour wasn't quite ready for Thévenet. The story at Pra Loup was less that Thévenet had taken the yellow jersey than Merckx had lost it. But the French public, who'd not seen a home winner of their race since Roger Pingeon in 1967, were about to find their new hero.

Thévenet wasn't confident of winning yet, however. Merckx attacked him the very next day, Bastille Day, on the descent of the Col de Vars, but he'd overestimated himself again and was caught at the foot of the Col d'Izoard. 'You have to know how to do two things in the Tour de France. One, take risks. Two, be very careful,' Thévenet says. 'You have to know where you can take a risk and where you have to be careful. You never really know if you are choosing the right option – it's easy to say afterwards, but at the time it can be very difficult to know.'

On the morning of Bastille Day, Thévenet had met his child-hood hero Louison Bobet, winner of the three consecutive Tours in the 1950s. 'It was like meeting God,' Thévenet recalls. 'He said to me, "If you want to be a great rider, you must cross the Izoard alone with the yellow jersey on your back."'

It was time to take a risk. Thévenet attacked, into a Bastille Day throng on the Col d'Izoard. 'There was an extraordinary crowd at the top. They were crazy, shouting, it was something approaching hysteria. There was a sort of communion between me and the public – they'd all gone there for me, to encourage and support me. It lasted only five minutes, but it was five minutes of madness. It marked me most, of everything that happened in that Tour. It was the best moment of my sporting life.'

By the finish, he'd gained another two minutes on Merckx. In spite of an ongoing but ineffectual campaign of harassment by the Belgian over the last few stages of the race – which might have been more dangerous had Merckx not crashed and broken a cheekbone – Thévenet defended his lead to Paris. Then he rode so many criteriums around France over the next couple of months that, in Daniel Mangeas's opinion, he ruined his next season.

Thévenet was incredibly popular in France at the time of his wins. The public nicknamed him 'Nanard', which bordered on the pejorative (*nanar* is French for 'junk') but became a term of endearment. However, despite having won two Tours, Thévenet has fallen between the gaps a little in terms of his celebrity since then. Even now, English-language cycling magazines feature regular articles about Bernard Hinault and Laurent Fignon, the last two French winners of the Tour, but Thévenet rarely gets a look-in. He's well known in France for his commentary work on television, but he's almost more known for that than for actually winning the race.

For Mangeas, this is down to Thévenet's lack of ego. 'Success never turned his head,' he says. 'I remember asking him and Bernard Hinault about how it felt to be cycling at the front of the race, with the crowds lining the roads and cheering. Thévenet told me that he loved it and that it gave him goosebumps. Hinault, on the other hand, said he didn't notice it, and that he was more concerned with beating his rivals.'

Paul Kimmage wrote fondly about Thévenet, who'd been his *directeur sportif* at the RMO team, in his book *Rough Ride*. He wasn't the most effectual team manager, but Thévenet, Kimmage said, always waited on the finish line for every one of his riders to come in, even on the mountain stages where they were 45 minutes behind the leaders. 'Thévenet had a quality which made up for his organizational faults – his sincerity,' wrote Kimmage.

Thévenet is even more an archetypal French hero than Hinault. Hinault was a Breton, and he made the French feel good about themselves in the same way that they felt good when they read *Astérix*, about the indomitable Breton holding out against the Roman invaders. But the French also recognized that Hinault wasn't quite like them – he wasn't enough of an underdog. Thévenet was more of a French everyman, not just because of his rural roots – he always looked slightly surprised to be in a position of celebrity. There was also a lot more vulnerability about Thévenet than either Hinault or Merckx, which further endeared him to the fans. For every good Tour, he seemed to have a bad one – 1971, 1973, 1975 and 1977 were good, while 1972, 1974 and 1976 were comparatively disappointing.

The French public's relationship with their sporting heroes is a complex and ambiguous one, illustrated in their reaction to the rivalry between Jacques Anquetil and Raymond Poulidor in the 1960s. Anquetil was the dominant rider – he won five Tours, while Poulidor won none, although he ran Anquetil particularly close in 1964, his last victory. Something always went wrong for Poulidor – he finished on the podium eight times, without ever wearing the yellow jersey. But Poulidor was much more popular than Anquetil, and to Anquetil's frustration, the more he beat Poulidor, the more they seemed to cheer for him. France was split into unequally sized camps, one supporting Anquetil, the other Poulidor, and there was very little crossover.

On one level, it was a question of world view. Jean-Luc Boeuf and Yves Léonard wrote in their book *La République du Tour de France* that Anquetil and Poulidor's rivalry played out across a struggle between modernity and tradition in France: 'Those who recognized themselves in Jacques Anquetil liked his priority of style and elegance in the way he rode. Behind this fluidity and appearance of ease was the image of France winning and those who took risks identified with him. Humble people saw themselves in Raymond Poulidor, whose face – lined with effort – represented the life they led on land they worked without rest or respite. His declarations, full of good sense, delighted the crowds; a race, even a difficult one, lasts less time than a day bringing in the harvest.'

In *The Tour de France 1903–2003: A Century of Sporting Structures, Meanings and Values*, Hugh Dauncey studies the French sociologist Paul Yonnet's argument that the Tour de France has both an 'official' competition, which covers the sporting aspects of the race, and also an unofficial competition for popularity, which don't necessarily favour the same riders. Interestingly, Dauncey lists not only Poulidor but also Thévenet as being especially successful in the competition for popularity.

Thévenet seemed to bridge the divide between Poulidor and Anquetil – he was both champion and plucky trier. Fans who liked winners could enjoy his two Tour de France wins, while fans who were more subjective about their sporting heroes could identify with his working-class roots or his biennial fallibility. But it doesn't explain why, despite enjoying the kind of universal popularity among cycling fans that Anquetil or even Hinault never achieved, his celebrity has not had the longevity that theirs has.

Ironically, when he was a young cycling fan in the 1960s, Thévenet was an Anquetiliste.

The 1977 Tour de France wasn't the race organization's masterpiece, in terms of route planning. Sending the peloton into the Pyrenees on the third day might have been in keeping with founding father Henri Desgrange's vision of the Tour as an attritional contest of endurance, but all it did was ensure that most of the peloton were out of the race by the end of the stage, with three full weeks to go. The route crossed the Col d'Aspin, the Col du Tourmalet and the Col d'Aubisque, and the 14 strongest climbers in the race finished in a group seven minutes clear of the next man. Then, with the Pyrenees out of the way, the race settled into moribund torpor – there was one brief shuffle of the general classification in the Bordeaux time trial, but the top order barely changed for the next 17 stages. In its favour, the route had kept suspense alive: the racing had been so controlled that with six days to go there were six riders still within two minutes of the lead.

Thévenet's Peugeot teammate Bernard Bourreau recalls that while his leader rode the 1977 Tour with more confidence, it was a harder race for the team: 'We knew Bernard was going well in 1975 but you could never be confident when racing against Merckx. However, in 1977, we started with the intention of winning the Tour. We were really set to do it.' The Peugeot riders' job was made harder by the fact that they were also riding for Jacques Esclassan to win the green jersey. However, they were helped by the fact that TI–Raleigh's

Dietrich Thurau had won the prologue and the first Pyrenean stage, and ended up defending the yellow jersey all the way to the Alps. TI–Raleigh were probably the strongest and best-organized team in the race, which also explains why the general classification hardly changed at all before the Alps.

Thévenet thinks he's more famous for winning in 1975 than in 1977, but considers 1977 the better victory. 'I was more relaxed and sure of myself in 1977. It was a harder win for me, even though the public seem to remember 1975 much more because I beat Merckx. Beating Merckx gave me confidence, because if I wasn't scared of Merckx, I couldn't be scared of anybody else.'

There's little doubt that Thévenet was the strongest rider in 1977, but he was almost outwitted by TI–Raleigh's Hennie Kuiper on the Alpe d'Huez stage, the hardest of the race. A mountain time trial to Avoriaz and a medium-difficulty Alpine stage to Chamonix hadn't done much to change the top order, which consisted of Thévenet in yellow, Thurau at 11 seconds, Van Impe at 33 seconds, Kuiper at 49 seconds and Zoetemelk at 1-13 (soon to be increased by 10 minutes following a positive doping test at Avoriaz).

In *L'Équipe*'s report of the Alpe d'Huez stage, Pierre Chany broke down the roles played by the leading actors: 'The star of the day was Van Impe. The hero was Thévenet. The hard-hitter, winner of the contest, was Kuiper. The others were simply the defeated. Galdós honourably, Zoetemelk, who contributed nothing, dishonourably. Thurau, painfully. And Merckx pitifully.'

Van Impe had attacked seven kilometres from the top of the Col du Glandon, the second of the day's climbs. By the foot of Alpe d'Huez, despite a strong headwind in the valley road, he led by almost three minutes. Behind, Thévenet chased with Kuiper and Zoetemelk on his wheel, refusing to contribute at all to the pace-setting, memorably described in Tim Krabbé's novel *The Rider*: 'Kuiper planned to lick Thévenet's plate clean before starting on his own.' Thévenet was more direct. 'They're small riders,' he said after the stage.

Thévenet's pace-setting pulled Van Impe back to a 1-20 lead with five kilometres to go, before chaos descended on the race. Kuiper attacked, and dropped Thévenet, while Van Impe was knocked off his bike by a television car, his wheel broken. As Kuiper's lead expanded towards the 49 seconds he'd need to take yellow, Thévenet embarked on the ride which should define his career, far more than his performances at Pra Loup or on the Col d'Izoard.

'On the Alpe I did an extraordinary last kilometre. I had somebody there with a kilometre to go, who shouted that I was in yellow by one second. The Dijon time trial was two days later and I absolutely wanted to keep the yellow jersey so that I could start last,' says Thévenet. 'In that last kilometre I took back seven seconds. I did a sprint but it absolutely wasted me. If the finishing line had been 50 metres further on I wouldn't have made it. I was incapable of more.

'Then I had to climb the three steps to the podium – *ooh la la*! Another col!' Thévenet's masseur had to half-carry him up the stairs in his hotel that evening. He was so tired he couldn't even eat, falling asleep without dinner, then waking, ravenous, in the middle of the night while team staff managed to rustle up a midnight meal consisting mainly of bread. He recovered well, however. 'The next day – fit as a fiddle!'

He'd saved the yellow jersey by eight seconds, and with two time trials, one long and one short, to come, Thévenet had won his second Tour.

Seeing Bernard Thévenet as a stopgap winner between Merckx and Hinault is to do him a disservice. The quality of the opposition he beat in 1975 made it one of the most competitive Tours in history. Five of the top six – Thévenet, Merckx, Van Impe, Zoetemelk and Gimondi – were past or future Tour winners, a result that is without equal in the Tour's history (Vicente López Carril, in fifth place, was the non-Tour-winning interloper). And 1977 was a hard Tour – only 53 of the 100 starters finished, with 30 riders eliminated on the Alpe d'Huez stage alone. That's a lower proportion of finishers than any Tour between 1957 and now, with the exception of the 1998 event, from which several teams withdrew in protest amid the chaos of the Festina scandal.

But it's true that Thévenet was never the same again after the 1977 Tour. His steady progression to the top of the sport was followed by a vertiginous descent into mediocrity. His body packed up first, closely followed by his morale: 'I never found the same level of form ever again. Hinault was coming, so it would have been difficult to win the Tour again, but I lost the will a bit as well, maybe. I couldn't do races or training all out any more. The problem started physically but I couldn't find the willpower to overcome it.'

Thévenet admitted in 1978 that he'd been suffering from health problems that were caused or exacerbated by having used cortisone for several seasons. His immune system was shot to pieces. 'I hope my experience will be educational for others,' he added after his confession. 'But I fear that it won't.'

2

Lucien Van Impe

1976

And did I know that a month before the start of this year's Tour, Van Impe put his watch on one hour? And whatever he did, whether it was going to bed, or eating his meals, or going out training, he did it an hour later than usual? In that way, when he came across the border, the rhythm of his daily life would not be put out by double French summer time. Well now, there was something interesting about a man who took such extreme precautions. Something curious, although not exactly heroic.

Geoffrey Nicholson, *The Great Bike Race*

Lucien Van Impe won the 1976 Tour de France in a time trial that was raced a whole year earlier.

With the mountain road stages completed in the 1975 Tour and Bernard Thévenet safe in the yellow jersey, there was one last sifting of the general classification to come before the final diminuendo of flat stages to Paris – a 40-kilometre time trial between Morzine and Châtel, in the Haute-Savoie Alps. The route left Morzine and went north along the Thonon road, running parallel to the rushing Dranse de Morzine river down the valley towards Lac Léman. Eight kilometres into the race, the riders tacked right following a sign for the Val d'Abondance, up one of those Y-junctions where the valley walls are so steep the two roads run parallel, at different gradients, for a short distance. The next six kilometres curved left and right uphill, crash barriers on one side of the road, overhanging trees shading it on the other, to the 1,235-metre-high Col du Corbier. Usually in the Tour, the Corbier is a second-category climb, but there were no mountains points on offer in the 1975 race – the only important thing was time gained and lost. Down the other side – fast at the top, then more technical with a ladder of five hairpin bends, almost dead turns, and a headlong plummet through the village of Bonnevaux to the junction with the D22 at La Solitude. From here, the road described a shallow S heading east, a shallow but persistent tilt up alongside the Dranse d'Abondance river to the finish 16 kilometres later at Châtel – real *rouleur* territory. The time trial had everything – a fast, slightly downhill start, a difficult six-kilometre climb, a technical descent and a power-cruiser's finish.

On the eve of the time trial, there wasn't much left to settle in the race. Thévenet led Eddy Merckx overall by 3-18, while Van Impe was the same distance behind Merckx in third, just 28 seconds clear of Joop Zoetemelk. Zoetemelk's time-trialling form was marginally better than Van Impe's – he'd beaten him by 44 seconds in a 37.5-kilometre time trial midway through the Tour, so race followers might have thought Van Impe's place on the podium was under threat. Van Impe was known as a climber. In 1975 he won his third of six King of the Mountains titles, and he'd achieved five top sixes in seven Tours, without ever getting closer than five minutes behind the eventual winner. But Van Impe not only defended his third place overall in Châtel, he won the time trial. Merckx was 57 seconds behind, Thévenet at 1-12. Van Impe ended the day only 1-46 behind Merckx.

Amid all the noise of a Frenchman having won the Tour, and of Eddy Merckx having been beaten in the race for the first time, somebody at *L'Équipe* noticed the other Belgian on the podium as the race finished, and ran a small story titled 'Could Van Impe Win the Tour?' They interviewed his team manager, Jean Stablinski, who said that he was convinced Van Impe could do it. 'His progression has been constant, and I always thought he'd be ready by the time he was 28. That's how old he is now,' said Stablinski.

It wasn't necessarily his riding skills that had held him back before. It was an ambivalent relationship with his own ambition. In the past, Van Impe had occasionally climbed as well as Merckx in the Tour, but always lost time in the time trials and on flat days when the race got tactical. In 1971, he came third overall behind Merckx. He had finished the final mountain stage only 2-19 behind his compatriot, and that included the two minutes Merckx had gained on an extraordinary escape on the downhill stage out of the Alps to Marseille. Yet Van Impe still contrived to eventually finish 11 minutes behind in Paris.

Going into the Bordeaux stage, Merckx was safe in yellow, but only led the green jersey competition by a handful of points, so he attacked and got away with a small group. Bordeaux cost Van Impe three minutes, then he conceded another five and a half minutes in the final time trial of the race. Van Impe suffered from the same apparent quashed ambition shared by almost all of Merckx's rivals in the early 1970s – stage wins and polka-dot jerseys papered over the fact that he didn't even try fighting for the general classification. On balance, Van Impe probably did the right thing – the cycling public remember six King of the Mountains jerseys and nine stage wins more than they might remember him finishing one or two minutes closer behind Merckx and one or two places higher in the overall.

Barry Hoban, who rode with Van Impe in the French Sonolor

team in 1970 and 1971, recalls that Merckx's dominance had a chilling effect on his rivals' ambitions. 'The problem Van Impe had was that he was brought up in the era of Merckx, who dominated and controlled the race. I don't think Lucien liked the responsibility of doing that. To win, the time comes when you have to control the race. Lucien's team didn't have to ride on the front, nor did Lucien. He could do what he wanted, win a couple of mountain stages, win the King of the Mountains, and he was quite happy with that. He was stopping short of the big prize.'

It looked like the King of the Mountains title and a decent overall position were the most he could hope for in any Tour, but the Châtel time trial in 1975 changed all that. 'I beat Merckx, Thévenet, Zoetemelk, all the big riders in that time trial. I immediately thought, "If I can time-trial like that, I can go to the Tour to win,"' Van Impe tells me.

There was one other moment which bolstered his confidence as a contender for the yellow jersey in 1976: the October 1975 announcement of the route of the race. The organizers had seen Thévenet dropping Merckx on the summit finishes of 1975, so they laid on a mountainous route, with stages to Alpe d'Huez, for the first time since 1952, and Pla d'Adet, the better to ensure a possible French victory. 'Thévenet won in 1975 and he was very strong in the mountains,' Van Impe explains. 'The French can be a bit chauvinistic, and they designed the 1976 Tour for Thévenet. But it was also a Tour for me. As soon as I saw the route in October, I thought, "I can win that."'

Lucien Van Impe came before my time as a cycling fan. I was three years old when he won the Tour, and the first Tour I watched on television – 1985 – was Van Impe's last appearance in the race. He finished 27th overall. I didn't notice his 20th place at Avoriaz at the time, nor did I know that two years previously he'd won his final Tour stage there, in a mountain time trial, on the way to his record-equalling sixth King of the Mountains title.

My introduction to Van Impe came a couple of years later, in Robin Magowan's book *Kings of the Road*. Even then, I'd only bought it because Greg LeMond and Bernard Hinault were on the cover, and there were pieces on Stephen Roche and Robert Millar. *Kings of the Road* was rooted in the bright primary colours of 1980s cycling, but Magowan also gave his readers a brief glimpse of recent history in the rearview mirror, with sections on Merckx, Van Impe and Zoetemelk.

What actually grabbed my attention, regarding Van Impe, were the photographs taken by Graham Watson. Van Impe was very photogenic, one of the few riders ever to look good in the Tour's polka-dot jersey. In Watson's photos, he had the beginnings of a windblown 1980s perm which flopped over an equally 1980s sweatband. In older pictures, a scruffily cut 1970s mop frames a younger, wolfish face. Van Impe wore his shorts higher than most other professional riders, and he had superb muscle development – thighs like ham hocks; long legs and arms for his height of five foot six. In short, he looked fantastic on a bike – classically elegant.

However, the interesting thing about photographs of Van Impe is how the still images differ from the reality. I've watched numerous clips of him racing on YouTube, and his riding style was a harrying, restless, nagging *agitato*. He punched and jabbed at the pedals, his rhythm erratic – standing on the pedals, sitting down, immediately standing up again. It was as if each pedal stroke was separate from all the others, and it's not relaxing to watch. I used to get the same not-quite-comfortable sensation when I watched Paula Radcliffe running. This pedalling style came from his teenage years.

'When I was 15,' Van Impe says, 'I told my father that I wanted to be like Charly Gaul and Federico Bahamontes – a climber. I wanted to climb the mountains like them, *en dansant* [dancing].'

Van Impe's father Josef was a keen cyclist and was equally keen on his son becoming one; keener, in fact, than Lucien himself initially. He supervised Van Impe's training, on the *bergs* and *monts* of Flanders. 'I'd ride five or six climbs, like Grammont [the Muur van Geraardsbergen] and the Kemmel, sprinting from the bottom to the top all the time, so I'd get better at climbing,' he says. 'The Muur is not a mountain, but when I was 16, I climbed it 20 or 30 times in a day, sprinting up. From my house to Grammont was 30 kilometres – I would ride 30 kilometres, then 50 kilometres of just climbing and descending the Muur, then back home.'

The climbs of Flanders are short and steep, and many are cobbled. The fastest way to climb them is with the same punchy cadence as Van Impe had on the bike, and he transposed that style into riding fast in the high mountains of the Tour. His father also took him to Spain to race and train in the mountains. Van Impe himself is not sure whether it was nature or nurture that made him such a good climber. It certainly wasn't ambition, aside from wanting to emulate Gaul and Bahamontes.

'I was born into a cycling family. My dad, brother . . . everybody cycled. We spoke about it all the time in the café my mum owned. Cycling, cycling, cycling!' he says. 'Me, I never loved cycling. I wanted to be a mechanic, but my dad wanted me to be a racer. He nagged me for a year to start. But you start winning bike races, and it's like a virus – it keeps on multiplying!'

Van Impe's path into professional cycling was an unusual one. He'd won a race in the Basque Country in 1966, at the age of 20, and his hero Bahamontes, who was at the race, told him he should turn professional as soon as possible. In 1969 his opportunity came in the middle of the year – he signed with

Sonolor, and a few days later he was taking part in his first race: the Tour de France. He came 12th in that race, almost an hour behind Eddy Merckx, but he was only four minutes from the top 10.

'He used to annoy people when he first turned pro, because he was so at ease when the pressure was on,' recalls Barry Hoban. 'He used to whistle while he rode.'

Modern training methods and racing tactics have blunted the powers of the climbers in cycling. These days, there are still riders who can climb extremely fast, but the speed of the racing in general means that their acceleration makes less of a difference than it used to. In the 1970s, however, climbers like Van Impe could take advantage of a generally slower pace in the mountains to make devastating attacks.

'He was so natural,' says Hoban. 'You can compare a climber to a sports car with a big engine and very light bodywork, which is what Van Impe was. He could explode away on a climb. Like Alberto Contador, but better. Merckx could climb, but he wasn't a climber – he had to follow a tempo. Van Impe could alter the pace all the time, he'd upset the rhythm.'

There's one more thing about Lucien Van Impe. He rose to the top in a sport where naked ambition is an asset, and a good proportion of the very successful can be psychologically complex, but he's very down to earth. Read through this book and draw your own conclusions over which of the yellow jersey club you'd like to go out and have a beer with, but Van Impe would be one of my choices, and not just because he's Belgian. When I spoke to him, he was expansive, accommodating and still seemed to be surprised and elated at having won the Tour. It was the reaction of a normal man, not that of an elite sportsman.

Van Impe likes to remind people that while his compatriot Eddy Merckx is the greatest cyclist in history, he remains the last

Belgian to have won the Tour de France. Van Impe is also regarded more fondly in his home country than Merckx ever was – he played Poulidor to Merckx's Anquetil back in Belgium.

Guy Fransen, the chief of Belgian newspaper *Het Nieuwsblad*'s sports section, sees Van Impe as the people's champion in a way that Merckx never was. 'We never expected Van Impe to win the Tour, because he was a climber,' says Fransen. 'We knew he could climb like a goat, but that he could do time trials and stay with the peloton in the flat stages, all that was a surprise. And later we appreciated Lucien more and more, as a rounded cyclist. I think we underestimated him. He was smarter than we thought.'

Fransen has a lot of Van Impe stories. Like the time famous Belgian cyclist Roger De Vlaeminck was invited to a gala event for Flandrian cycling. De Vlaeminck isn't the easiest man to get on with, and Van Impe offered to pick De Vlaeminck up in his car and drive him to the gala. The subtext was that not many people were prepared to spend an hour in the car with De Vlaeminck. 'He went 60 miles out of his way to pick Roger up,' says Fransen. 'Lucien is everybody's friend. He's the guy next door.'

'When I'm at an event and see Lucien,' Fransen continues, 'I can speak to him as a friend. But with Merckx, I hesitate to talk to him. He is the paterfamilias.'

For the first six years of his career, Van Impe won stage and mountain jerseys. But even when the fire of his ambition to win the Tour flickered into life in the second half of 1975, he couldn't just change his personality into that of somebody who could control the Tour de France. He would need somebody else to do that.

It's almost 40 years since Van Impe and Cyrille Guimard won the Tour together, one as the rider, one as his manager, but they still don't agree on how it was done. It's fair to say that the process of winning the race caused a rift between them that never healed – sometimes the same creative tension that results in success causes relations to break down.

Are you friends? I ask Van Impe. 'Well, you have to remember that Guimard doesn't have friends,' he says. 'As a team manager, *ça va*. When we spoke about tactics, he was good. But as a man, to live with, it didn't work.'

There's a chapter in Guimard's 2012 book *Dans les Secrets du Tour de France* which is called 'Victory While Cursing: How to Win the Tour With a Rider Who Doesn't Want to', and another called 'Lucien Van Impe: the Man is Not Always as Worthy as the Champion'. When I speak to Guimard about Van Impe he damns him with the faintest of praise. 'He was an intelligent rider, in a way, but he was in his groove, and it was difficult to get him out of that,' he says. 'He was one of the best climbers of all time, but he felt he couldn't beat Merckx, so he was happy to focus on the climbers' classification. The way he rode, he was a natural teammate for Merckx.'

You wouldn't think that they'd managed to work together at all.

Guimard is one of the most successful managers in Tour de France history – he won the Tour with Van Impe in 1976, worked with Hinault in his first four wins, and with Laurent Fignon for his two Tours. He also coached Greg LeMond when he turned professional, and even managed Bjarne Riis at Super-U and Andy Schleck for his last season as an amateur. Riders he has coached at one point or another have won 13 Tours, which is a matchless record in cycling, even if the sport seems to have left him behind a little in the last decade.

Guimard's man management was abrasive and autocratic, but very effective, although his biggest skill might have lain in identifying talent in the first place. He was also very strong tactically – when he'd been a rider, he'd punched above his weight and won eight Tour stages, coming within a whisker of finishing second overall to Merckx and winning the green jersey in 1972 before tendonitis forced him out of the Tour with a few days remaining. He retired young from racing in early 1976, winning one last race, the National Cyclo-Cross Championships, before taking up the job as Gitane's team manager. He was younger than several of the more experienced riders, including his team leader Van Impe.

The way Guimard tells it, he had to chivvy and nag Van Impe into seeing himself as a yellow jersey contender. In *Dans les Secrets du Tour de France* he wrote at length about their different outlooks. 'He had to convert my aim, which was for him to win the Tour, into ambition for himself,' he said. 'I put it into his head that he could win. The hardest thing wasn't me believing in him, but that Lucien would find the idea credible. I said to him, "Lucien, you are going to win the Tour, and I'm going to tell you how you are going to do it," and he answered, "Yeah, sure," like he always did.'

Guimard hated that. The problem with Lucien, he wrote, was that he always answered, 'Yeah, I'll do it tomorrow.' Some of the other riders on the team even used to call Van Impe, 'Mr Yeah-I'll-Do-It-Tomorrow'.

The 1976 Tour started and finished as the Freddy Maertens show. The Belgian sprinter, who rode for the Flandria team, won three out of the first four stages, including the prologue, a bunch sprint and a 37-kilometre time trial, and wore the yellow jersey all the way from the prologue to the Alps. In the first 10 stages, his lowest finishing position was ninth. After the Pyrenees, he took four more stage wins to achieve a record-equalling eight stage wins in a single Tour. Maertens' sprint dominance suited Van Impe perfectly – Flandria did the work of controlling the race up to the Alps, to keep Maertens in the yellow jersey and to keep him in the hunt for stage wins. Geoffrey

Nicholson, in his book about the 1976 Tour, *The Great Bike Race*, wrote that Flandria had not given an inch in the first week: 'Maertens and the Flandria team have smothered the race. Their ideal has been an uneventful stage and a mass sprint finish – led in by Maertens, like lightning outrunning a storm.'

Van Impe and Guimard were also lucky to an extent that in 1976 many rivals eliminated themselves. Merckx, who had never been the same since he'd been defeated the year before, had flogged himself round to eighth place in the Giro d'Italia suffering from a saddle sore, but had to pull out of the Tour. Defending champion Thévenet was out of sorts and wouldn't finish the race; 1973 winner Luis Ocaña was another rider whose best years appeared to be behind him, and Van Impe's young teammate Bernard Hinault was still two years away from entering the Tour. Only Joop Zoetemelk, on the comeback from a horrific racing accident in mid-1974 (see Chapter 4) seemed to have timed his form right for the 1976 race.

On the morning of the Alpe d'Huez stage, Guimard told Van Impe to concentrate solely on gaining time in the general classification. 'You'll see at the top who is capable of staying with you,' he said.

It turned out that only Zoetemelk could live with Van Impe in the mountains. Van Impe set the pace all the way up the climb, with Zoetemelk sitting on his wheel. Zoetemelk won the stage, three seconds clear of Van Impe, who took the yellow jersey.

'Zoetemelk stayed behind me, saying that Poulidor [his team-mate] was not far behind. He started to ride a little with two kilometres to go,' says Van Impe. 'It was the first time I took the yellow jersey, and I said that evening I would win the Tour.'

Van Impe was so pleased with taking the yellow jersey on Alpe d'Huez that he later named his house after the climb. But Guimard wasn't happy. 'It was the worst possible thing that could have happened,' he wrote in his book. 'My team was not capable of defending the yellow jersey in the high mountains. I knew we were riding towards doom – my plan had been completely derailed. I knew that under no circumstances should we start the key stage to Pla d'Adet in the race lead.'

At Alpe d'Huez, Van Impe led Zoetemelk by eight seconds. The Dutchman gained another second the next day on the finishing climb to Montgenèvre. It was the worst of both worlds for Guimard – Van Impe's already small lead was being reduced further, and Gitane were still having to control the race. So he concocted a plan.

Running a finger down the general classification on the eve of the first Pyrenean stage to the Pyrénées 2000 ski resort, he saw the name Raymond Delisle, in eighth place, 4-17 behind Van Impe. Delisle was a stayer, a respected and popular professional who'd finished 11th three times in the Tour, won the French championships and been in the top 10 of some big races, but at 33 wasn't a big threat for the yellow jersey. Guimard got hold of Delisle and hinted to him that if he went on the attack to Pyrénées 2000, Gitane wouldn't chase too hard. Van Impe wasn't keen, and Guimard alleges that when Delisle got away the next day, Van Impe had marshalled the Belgians in the team, Willy Teirlinck and René Dillen, to keep his lead in check. There was even a rumour that Van Impe didn't want to lose the jersey because his wife Rita was about to arrive on the Tour.

In the end, Delisle won the stage by five minutes to his nearest rival, and just under seven to Zoetemelk and Van Impe. The responsibility of defending the race lead would fall for a couple of days to Delisle's Peugeot team.

What happened on Col du Portillon, during the Pla d'Adet stage, two days later, depends on who you listen to.

Lucien Van Impe: 'I knew I could take the jersey back at Pla d'Adet. I attacked 90 kilometres from the finish, all alone, behind the break. Zoetemelk thought it was too early and waited too long to follow. Guimard always takes credit for it.'

Geoffrey Nicholson: 'Guimard wants his man to make a frontal attack in the middle of the stage and win back the yellow jersey by minutes, not seconds. When Dillen drops back to the team car for water bottles he returns with a message for Van Impe: "Guimard asks you to attack." Van Impe whistles through his teeth and says it's mad. Nor does he budge when Ocaña strikes away. Then Raymond Martin [Van Impe's Gitane team-mate] arrives with a more emphatic message: "Guimard says you must attack now." "If he wants me to attack," says Van Impe, "he must come and tell me himself." And that is what Guimard does, driving up the narrow road beside the peloton, klaxon going, to deliver his ultimatum.'

Cyrille Guimard: 'I drove up to Lucien. He still had doubts: "Cyrille, you don't understand, there are 80 kilometres to go, I'll never do it." I was purple with rage. He was about to lose the Tour and there was nothing I could do about it. Just then, the *Het Volk* newspaper car drove up and I shouted to them, "Tell him in Flemish, seeing as he won't listen to me, that if he doesn't start riding, he's going to lose the Tour, the idiot!" No sooner said than done. Guess what? Van Impe turned on the after-burners. It was a miracle.'

Though neither man will let the other take credit for it, Guimard and Van Impe concocted a race-winning plan on the Pla d'Adet stage, and whether he was convinced or not, Van Impe still had to ride over three mountains on his own. Rather than wait until the last climb to the summit finish, where Zoetemelk would probably have matched Van Impe closely enough to threaten his Tour win, Van Impe attacked with the Portillon and Peyresourde still to go. Van Impe, at this point, still had the reputation of a King of the Mountains classification points hunter, and Zoetemelk initially thought that was his aim.

The Dutchman's manager, Louis Caput, saw the danger and told him to chase Van Impe, but Zoetemelk left it to Delisle's Peugeot team, who weren't up to the job, to take responsibility for keeping Van Impe under control. By the time he realized it was too late, Van Impe had linked up with previous escapee Ocaña and was three minutes up the road. At the finish, Zoetemelk was 3-12 behind, and only two more riders got within seven minutes of Van Impe. The Tour still had well over a week to go, but Van Impe had built an insurmountable lead.

Zoetemelk took a final summit stage win at Puy de Dôme. It was ironic that the Dutchman, who was famous for coming second, actually won three summit finishes during the 1976 Tour, but his time gain over Van Impe at these finishes was only 16 seconds. Van Impe's final margin of victory was 4-14 over Zoetemelk, more than the time he'd gained at Pla d'Adet. There was little doubt that he was a worthy winner of the yellow jersey.

Or maybe he was just lucky. A year later, Van Impe embarked on a similar long-range attack, this time in the Alps. At the beginning of the final mountain stage of the 1977 Tour, to Alpe d'Huez, he lay just 33 seconds behind yellow jersey Bernard Thévenet. Van Impe attacked on the Col du Glandon, with 60 kilometres still to go, a lot of it into a headwind. He led by almost three minutes at the bottom of the final climb to the Alpe, but, as we have seen, the brave rearguard effort by Thévenet, a determined chase by eventual stage winner Hennie Kuiper and a television car knocking Van Impe off his bike with just a few kilometres to ride all conspired to kill his effort. It was one of the most exciting Alpe d'Huez stages in the race's history – a really unpredictable and constantly evolving three-way battle, ultimately won by Kuiper, with the war of the general classification won by Thévenet. That's the way cycling goes – one year, you go on a long-range attack in the mountains and you win the race and are hailed a tactical genius, the next year you do the same thing, and it amounts to naught.

Guy Fransen thinks that Van Impe probably won the right number of Tours. 'Of course, Merckx was so dominating, and Merckx's best years, 1969 to 1975, were Lucien's golden era too. Maybe he could have won two or three Tours, but you could say that of a lot of riders in Merckx's era,' he says.

'I could have won the Tour three times,' Van Impe tells me. But that's why I think he has such a hard time letting Guimard take the credit for the Pla d'Adet attack. He was denied in 1975 by not realizing until it was too late that he was a yellow jersey contender, and in 1977 he had the confidence and form to mount a challenge, but he was thwarted by the wind, bad luck and a very strong and determined rival in Bernard Thévenet. So he's left with 1976. Considering the legwork he put into winning that race, he's reluctant to share it with anybody.

3

Bernard Hinault

1978, 1979, 1981, 1982, 1985

The Blaireau *was a weird fellow: he frightened me . . . Sometimes he would attack, and the bunch would string out in a long line behind him. Then he would sit up and start laughing at us, mocking us. He had a certain presence, a sort of godlike aura. He was a great champion, but I didn't like him.*

Paul Kimmage, *Rough Ride*

Less than a page into Bernard Hinault's autobiography, *Memories of the Peloton*, the teenage future Tour winner has already fallen out with his family and run away from home. The falling-out this time (the presumption is that arguments were a common occurrence in the Hinault household) was over the young Bernard's preference for cycling over working.

The stand-off lasted three days, during which Hinault slept in barns and haylofts and spent his time roaming the country-side, in his words 'free as a bird', before going back to have it out with his father Joseph. Hinault decided he would bluff his father: he said he would be leaving home and giving up cycling. 'What I wanted, above all, was to be at nobody's beck and call, least of all my father's,' wrote Hinault. 'He lowered his gaze and said, "No, you carry on cycling." From that day onwards it was never questioned again.'

There's something almost frightening in Hinault's triumph over his father, a sense that family ties weren't as strong as his desire to impose himself on people. A lot of cycling fans and some journalists lap up this kind of story, because it fits so well with our perception of Hinault. It's primary evidence, we think, of the immense willpower champions supposedly have. We extrapolate from this early encounter with his father to Hinault winning this or that Tour de France and conclude that great champions are born, not made. The wilful 17-year-old who faced down his father became the belligerent Tour debutant who stood on the front line of a riders' strike in Valence-d'Agen in 1978 protesting over too many split stages, his chest puffed up, his jaw set, looking down his nose at anybody who dared challenge him. The teenage Bernard Hinault is indistinguishable from the five-time Tour winner, the man who waged psychological warfare on Greg LeMond in the 1986 Tour.

Or maybe Joseph Hinault was just not very good at bluffing. What seems certain is that Bernard Hinault was not very easy to live with, and whether this made him better or worse at winning bike races is anybody's guess. The real Bernard Hinault is buried so far underneath a lacquer-hard exterior of bluff, defensiveness and pugnacity that it's far easier to assume that with the Breton, what you see is what you are going to get.

There's a certain level of emotional detachment needed to maintain such a persona, although Hinault plays up to the stereotype naturally and easily, as if on autopilot. On the one hand he is a reliable rent-a-quote for what any given rider in any given race needs to do in order to win, which is attack. On the other, he remains as stubbornly insistent now as he was in 1986 that he was not trying to undermine LeMond in that year's Tour. Either way, no matter how many times he says something, you wonder if he'll ever say or even think that the truth is more complex than he's previously been willing to admit. Hinault's world sometimes seems as black and white as the flag of his native Brittany.

Hinault won the Tour at his first attempt, in 1978, then dominated the race in 1979. A knee injury saw him pull out of the 1980 Tour, but he came back to win the next two races at a canter. He didn't start the 1983 race, having damaged his knee again, was beaten into second place by Laurent Fignon in 1984, then won his fifth Tour in 1985, before coming second in his final Tour in 1986, during which it was never quite clear whether he was working for or against his teammate, and eventual winner, Greg LeMond. I think Hinault was the best Grand Tour rider in cycling history. As well as five Tours, he won the Giro d'Italia three times and the Vuelta a España twice – in 12 Grand Tour starts, he won 10, and came second twice. Not even Eddy Merckx (16 starts, 11 wins, one second but three minor placings and a disqualification) or Jacques Anquetil (16 starts, eight wins, two seconds, three thirds, three abandons) can match his consistency, although Merckx won one more in total.

Hinault built his first four Tour wins on a solid base of formidable time trialling and strong but defensive climbing. Occasional bursts of dynamic flair – Hinault wasn't above getting involved in bunch sprint finishes and, what's more, winning them – were tempered by a general feeling of tactical conservatism.

Laurent Fignon, the old teammate who eclipsed Hinault in 1983 and 1984, had a complicated relationship with the public – he wasn't universally liked, but he did ride with a lot of panache. And in the last three years of his career, Hinault picked up on the prevailing wind, and rode much more aggressively, which won him a lot more fans than his earlier wins had. Paradoxically, it was his Tour defeats in 1984 and 1986 which saw him at his most popular. 'They never liked me so much as when I was losing,' he ruefully admitted. Ironically, when he did win one-day races, such as the 1980 world championships, 1980 Liège–Bastogne–Liège or 1981 Paris–Roubaix, he was much more aggressive and exciting in his tactics. And in his two losing Tours, he attacked far more so than in his winning years, a flamboyant and televisual showman, clad in the Rubik's Cube team colours of La Vie Claire.

Physically, Hinault was as gifted as any cyclist has ever been. Cyrille Guimard, who was his first manager as a professional, says, 'In terms of his physical potential, he's the best of all time. Above Merckx.' Mentally he was unusually strong too, although Guimard qualifies this as more complex. 'He was a hunter of big races. He only wanted to peak in big events, not secondary events,' he says. This differentiates him from Merckx, who wanted to win anything and everything. But while Merckx just liked to win, Hinault needed to make things more personal in order to bring out the race-winner in him. 'Hinault is a boxer. He needs somebody opposite him to hit,' says Guimard. 'It could be other riders, it could be journalists.'

Hinault needed to face people down, or to prove them wrong, or at least to feel like he had. He entered his first race as a 16-year-old without even having done any real training or group riding, promising his mother he'd bring back the winner's bouquet as he left the house. Her response, according to Hinault, was sceptical. 'Don't be such a clever dick, or you'll end up in a ditch,' she said. Despite his inexperience, Hinault won the race, and duly presented his mother with the flowers that afternoon. 'Promises are made to be kept,' he reflected.

It's interesting that Hinault dedicated *Memories of the Peloton* to 'all those who believed in me'. It might have been more accurate, given his need for external motivation and enemies real or imagined, to dedicate his wins and success to those who hadn't.

As Hinault's career developed, so his reputation and myth grew. He suffered a spectacular crash in the 1977 Critérium du Dauphiné Libéré, disappearing over a steep precipice on a mountain descent while television audiences gasped in horror. The footage of him scrambling out of the ravine to not only carry on but also win the race gave him an aura of indestructibility. In the Valence-d'Agen riders' strike of 1978, when he was only 23, Hinault had tried to explain the peloton's grievance to the local mayor. He felt the mayor wasn't listening to him, so he told him to 'shut up and listen'. A few years later, in 1984, a group of shipyard workers blocked the road in their own protest during Paris–Nice and Hinault got off his bike and waded in, throwing punches. Hinault, it was agreed, was tough and stubborn. He could be a hothead too, although this doesn't square easily with the conservative approach to stage racing between 1978 and 1982.

Hinault was perceived as a typical Breton, and this was a matter of pride for him. 'I was the true Breton in our family: stubborn, belligerent and afraid of nothing,' he said. In early 1982, at the Breton Tour de l'Armor, he enlisted his teammates for a mid-race bender at the team hotel. Laurent Fignon wrote in his autobiography *We Were Young and Carefree* that Hinault went to his nearby house to pick up some wine. 'After dinner I'll come back with a few bottles. We'll toast Brittany,' Hinault had said.

He was given the nickname *le Blaireau*, the Badger. Originally, fellow Breton cyclists Maurice Le Guilloux and Georges Talbourdet used '*blaireau*' as a general term between themselves, in the same way they might call each other 'mate' or 'pal'. In the patois of their chain gang, Hinault became known as '*Petit Blaireau*'. But at some point he morphed from being just *a* badger to '*the* Badger', and the name stuck. Of course, it helped that Hinault's character fitted the nickname perfectly

– just like a badger, he was most dangerous when cornered.

What Guimard says about Hinault's mental strength being as important a part of his armoury as his physical strength is revealing. It wasn't so much that Hinault was invincible in the first half of his career, but there was a *perception* that he was invincible, and that was indistinguishable from the real thing. He provoked a similar level of lethargy in his rivals' ambitions as Merckx did. In fact, there seems to be an entire lost generation in the first part of Hinault's career. The same people who came second to Hinault between 1978 and 1982 – Joop Zoetemelk and Lucien Van Impe – had been among Merckx's biggest rivals. It wasn't until 1983 that a new generation of young riders emerged who were capable of rivalling Hinault.

It took two Tours for Hinault to build that perception of invincibility: 1978 and 1979. He didn't dominate at all in 1978 – for most of the race it looked like a hard-fought and close battle, yet he still won comfortably in the end. By 1979 he'd gained in confidence and experience, and it's possible that in terms of his Tour-winning powers, 1979 was Hinault's peak.

Guimard and Hinault had decided against entering the Tour de France until he could ride it to win it. Although his background and upbringing in rural Brittany, and then his development as a rider, had been rooted in tradition, Hinault was perhaps the first modern professional cyclist in terms of his understanding of peaking, rather than simply racing week in, week out. He always saw cycling as something to be enjoyed, rather than as a chore. 'I make money for my wife and son. I *race* for me,' he once said. He was prone to taking his training in the off-season remarkably lightly, even by the standards of the time. Guimard used to poke fun at him at early-season training camps, blowing out his cheeks and hinting that Hinault's winter weight gain made him look like a pig. This explains why his wins were as impressive as Merckx's in quality, yet lagged behind in quantity. But it also explains how he was able to bring himself to form for what he called his 'appointments' – the target races he aimed to win. Instead of throwing him into every race, to see how much he could win, Guimard devised a more gradual and logical route to winning the Tour at Hinault's first attempt. He picked and chose his victories, right from the start.

Hinault was also lucky with his timing in 1978, because the field looked comparatively weak. Defending champion Bernard Thévenet was riding poorly, and Merckx, also a shadow of his former self, had retired. Zoetemelk was strong, but he'd not managed to shift the perception that he wasn't aggressive enough to win the Tour. In a race with two very long time trials, Zoetemelk was unlikely to gain enough time in the mountains to contend with Hinault. Apart from the Dutchman, Hinault's main competition was Michel Pollentier, a wizened-looking Belgian with a comb-over and a riding style and general comportment that made his clothes and bike look one size too big for him, and Jos Bruyère, a former *domestique* of Eddy Merckx who got into a soft break in the first week and gained three minutes, then finished runner-up to Hinault in the long time trial through the vineyards of Bordeaux, giving him a head start that he spent the rest of the race killing himself to maintain.

But there was an air of inevitability about Hinault winning, and he'd already won his debut Grand Tour, the Vuelta a España, that spring. He comfortably won in the Bordeaux time trial, then finished second in the main Pyrenean stage to Pla d'Adet. At this point, roughly the halfway point of the Tour, Bruyère led Hinault by just over a minute (already down from four minutes at the end of the first week), and Zoetemelk was almost another minute in arrears. Hinault then had a mid-Tour wobble, at the long time trial which finished at the summit of the Puy de Dôme, just two days after the riders' strike at Valence d'Agen.

According to Robin Magowan, who followed the 1978 Tour

for his book *Tour de France*, Hinault took quite a battering in the press for having been one of the ringleaders of the strike. Magowan speculated that the pressure was getting to Hinault at this point in the race: 'His off-day may be a matter of fatigue and loss of confidence induced by the shellacking he has taken at the hands of the press.' Instead of taking the yellow jersey, Hinault was beaten into fourth by Zoetemelk, Pollentier and even Bruyère – the Belgian rider defended his yellow jersey, only now it was Zoetemelk lurking a minute behind, with Hinault back to two minutes in arrears.

At Alpe d'Huez, Pollentier entered cycling infamy by winning the stage, taking the yellow jersey, then failing to produce a sample at doping control in tragicomedic circumstances. He'd engineered a Heath Robinson contraption involving a bulb of urine under his armpit, to be delivered through a tube, but was caught red-handed and, one presumes, red-faced, then summarily ejected from the race the same evening.

And still, Hinault was not in yellow. Zoetemelk inherited the race lead, but the Breton was now only 14 seconds behind. With third-placed Hennie Kuiper over five minutes behind, Hinault went into full defensive mode, finishing with Zoetemelk in Morzine and Lausanne, knowing that Zoetemelk had little chance of defending his slim lead in the 72-kilometre Nancy time trial. Hinault duly won the time trial, with Zoetemelk crushed, four minutes behind. With only two days to the end of the race, Hinault had played a blinder. It hadn't been particularly entertaining, save for the brief sideshow at Alpe d'Huez. Nor had it been that obvious how dominant Hinault actually was – Zoetemelk finished 3-56 behind, and only two more riders, Joaquim Agostinho and Bruyère, were within 12 minutes of the winner.

A year later, Hinault went into a Tour that could have been designed for him, so well did it suit his strengths. It started in the Pyrenees. Stage one crossed the Col de Menté and Col du Portillon. Stage two was a long time trial finishing at the top of the Superbagnères climb, which is one of the hardest ascents in the Pyrenees. This was followed by a multiple mountain stage over the Col de Peyresourde, Col d'Aspin and Col du Soulor. It was the hardest ever start to a Tour de France. After three days in the mountains, two team time trials, each around 90 kilometres long, sandwiched a series of flat stages up the west of France from the Pyrenees to the English Channel.

Hinault was rampant – his results for the opening stages of the race were: fourth, fifth, first, first, fifth (in the team time trial), fifth, second. After the second team time trial, where Renault were second, Hinault led Zoetemelk by a surprisingly narrow margin of 1-18, but only two more riders were within four minutes, and only another four within six minutes.

But it almost all went wrong on stage nine, which crossed the cobbles of northern France and finished in Roubaix. The day went disastrously for Hinault – he punctured mid-stage, just at the point where Zoetemelk was attacking with a group of general classification contenders, including Pollentier, Johan van der Velde and Dietrich Thurau, all stung by their time losses in the first week. Zoetemelk didn't hang back, and Hinault had to chase for 100 kilometres. *Cycling Weekly* described the effect of the cobbles on his pursuit: 'Now the *pavé* was coming more regularly, bone-shattering, morale-breaking, great cottage loaves that juddered and jarred, thin ribbons threading their dusty way through ripening corn fields, every now and then a deep pot hole to catch the unwary.'

Hinault had been caught out, and another puncture at Hem, with 10 kilometres to go, could have cost him the Tour. He rode into the Roubaix velodrome to boos from the crowd and reportedly in tears, 3-45 behind the stage winner Ludo Delcroix, and 3-26 behind Zoetemelk. The Dutchman now led the Tour, two minutes ahead of Hinault.

The Breton's usual reaction to being attacked was to attack right back, whether his adversary was stronger or weaker than him. He could have waited six days, for the Avoriaz time trial, but he saw the intervening five stages as opportunities to jab and jab at his opponents, as well as give vent to his anger at what had happened. He described his reaction in the cycling training book he wrote with Claude Genzling, *Road Racing, Technique and Training*: 'I had found myself virtually alone on the cobbled section after a flat, behind five strong riders who were pacing each other ahead of me. In the following days we were at each other's throats. The day before the Avoriaz time trial my whole team and I gave them an unbearable day. There were five intermediate sprints for time bonuses and I fought for each one of them. It was sheer hell for the others.' Modesty doesn't temper the conclusion Hinault professes to have drawn from the 1979 Tour: 'I must confess I was in really super shape that year.'

Hinault nipped 36 seconds out of Zoetemelk's lead in a mid-distance time trial in Brussels. Then three seconds on the summit finish at Ballon d'Alsace. In the Évian stage, on the eve of the Avoriaz time trial, he gained a minute in time bonuses, while Zoetemelk picked up only 20 seconds. The general classification on the eve of the time trial was: Zoetemelk in the yellow jersey, Hinault 49 seconds behind (down from 2-08 after the Roubaix stage) and Kuiper in third, 7-48 behind. Then, at the time trial, Hinault put over two and a half minutes into Zoetemelk. He was dominating the Tour with insouciant ease.

This was probably the high water mark of Hinault's popularity, until he reinvented himself as an attacking underdog in the last three years of his career. He was still a relative novelty, so the public were excited at his wins, without being jaded by his tactical predictability and the smothering effect his strength had on races. Ex-Tour speaker Daniel Mangeas thinks Hinault as a winner was popular, but that this popularity came with a qualification. 'The public liked Hinault for his force of character,' he says. 'They never imagined themselves doing what he did, but admired what he could achieve, whereas they identified more easily with someone like Thévenet.'

In an article entitled 'French Cycling Heroes of the Tour: Winners and Losers', however, Hugh Dauncey argues that the French public didn't have much choice, although Hinault had several attributes which made him accessible to fans. 'Hinault in the early 1980s was the only champion present in the French market, and could therefore capitalize on his "scarcity" both in terms of financial reward and in terms of his media image,' wrote Dauncey. 'Hinault appealed to the French cycling public because of his origins, because of his behaviour in racing both ethically and athletically, and because of his resourceful and charismatic personality. Hinault came from modest origins in Brittany, thus fulfilling the first requirement for true French champions, namely that they are "popular" (that is, working-class men-of-the-people, and generally rural). Although from a rural and agricultural area, Hinault was not from an agricultural family, since his father was a railway employee. Thus he appeared as someone with whom both rural/agricultural and urban/industrial France could proudly identify.'

Who knows how popular Hinault would have been if he'd attacked more in the first half of his career, or been beaten more often?

After Avoriaz, the 1979 Tour didn't get any easier – there was a summit finish at Les Menuires, then two consecutive days finishing at Alpe d'Huez. This might look today like a piece of sadistic route planning by the Tour organizers, but it was actually supposed to be even harder. Following the Les Menuires stage, the original Tour route had the riders crossing the Col de la Madeleine, Col du Télégraphe, Col du Galibier, Col d'Izoard before a summit finish on the Col de Vars. Then the next day the race would cross the Col du Lautaret to finish at Alpe d'Huez. But three weeks before the Tour, a dispute between the mayor of Vars and a real-estate developer who'd offered accommodation to the teams and Tour entourage meant the Vars finish fell through. The organizers swiftly concocted a plan B – two finishes at Alpe d'Huez, with the Izoard and Vars cut out of the route.

Not that it made much difference to Hinault – on the second day at the Alpe, he allowed Zoetemelk to sneak off and gain the best part of a minute, but took it all back, and more, in the final time trial of the race, to lead by three minutes (this would later expand to 13 minutes as Zoetemelk was penalized 10 minutes for a positive doping test). Third-placed Agostinho was an incredible 24 minutes in arrears. Hinault won the penultimate stage of the race in a bunch sprint. Then he broke away with Zoetemelk on the final stage into Paris, and won the stage in a two-up sprint, two minutes clear of the peloton. Only Merckx had dominated any Tour in the same way Hinault did in 1979: the Frenchman won seven stages, the yellow jersey and the green jersey; he was second in the mountains classification; his team-mate Jean-René Bernaudeau won the white jersey; and Renault won the team classification.

Sometimes you wish that Hinault could have enjoyed his wins a bit more. He professed to enjoy racing, but seems incapable of looking backwards, either to enjoy a spot of pleasant nostalgia or celebrate his achievements, or to examine mistakes and indulge regrets. Tellingly, in *Memories of the Peloton*, he spent one single paragraph on stages one to 19 of the 1978 Tour, two whole pages on the events of Valence-d'Agen, and barely a page on winning the final time trial and the yellow jersey. Incredibly, the 1979 Tour, his peak as a rider, doesn't even merit a mention. The book skips from the 1979 Flèche Wallonne to the 1980 Liège–Bastogne–Liège.

But that's the point about *Memories of the Peloton* and about Hinault as a person. His primary motivation in life was to settle scores and impose himself on people – winning bike races was just the method he happened to use. He didn't seem to care what people thought of him at all, except when he could use it as fuel for his competitive fire. Yet he possessed a large ego. When he pulled out of the 1980 Tour de France with a knee injury, he decided his revenge would take place at the world championships later that year. The winner of the rainbow jersey, he wrote in *Memories of the Peloton*, 'would be a French rider whose honour had been sullied time and time again in the newspaper columns'. His comeback win there was as defining as any of his Tour wins, and you get the impression that he enjoyed it all the more for proving his critics, real or imagined, wrong. 'A few weeks earlier, nobody had given a fig for my chances. I'd been insulted, jeered during criteriums, buried alive. I was reborn,' he said.

With two more straightforward Tour wins in 1981 and 1982, Hinault was on the verge of equalling Anquetil's and Merckx's record of five Tour wins, with four years of his career still to run – he'd promised to end his career on his 32nd birthday, and as he'd said on presenting his mother with the winner's bouquet after his first race, promises are made to be kept. There was no sign that he was falling away from his peak. But the strained knee that saw him miss the defence of his title in 1983 was a good metaphor for the challenge he was now facing in holding on to his position as the world's best Tour rider. Hinault's team-mate Laurent Fignon won the 1983 Tour at his first attempt (helped in part by Pascal Simon having to pull out of the race with a broken shoulder sustained in a crash while looking like the strongest rider and wearing the yellow jersey). What's more, in Hinault's absence, a younger generation of riders was coming through, including Fignon, Greg LeMond, Stephen Roche and Phil Anderson – all attacking, ambitious riders, none of whom came from cycling's traditional feeder system of the European working class.

But Hinault responded to the challenge by reinventing himself. First, he left the Renault team – with Fignon in the ascendancy, and his relationship with Guimard having cooled considerably, he could do without an intra-team struggle for supremacy. Daniel Mangeas recalls travelling to a race in a car with Hinault and Fignon in 1982, and he says he could already see that the Renault team would soon not be big enough for both of them: 'Fignon was a city boy and Hinault was the rural boy, but it wasn't that they were different – I could just see already that they couldn't be on the same team. Both wanted to win. I sensed from the conversation that it would be impossible for them to work together.'

Hinault joined a new team being set up by the controversial and publicity-hungry French businessman Bernard Tapie to advertise his chain of health-food shops, La Vie Claire. It was a self-consciously modern team, perhaps the first truly modern bike team, in terms of the salaries Tapie was paying, and in the scientific approach of the team manager Paul Köchli. Their team kit was based on the art of Piet Mondrian – bright primary colours arranged in modernist blocks, although one of their early designs was reportedly for an all-black kit, presaging Team Sky by a quarter of a century.

Hinault was known for being a cunning, clever rider; Guimard describes him as having extremely instinctive intelligence. My own impression was that Hinault was very clever – on quite a narrow bandwidth. He wasn't academic-smart, but he under-stood people and he knew exactly how to assert himself to maximum advantage. However, when he went up against a clearly stronger Fignon in the 1984 Tour, any tactical nuance he might have displayed in the defensive Tours of 1978 to 1982 was lost. He simply didn't know what to do, so he attacked, even though it hurt his own chances, and made Fignon look even better in the process. When his primary weapon – being the strongest rider in the race – was no longer available to him, he had no plan B.

But in his three seasons at La Vie Claire, he'd shown a more profound understanding of the shifting currents of cycling than his riding might have suggested. He embraced Köchli's new training methods, and was an early adopter of Look's new clipless pedals, which became ubiquitous by the 1990s. The mid-1980s were a time of great change in professional cycling in terms of the technology and tactics, and though Hinault's career and background were rooted in tradition, he'd been smart enough to manoeuvre himself into the sport's vanguard in his final years. He was also clever enough to see that up-and-coming rider LeMond was signed to his team to bolster his challenge in the 1985 Tour and, by taking the initiative early in the Tour, he kept the American's ambitions perfectly curtailed for that season at least.

Despite 1984, 1985 and 1986 being atypical of Hinault's history in the Tour, it's those three years he tends to be remembered for, rather than the previous six. In his last two Tours he knew full well that the greatest threat was within his team, and took advantage of LeMond's more passive racing style to establish himself as the dominant rider in both years.

Hinault won five Tours, and there was something elemental and impressive about both his physical abilities and the need he had to win. But it was the nature of his defeats that were more revealing of his character: 1984 revealed how one-dimensional his tactics could be when he wasn't the strongest rider, but his refusal to give in, to fight when the battle was lost, kept the race interesting, where his own rivals in the late 1970s and early 1980s had been far less willing to give it a go. But 1986, when he pushed LeMond relentlessly, both physically and psychologically, showed that in the end Hinault was not the master of his own ambition. Life cannot always be easy when it's a constant series of battles, and if any rider looked unprepared for the real world, it was Bernard Hinault on his 32nd birthday.

But then he settled into a happy second life – what he termed *la vie active* (the working life) – as a farmer and a ubiquitous and good-natured presence at the Tour de France in his role of presentation manager. The Badger wasn't quite tamed, but seemed happy in his cage.

4

Joop Zoetemelk
1980

They all tried to duel with Eddy. He killed them. I was smarter.
I knew exactly how far my possibilities reached.

Joop Zoetemelk

They used to tell a joke about Joop Zoetemelk. Why did he keep his milky complexion right through to the finish of the Tour de France? Because he spent the whole race riding in Eddy Merckx's shadow.

Poor Joop. Raymond Poulidor came second in the Tour and was loved for it, while Zoetemelk was pilloried. The Frenchman might have got first dibs on the nickname 'the Eternal Second' but Zoetemelk was runner-up in the Tour more often than Poulidor – six times, to Poulidor's three. Typical Poulidor – he was even second-best at being the second-best. Poulidor's long career saw his Tour ambitions thwarted by five-time winner Jacques Anquetil, then by five-time winner Eddy Merckx. Zoetemelk had it even worse. The first years of his career more or less coincided with the best years of Merckx, then his ambitions bumped up against those of Bernard Hinault, who also won five Tours. Zoetemelk even raced against the next

52

five-time winner, Miguel Indurain, in three Tours in the mid-1980s, when Zoetemelk was past his best, and Indurain well before his. It's ironic, or perhaps telling, that Poulidor and Zoetemelk actually spent four seasons riding together for the same team, Gan–Mercier (then Miko–Mercier) between 1974 and 1977.

In a different era, with the physical gifts he had, Zoetemelk might have been a multiple Tour champion. Instead, the perception is that he was damned lucky to even win one, in 1980. The experts agreed, if Hinault hadn't pulled out that year with an injured knee, Zoetemelk would have been second again, no question. Zoetemelk even had a disparaging nickname, 'the Wheelsucker'.

Nobody likes a wheelsucker, whether it's in a fourth-category race or the Tour de France. The unwritten constitution of cycling dictates that a certain amount of work must be shared between rivals, because of the inherent unfairness built into the sport by the laws of physics. Depending on the speed, and the direction and strength of the wind, cyclists who ride behind another cyclist save a significant amount of energy. Some riders, through a kind of vegetable obstinacy, naïvety, machismo or a sense of fairness (these last riders don't get very far) find themselves taken advantage of by wheelsuckers again and again. There's only one thing worse than a wheelsucker, and that's a wheelsucker who wins.

But isn't wheelsucking the point of road cycling? Professional cyclists win races through selfishness, not generosity. Zoetemelk happened to be criticized for it, but anybody who has done anything in cycling has wheelsucked. Sprinters are wheelsuckers; Tour de France winners are wheelsuckers. The point is not to do it too obviously or obnoxiously.

Paradoxically, Zoetemelk probably wouldn't have had such a hard time from the cycling public if he'd done the same amount of sitting in, but won more races. What Zoetemelk was actually being criticized for was a *lack of ambition*. Cycling fans are very forgiving of defeat – there's even a tradition of celebrating the last-placed finisher in the Tour de France, the *lanterne rouge,* which is not at all the equivalent of rugby's wooden spoon. There's a recognition, absent in most other sports, of the level of effort involved in just getting around a bike race, and also of the team dynamic that relies on the willing sacrifice of foot soldiers. But there's one proviso in this – it's fine to lose, but only if you've tried to win. That partly explains the difference in the public reaction to Poulidor and Zoetemelk. Poulidor's career might have been a tactical disaster area, but at least he tried. (It's also important to note the difference in their personalities: Poulidor was friendly, smiley and sociable; Zoetemelk was quiet, solitary and taciturn.)

Zoetemelk saw things differently. He turned professional in 1970, when Eddy Merckx was already dominating the sport. Merckx was stronger than Zoetemelk – stronger than everybody, in fact – so Zoetemelk accepted that the best he was going to do in most races was finish second to the Belgian. He had no interest in coming second spectacularly, or risking second place in order to possibly get first when the odds of success were vanishingly small. Zoetemelk looked at the situation pragmatically. In the first half of the 1970s, Merckx was the strongest, Zoetemelk the second-strongest, so second was the best he could do. In the late 1970s, he made much the same calculation with regard to Hinault.

It's easy, from the perspective of our self-appointed roles as armchair team managers, to forget that Merckx was more or less unbeatable at the height of his career. 'No one could follow Merckx,' says Zoetemelk's Gan–Mercier teammate Barry Hoban. 'Anyone who could was doing pretty well. It wasn't a question of sitting on Merckx's wheel and being stronger. Joop was hanging on for grim death.'

'I was six times second, and second is already pretty good,' Zoetemelk says. 'Merckx was above my level. Then I fell on Bernard Hinault, who had the same level as Merckx.'

The Dutchman's reputation as a runner-up obscures the fact that his Tour de France record was extraordinary. He started and finished 16 Tours, a record which still officially stands (Jens Voigt, Stuart O'Grady and George Hincapie all started 17 Tours, but none completed them all; O'Grady finished 15 and Voigt 14; Hincapie did finish 16 but three were later annulled for doping offences). Zoetemelk took part in every Tour between 1970 and 1986 except 1974, when he was injured. He finished in the top five in 11 of his first 12 Tours (the only blemish was his eighth place in 1977, when he was penalized 10 minutes for a positive doping test). He also won the Vuelta a España, Paris–Nice three times, Paris–Tours twice, Tirreno–Adriatico and the Tour of Romandy. In 1985, when he was 38, he won the world championships road race, and in 1987, at 40, he won the Amstel Gold race. Not bad for a wheelsucker.

It is tempting to draw a straight line from Zoetemelk's humble background and upbringing, through his undemonstrative personality, all the way to the apparent lack of ambition in his racing career. The son of a pig farmer, he was brought up in rural Holland near the town of Leiden, which lies a few kilometres inland from the North Sea coast between Rotterdam and Amsterdam. Leiden is where the 1978 Tour de France started (Zoetemelk's final position: second). The sound of his childhood was the percussive thump of the windmills powering the drainage pumps. He described the area and its people in an interview with *Cycle Sport* magazine: 'The part of Holland I grew up in is made up of polders, drained marshes that men turned into fields so that they could farm them. They had a constant battle and that shaped the people there; it made them resolute, obstinate. For the early farmers it was a constant battle with water – their land was flooded regularly. Up there, nothing was given. People had to persevere.'

You can see why Zoetemelk's attitude to his career is one of contentment to have been there, up in second place, rather than regret over what he didn't win. Other cyclists, even when they include Eddy Merckx, are still far less implacable and hostile opponents than the ever-encroaching sea.

Zoetemelk isn't exactly a people person, and he tells me he is happiest when he's out walking in the forest on his own, but it's a mistake to think that he's antisocial. I was in a hotel lobby at the Tour du Haut Var a few years ago, and Zoetemelk was sitting there in an armchair, with Bernard Hinault next to him, both waiting to go out to dinner. Neither spoke to one another, but neither looked uncomfortable in the silence. They looked like old friends who knew each other too well to need to indulge in small talk. 'I'm a bit solitary,' Zoetemelk says. 'I don't need lots of people around me. In the Tour, I never minded rooming alone.'

In some ways remoteness of character can be an asset for an endurance athlete. The long hours of training are easier to bear if you wouldn't rather be socializing with friends. On the other hand, it meant that Zoetemelk wasn't a natural team leader.

'I used to control the race for him,' says Barry Hoban. 'He didn't do it, so I was captain on the road for him. A rider like that needs a ganger. It was the same with Jacques Anquetil, who had Jean Stablinski ride for him, because Anquetil would never shout at anybody. Zoetemelk wouldn't either, but I would.'

Zoetemelk's career could have been a lot better, however. Not because of his riding style and personality, although Hoban used to joke to Joop's late wife Françoise, who was a lot more extrovert than her husband, that if Zoetemelk had her character, he'd have won a lot more big races.

Zoetemelk was a year younger than Merckx, but while the

Belgian turned professional at 19, in 1965, Zoetemelk didn't do so until 1970, when he was 23. Merckx had decided he wanted to be a professional cyclist as a child, but Zoetemelk discovered the sport later, starting out as a speed skater, training on a bike during the summer months, and discovering that he had an aptitude for it. He won an Olympic gold medal in 1968, in the team time trial, then easily won the Tour de l'Avenir, the amateur version of the Tour de France, in 1969. Incredibly, he came second in the Tour de France as a new professional, in 1970, although he was almost 13 minutes behind the winner, Merckx. No new professional has repeated or bettered that achievement since – riders like Hinault and Fignon have won the Tour at their first attempt, but not as first-year professionals. The following year, Zoetemelk was second again, then fifth in 1972, and fourth in 1973. Along the way, he picked up a sixth place in the Vuelta and third places in Paris–Nice and the Critérium du Dauphiné Libéré. Placing highly and not winning seemed to be becoming a habit.

Then came 1974. Zoetemelk thrashed Merckx at Paris–Nice, dropping him on the Mont Faron stage, then winning the Col d'Èze time trial. Two weeks later, he beat Merckx again in the mountainous Catalan Week race. Hoban says that Zoetemelk was in a class of his own in that event. Merckx had been suffering from ill-health that spring, but the Belgian even admitted himself that his beatings at the hands of Zoetemelk made him fear that his career was about to start on a downward trajectory.

'Joop annihilated Merckx on the final stage to Andorra,' Hoban recalls. 'They were together, side by side. Merckx geared down, Joop changed up a gear and jumped him, and Eddy couldn't move. He left him for dead.'

'That Zoetemelk,' Hoban adds, 'never really came back again.'

On the opening stage of the Midi Libre, to Valras-Plage, the bunch approached the finish in a long, very fast-moving line, pinned by a strong cross-tailwind to the right-hand side of the road, in hot pursuit of a trio of late escapees. Only the few riders at the front would have seen the car, which belonged to a British tourist, parked in the road, right in the path of the peloton, and they tacked round it, probably flicking their elbows and shouting the warning. But at that speed, the bunch is moving forwards faster than any communication can move in the other direction, and about a dozen riders piled into the car. Zoetemelk was in the crumple zone at the front of the bunch and he was knocked unconscious.

He pulled out of the race, complaining of a bad headache, and travelled home after a doctor at the local hospital found nothing untoward in his X-rays. When he got home, the headaches got worse, he could neither eat nor sleep and he started losing weight, going from an already spare 63 kilogrammes down to 53 in 10 days. He was rushed back to hospital, where he was diagnosed with a double skull fracture and meningitis. He didn't race again until 1975, and even then he was suffering from severe anaemia. The illness and recovery killed his sense of taste and smell – to the extent that Hoban once found him after a race knocking back glasses of white wine, which he'd mistaken for water.

Zoetemelk reckoned he was never the same again after the crash. He was still strong enough to win Paris–Nice for a second time in 1975, and he was second behind Lucien Van Impe in the 1976 Tour de France. But when Hinault came along and started dominating the race like Merckx had, it looked like bad luck had robbed Zoetemelk of his chance at winning the yellow jersey.

Maybe Zoetemelk's run of near misses at the Tour deceived us. Second is only one place from first, but he habitually conceded huge time gaps to the winner. He never got closer than nine minutes to Merckx. In 1973, when Luis Ocaña won, Zoetemelk was 26 minutes down, in fourth place. He got closer to Van Impe and Hinault, in the late 1970s – Van Impe beat him by four minutes in 1976, and Hinault put just over three minutes into him in both 1978 and 1979.

And considering how straightforward and comprehensive most of his defeats were, it's ironic that when he did win the Tour, in 1980, it was almost at a canter. Little went wrong for him after a shaky start, and he confidently saw off his rivals, one at a time. It might just have been his turn. That said, probably the most important factor in his Tour victory was his switch to the Dutch TI–Raleigh team, managed by Peter Post. Post was an ex-rider with an autocratic streak, and he brought a level of organization and philosophy of team ethos to cycling that mirrored the Total Football method of the Dutch football team in the 1970s.

For most of his career, Zoetemelk rode for French teams, and he'd settled in France, with a French wife. Hoban points out that there was a cultural difference between French teams and the more organized north-European squads. To some extent, you could make the same generalization even now. 'French teams always had two or three leaders in the team. That means more equations, and the spreading of loyalties meant they often missed out on the big prize,' he says. 'When it came to the Tour, Peter Post said, "We've got Joop, and he is our one plan." The year he won, he had a very good team behind him.'

Zoetemelk was clear about his reasons for going to TI–Raleigh, and it had little to do with sentiment: 'There were more team time trials in those days, and Post's teams were always good at them. Post was a strong leader, not a friend. But I rode well with him.'

There were two team time trials in the 1980 Tour – one on the afternoon of the second day, and one on stage seven, followed the same day by another flat stage. TI–Raleigh duly won both – they beat race favourite Hinault's Renault team by 44 seconds in the 45.8-kilometre stage in Frankfurt, then beat Peugeot into second on a 65-kilometre run to Beauvais by 37 seconds. Renault were fourth, 51 seconds behind.

Despite a theoretical 95-second beating of Renault over the two stages, the rules for the team time trial that year awarded time bonuses for position, rather than simply adding time. To make things more complicated, the bonuses were different for each of the two team time trial stages. In the first, TI–Raleigh received a 2-15 bonus, subtracted from each of their riders' times, while second-placed Renault received 1-50. In the second, TI–Raleigh's bonus was 3-15, while Renault got 1-40 for their fourth place. Ironically, TI–Raleigh had only beaten Renault by 51 seconds in real time, but the bonuses meant the French team conceded much more. Zoetemelk took two minutes on Hinault just in the team time trial bonuses. In comparison, eventual runner-up Hennie Kuiper conceded 1-25.

TI–Raleigh's strength in the team time trial had put Zoetemelk in a strong position in the first week, which was just as well, because Hinault, during this period, was rampant. The Frenchman had won the prologue (putting 27 seconds into Zoetemelk), then beaten Zoetemelk into second place in the time trial on the Spa motor-racing circuit, by 1-16 over 33 kilometres. On the stage to Lille, which covered several cobbled sections of road, he'd escaped with Kuiper and Belgian rider Ludo Delcroix and gained 2-11 on Zoetemelk. Going into the long time trial in Laplume, Hinault was third overall, but led Zoetemelk by two minutes. Kuiper was 24 seconds behind Zoetemelk. The team time trials had kept Zoetemelk in a comparatively strong position – as a comparison his old Miko–Mercier team would have conceded an extra 90 seconds to Hinault and 2-05 to Kuiper.

On the surface, it looked like 1980 was shaping up much like 1978 and 1979 – Hinault first, Zoetemelk second, the rest nowhere. But in the Laplume time trial, over 51 kilometres, the winner was Zoetemelk. Hinault was in fifth, 1-39 down. Hinault went into the yellow jersey, but his buffer over Zoetemelk was only 21 seconds.

'I wasn't good in the first part of the 1980 Tour,' says Zoetemelk. 'I'd suffered gastroenteritis at the end of the Tour of Switzerland and it meant I started the Tour in bad shape. The cobbles stage was difficult, and Hinault was in good form. But I started to get better, and when I beat Hinault in the time trial I started to get more confident.'

Zoetemelk's steady improvement was merely the backdrop to a much bigger story, however. As the race approached the Pyrenees, it became clear there was something up with Hinault's knee.

Hinault's knee received the same kind of coverage – one-third forensic science, one-third soap opera, one third obituary – from the French press as David Beckham's second metatarsal did in the English media in the run-up to the 2002 World Cup. The weather had been terrible over the first week, and Hinault had overreached himself in the cobbled stage, developing tendonitis. He'd been nursed round the second team time trial, and was obviously below par in Laplume. Faced with the looming Pyrenees, Hinault pulled out of the race and temporarily disappeared, leading to a comedic search for him by the press before he was eventually tracked down to his teammate Hubert Arbès's house near Lourdes. Hinault's manager Cyrille Guimard was left to explain to reporters why the defending champion couldn't continue. There were no press conferences in those days – Guimard hosted the media in a café, a smouldering Gitane burning down between his fingers providing an appropriate metaphor for Hinault's Tour hopes.

With Hinault out, Zoetemelk suddenly looked like a Tour winner. Post's original plan had been for Zoetemelk to limit his deficit in the opening two weeks, then attack through the one Pyrenean stage and the three Alpine stages, which came bunched together deep in the last week. Instead, Zoetemelk entered the Pyrenees in the race lead and, of the realistic challengers, only Kuiper was within five minutes of him. Zoetemelk switched to a more defensive plan. He contained Kuiper in the Pyrenees and the first Alpine stage, then spent the next two days adding another four minutes to his lead. A win in the final time trial, in St-Étienne, gave him the overall win by almost seven minutes. It was a glimpse of how things might have been if his crash in 1974 hadn't had such a catastrophic effect on his form and health.

1980 was seen as a lucky win but, as Zoetemelk himself pointed out, one of the prerequisites for winning the race was enduring the full three weeks: 'I stood up to the race and survived, and Hinault's knee didn't.'

Could Zoetemelk have won more Tours? The 1974 crash made it a difficult prospect. But apart from that, Zoetemelk seemed to be in his comfort zone in the races won by Merckx and Hinault. Whatever aspect of their personalities made Merckx and Hinault need to dominate bike races wasn't present in Zoetemelk. Thévenet once said of Zoetemelk, 'He didn't care if he won by 20 minutes or one second.' Zoetemelk had watched riders like Luis Ocaña and Bernard Thévenet go head-to-head with Merckx – each came away with at least a Tour win, but their careers were comparatively short. Zoetemelk put his career longevity down to not going beyond himself in trying to beat Merckx, something he considered unrealistic.

But even when Merckx and Hinault weren't a factor, Zoetemelk still found it difficult to know what to do to win the Tour. In 1976, he didn't consider Van Impe a threat and it cost him the race. In 1977, he conceded time early, but rode negatively behind Thévenet. In the end, it seemed like he didn't know what to do when there was a really strong race leader, nor when there wasn't. The difference in 1980 was that Hinault was around for just enough of the Tour to impose order on it – but on that occasion Zoetemelk was the beneficiary, not the victim.

5

Laurent Fignon
1983, 1984

All Gaul is divided into three parts concerning Laurent Fignon: those who don't like him, those who don't like him but are willing to overlook their feelings as long as he wins, and those who don't like him but are willing to overlook their feelings as long as he loses. The third group is by far the largest.

Sam Abt, *Tour de France, Three Weeks to Glory*

I can't look for too long at photographs of the 1989 Tour de France podium. They're portraits of awkward misery, frozen moments of sporting humiliation, painted in incongruous primary colours, the bright reds, yellows and blues of the riders' sponsors. The pictures are intrusions into Laurent Fignon's private shock at having lost the race in the most mortifying fashion, on the final day of the race, in his home city, by the narrowest margin ever, in the year of the French republic's bicentenary. Maybe somebody else has suffered a more ignominious defeat in cycling, but I doubt it.

In the middle of all the pictures is Greg LeMond, who is justifiably ecstatic at having just won the race by eight seconds in a final-day turnaround that still ranks as one of cycling's greatest ever upsets. On his left, Pedro Delgado is also wearing a wide grin. Typical Pedro, he's an easy-going guy, good company, and pretty happy to be there – he's had a great Tour, apart from a poor opening weekend. On LeMond's right: Fignon.

If you're into sporting rarities, there's a lot to like about these photographs. For the only time in cycling history, the Tour de France podium consisted of the Tour winner (obviously), the Giro d'Italia winner (Fignon) and the Vuelta a España winner (Delgado) from that year. It's also the only time in cycling history that three previous winners of the Tour had all stood on the same final podium together. There have been more occasions – 10 in all, the most recent being 2012 – that the top three riders would be current or future winners, but 1989 represents the greatest clash of champions in the race's history.

Fignon had started the final day in the yellow jersey, 50 seconds clear of LeMond. For the first time since 1971 the race had finished with a time trial, which made Fignon's defeat more immediate, and totally irreversible. It was the first time since 1968, and only the fourth time in Tour history, that a rider had lost the race lead on the final day. The size of the gap between LeMond and Fignon, eight seconds, remains the narrowest margin between first and second in the Tour. But who cares about stats, in a situation like this? The story is the thing. It's only sport, but it's hard to imagine just how bad Laurent Fignon felt on that podium. Imagine the confused sense of self-consciousness he must have felt with every movement, the stabbing jolt of adrenalin in his chest, the jelly weakness of his legs, the knowledge that if he could just do the day over again, there's no way he'd lose the yellow jersey.

There's one picture in particular, taken by the Italian photographer Roberto Bettini, which is unbearable. It's understandable that Fignon looks utterly miserable in most of the pictures, but in this one, he's attempting to smile. Next to LeMond and Delgado's natural, infectious and beaming grins, Fignon's smile looks desolate. Even behind his wire-framed glasses you can see that his eyes are wet. Where else can his sadness escape, except through his eyes? Even though his glasses are his last defence against the world, I feel like I can see uncomfortably deep into Fignon's soul in this picture. No cyclist deserves to have his dignity stripped in such a public way, not even Laurent Fignon.

Fignon was never hugely popular when he was racing. He won the *Prix Citron*, the award given by journalists and photographers to the rider they consider to have been the least co-operative with the media over the course of the Tour, in 1989. The bright yellow of the lemon with which he was presented was a chromatic reminder of the jersey he'd lost on the final day, although Fignon did manage to see the funny side. 'At least I won something,' he said. In previous Tours, Fignon had scowled, snarled and sworn at the intrusive journalists, saving his deepest ire for the photographers. When they buzzed around him like wasps around a jam pot as he struggled through the 1988 Tour, their flashes stinging his eyes and pride, he'd thrown his water bottle at them. It was a great picture.

Fignon was too good to be likeable in 1984, the year he'd humiliated Bernard Hinault in the Tour by beating him easily. Then, when he was struggling with injuries and poor form between 1985 and 1988, he was too dislikeable to be likeable. Fame, and the pressure of professional cycling, were bad for him in some ways. Greg LeMond once said of Fignon, 'He's easier to like when he's not winning.'

He was chronically shy when he was young, and although he says in his autobiography, *We Were Young and Carefree*, that he overcame this as he left adolescence, it followed him into his adult life, manifesting itself as a protective carapace of prickliness and defensiveness. He was stereotyped as proud and haughty, a typical city boy, even though the reality was that he grew up in the countryside just outside Paris, rather than in the city itself. He had no humility, compared to far more popular riders, country boys like Bernard Thévenet and Raymond Poulidor. It can't have helped that Fignon was instantly successful as a cyclist – he won the Tour in his second season, at his first attempt, in 1983. Maybe the early wins gave him a sense of entitlement which made his reaction to disappointment in subsequent years much like that of a spoiled child whose favourite toy has been taken away.

Fignon looked easy to understand on the surface, but a lot of people got him wrong. *We Were Young and Carefree*, which was published in 2009, surprised the cycling world. It exudes *joie de vivre*, energy, emotional balance and the wisdom of hindsight. The melancholy that springs from knowing that both Fignon and his best friend, Pascal Jules, his teammate from their first days as professionals, died young – Fignon in 2010 at 50, and Jules in 1987 at 26 – makes the book a poignant one.

I couldn't help liking Fignon when he was riding. When he won races, he looked ecstatic – I'm always suspicious of a rider who affects coolness when he or she wins. Fignon's riding style was exuberant – he liked to attack, with panache; he had both punch and flow – and his power emanated from his thighs, which looked a size too big compared to the rest of him. He simultaneously looked stronger than the cyclists who rode with class and grace, while riding with more class and grace than those who relied on power. But the main attraction was that he was so terminally uncool and freaky, with his wire-rimmed glasses, wispy hair and sweatband – he stood out a mile from his peers. His eyes were a watery blue, and there was a permanent shadow of stubble on his face, darker than the flaxen blond of his hair. When he wasn't sulking, Fignon's face defaulted to a cheerful, slightly cheeky expression – the corners of his mouth turned up, his eyebrows slightly angled, but he still had an air of melancholy.

The reason the French seemed to get so hung up on him – his refusal to tick their boxes – were the same reasons I found him so compelling. His nickname, which carried the slightest hint of anti-intellectual mockery, was '*Le Professeur*', but it was a distraction – they'd have found another nickname for him if only he hadn't worn glasses.

Is Laurent Fignon the double Tour winner or the Tour loser? His autobiography makes it clear that his self-perception was more the former than the latter. The opening lines of the book are a conversation, real or imagined, with a stranger: "'Ah, I remember you: you're the guy who lost the Tour de France by eight seconds!" "No, monsieur, I'm the guy who won the Tour twice.'"

He's both, though. Otherwise, why start the book with a chapter about 1989? The pretext is that he'd like to get it out of the way, so he can get on to the more interesting stories, but it's telling that apart from the section of the book which deals with Pascal Jules' death, the writing about 1989 is more immediate and passionate in its exploration of his defeat than it ever is about his victories.

It's hard to imagine, from the perspective of the twenty-first century, when there are fewer surprises in the Tour de France, how open the 1983 race was. Bernard Hinault had won four out of the last five Tours, and his margins of victory in 1981 and 1982 were 14 minutes and six minutes respectively. He looked untouchable. But there was no gradual tailing off of his powers in 1983, no up-and-coming riders realizing that he was vulnerable, in the same way that Merckx and Anquetil's runs of victories came to an end. Hinault strained his knee in winning the spring's Vuelta a España, and that was it, he was out of the race. His runners-up in '81 and '82, Lucien Van Impe and Joop Zoetemelk, were too old to really be considered outright favourites for 1983, while all the other possible contenders seemed to be too young. Fignon wasn't even included in the latter group – he was a second-year professional, 22 years old, although handicappers might have noticed the 15th place he achieved in the previous year's Giro d'Italia and the seventh place in the 1983 Vuelta, and seen the logical potential for improvement. In Hinault's absence, the Renault team had nominated Marc Madiot, not Fignon, as the leader.

Fignon didn't start the race particularly well. He contracted conjunctivitis in the first few days, and rode an early cobbled stage holding the handlebars in a panicked death-grip, which gave him painful blisters. Renault were seventh in the team time trial, which cost them 2-15 to Zoetemelk's winning Coop–Mercier team, and 1-30 to Peugeot, whose riders Pascal Simon, Phil Anderson, Robert Millar and Stephen Roche were all ambitious for the general classification. And Fignon only managed 16th in the long time trial in Châteaubriant. If Hinault had been riding, Fignon would probably have been four minutes down by this point. But the curious thing regarding that absence of a *patron*, somebody to dominate the race, was that not only was there no particular favourite, nobody strong enough to win, it was more the case that nobody knew *how* to win. Remember that even Hinault held back until the final week during his first Tour victory.

Fignon still looked no more like the eventual yellow jersey after the main Pyrenean stage to Bagnères-de-Luchon, which was won by Scotland's Millar. Peugeot's leader Pascal Simon had accidentally-on-purpose left his teammate, third-placed Anderson, behind when he'd suffered a mechanical, and while Fignon concentrated on losing as little time as possible in order to take the white jersey (best young rider), Simon had suddenly gained what looked like an unassailable lead. Before Bagnères-de-Luchon, the general classification had shown little coherence or shape. Afterwards, the race looked to be over. Simon had the yellow jersey; Fignon was second, four minutes behind.

But winning the Tour doesn't involve simply being the strongest in the race. You have to finish it, too. Simon's aura of invincibility lasted but one day, as he crashed and seriously injured his shoulder in the very next stage. Fignon's manager Cyrille Guimard counselled caution and advised his rider to spend the next few days gathering his forces. 'If this injury of his is as bad as they say, the *maillot jaune* will come to you sooner or later. Then there will be a lot of work to be done, so save yourself for the moment,' Guimard told Fignon.

An uneasy truce settled on the race while Simon battled through, the crack in his broken shoulder symbolizing his shattered hopes of making it to Paris in yellow. Even so, he held on to the lead for six more days, through the time trial up the Puy de Dôme. The result couldn't have suited Fignon better – as the race went into the Alps, he was in second, 40 seconds behind Simon. Simon packed on the stage to Alpe d'Huez, and Fignon rode defensively, while different rivals came at him through the Alps. Peter Winnen gained time on him at Alpe d'Huez and the Avoriaz time trial, but had been starting from a position several minutes down on Fignon. Pedro Delgado moved up into second after the Alpe, but subsequently got food poisoning and dropped out of contention. After three days in the Alps, Fignon had been challenged, but still emerged in first place, and with a long time trial in Dijon to come, his rivals had run out of road.

In Dijon, Fignon rode for the first time like a Tour winner, rather than somebody trying not to lose it, and won the stage.

While pundits and fans wondered out loud what would have happened if Hinault had been fit, or Simon hadn't crashed, or Delgado hadn't got ill, *L'Équipe*'s senior writer Pierre Chany had spotted a worthy winner in Dijon. 'The morning of the final time trial on Saturday, there was a caveat on the judgement to be made of a lad who'd admittedly been convincing through the race and whose limits are still unknown. He won the Tour, his first, just like Coppi in 1949, Koblet in 1951, Anquetil in 1957, Merckx in 1969, Hinault in 1978, and this company enhances his win, but he also evoked the less glorious winners who'd taken their Tour without recording a stage win . . . He was able to settle the issue in the authoritative style of a man functioning in perfect harmony of body and mind. Fignon made it clear that he was the best of all the contenders who were there and none of the famous non-starters could claim he might have been better.'

Others might have been less convinced, however. In 1984, Hinault was going to be back, and this time he was mad.

I'd always wanted to interview Fignon, and when I was working at *Cycle Sport* magazine I managed to get his number from somewhere or other. I used to call every now and again, but the conversation would inevitably be a short one. Interview requests were politely and apologetically rebuffed. It was only when I went to Paris to interview Jean-François Bernard, who did a bit of commentary work with Fignon from time to time, that I spotted an opening. Bernard told me that he enjoyed the occasional round of golf with Fignon, but that Fignon took it a lot more seriously than he did. The next time I phoned Fignon, it was to invite him to the UK to play a round. We'd sort the hotel, the meal and the green fees. In exchange, I'd get my interview. The only condition he made was that there was to be no talking about cycling during the golf.

Fignon was great company. The touchy, arrogant, over-sensitive double Tour winner/Tour loser seemed to have been left behind in the pages of old newspapers and magazines. He manfully struggled through a traditional British roast beef and well-done cabbage at Simpson's in the Strand, telling me, 'The meat is overdone, I prefer my steak *bleu*,' and no subjects were off limits. He had an infectious high-pitched giggle that seemed to be so much part of his speech pattern that I left it in my notes when I wrote up the interview. He invariably slipped into the present tense when reminiscing, which added immediacy to his stories. There were only brief glimpses of the Fignon I thought I knew on the golf course, when his game occasionally went to pieces, and he'd berate himself angrily, and swear. Then he'd be back to normal, almost immediately. I think that's what the media missed first time round. He was touchy, and prone to snapping – photographers and journalists got a rise out of him easily, whether it was deliberate or not. But it was that which tended to get reported, while his return to a more relaxed mood did not.

He'd also grudgingly accepted the notoriety he'd got from finishing second in the 1989 Tour, and came to regard the fact that he was never so popular as after that defeat with amusement. 'I'm a winner. I like competition, it's the only thing that interests me,' he said. 'When I trained I was never so strong, but in competition it was different. I stopped riding my bike because I wasn't able to win any more. Winning comes first. What does history remember? The winner, before everything. History remembers the winner and forgets the circumstances.'

But Laurent, I said, you will never be forgotten by cycling history, because—

'Because I lost a race,' he admitted. 'People remember the Tour of 1989 because it was a nice fight, a good scrap. It was an interesting Tour, as Tours go. Today, and it is with great regret that I say this, in France it is sometimes better to have lost than to have won. It is indicative of the French attitude to sport that I am remembered as the guy who lost the Tour de France by eight seconds.'

In *Something to Declare*, his collection of essays about France and French culture, the novelist Julian Barnes tells a story about the time he watched the French football team playing a World Cup qualifier against Bulgaria in 1993, in the company of two off-duty French waiters. As the game drifted towards a draw, Bulgaria scored against the run of play, denying France, in the last minute, a trip to the USA the following summer. 'In Britain, this might have led to domestic violence, or the torching of any nearby Bulgarian car or restaurant, if one could be found. There, one deeply despondent French waiter said to another, "It was a pretty goal."'

No wonder it took until 1989 for the French to appreciate Laurent Fignon, not that he appreciated the sentiment in return. The interesting thing is that Fignon had already done plenty of losing by that point. An operation on his Achilles tendon in early 1985 cut his career cleanly in two with a scalpel-sharp slice. But, if anything, his poor form exposed him to more ridicule than sympathy. Even during 1987 and 1988, when his form started to return, with a mountain-stage win and seventh overall during the 1987 Tour, and a win in Milan–San Remo in 1988, Fignon could still expect to spend the summer at loggerheads with the French press.

According to Daniel Mangeas, Fignon's unpopularity went back to the Alpe d'Huez stage of the 1984 Tour, and a throwaway comment Fignon made about Hinault's relentless but ineffectual attacking. Hinault had been aggressive in some tactically questionable places, and Fignon told the press afterwards that the move had made him laugh. Later he explained that he hadn't meant his comments to mock Hinault, more to acknowledge his indefatigability. After all, Hinault was at least providing entertainment and paying lip service to the idea that the Tour wasn't over, despite Fignon's large lead. 'Fignon was untouchable in 1984,' says Mangeas. 'But when he said he laughed at Hinault, it was taken very badly by the public and that played badly in terms of his popularity. It blighted the rest of his career.'

The 1984 Tour was a classic example of how the greater narrative of the race can sometimes cover up the fact that sporting intrigue is minimal. Despite the fact that from the first long time trial onwards the final result was not in doubt, the battle that Bernard Hinault made of the race, and the story of the apprentice beating the master, made it appear exciting.

Both Hinault and Fignon were making comebacks of a sort. Hinault wanted to reassert himself as the Tour champion after his year away from the race in 1983; Fignon had been stung by the perception that some had considered his win the previous year as lucky, that if Hinault had been there . . . Fignon was also seething after the 1984 Giro d'Italia, where he'd come a narrow second to Francesco Moser. Fignon's opinion was that the Giro organizers had done Moser a huge favour by cancelling a high mountain stage because of a vague and non-specific threat of landslides. He also railed against the local fans, who he alleged were pushing Moser on the other mountain stages, and claimed that a television helicopter was hovering in front of him during the final time trial and creating a strong draft for him to have to ride into.

The 1984 Tour is usually presented as Fignon versus Hinault, but it was more complex than that. Hinault had left the Renault team over the winter to join Bernard Tapie's new team, La Vie Claire. That meant the sides were a little uneven – Fignon had the advantage that his manager Guimard knew Hinault very well. Renault also had Greg LeMond in their team, riding his first Tour, before Hinault poached him for La Vie Claire in 1985. La Vie Claire might have developed into the strongest team in the world by 1986, able to fill five of the final top 12 spots in the Tour, but in 1984 they were still comparatively weak, and Fignon and Renault were at their strongest.

Though Hinault had pipped Fignon in the prologue, Renault gained almost a minute on La Vie Claire in the team time trial. While the race was distracted by the sideshow of Fignon's team-mate Vincent Barteau taking the yellow jersey after getting into a first-week break and gaining 17 minutes on the field, Fignon started to hammer Hinault. In the long time trial at Le Mans, he put 49 seconds into him. He picked up another minute or so in the Pyrenees. Then, in the Alps, he started winning stages, and it was as if he couldn't stop.

'When I won the Tour in 1984, it was easy,' Fignon told me. 'Every day, easy. No problem. My legs didn't hurt.'

He won the uphill time trial to La Ruchère, then came second to Luis Herrera on Alpe d'Huez, but finished almost three minutes ahead of Hinault. He won again at La Plagne, by over a minute, and again in the last Alpine summit finish at Crans-Montana. A victory in the final time trial in Beaujolais meant that Fignon finished the 1984 Tour 10 and a half minutes ahead of Hinault, and almost 12 ahead of his teammate LeMond, who'd been suffering from bronchitis. He'd won five stages, Renault had won 10, LeMond won the white jersey and Renault the team classification. Fignon had humiliated Hinault, and the impression he gave was that he enjoyed it. 'I had Guimard at my side,' he wrote in *We Were Young and Carefree*. 'We both knew that Hinault was an impulsive, angry rider who didn't have the best tactical awareness. He would return blow for blow or simply knock everyone senseless, but when he needed to calculate, hold back and race with his head, Hinault had dire need of Guimard.'

Hinault's tactical vulnerability was revealed in the Alpe d'Huez stage. 'We're on the Laffrey,' Fignon told me, his speech slipping into the present tense. 'It's a very difficult climb, and he attacks. I bring him back. He attacks again. I bring him back. He attacks again, I bring him back. It's pissing me off, so I attack, and leave everybody behind except Herrera, and off we go.'

Fignon and Herrera made good their escape over the top of the Côte de Laffrey, and it was only a hard chase by Hinault that enabled him to finally close the gap in the valley road to Alpe d'Huez. 'Hinault comes back to us in a little group, maybe three or four kilometres from the bottom of Alpe d'Huez, and he attacks right away. I said it made me laugh, because it was a tactical error – I'd get him three or four kilometres into the mountain and put three minutes into him. The journalists were trying to make a big Hinault–Fignon rivalry at the time, so they blew it all up. I wasn't mocking him – I was naïve.'

Remember that Fignon was still only 23 in 1984, with the feeling of invincibility that comes with never having had to face a major setback. Setbacks would come in the future, and you get the impression that the Fignon of 1989 onwards regrets telling the press that Hinault's relentless and futile attacking made him laugh. But the Fignon of 1984 seemed quite comfortable about it.

Fignon had two extraordinary seasons, 1984 and 1989, and a lucky one in 1983. The rest was a mix of decent form, unfulfilled promise and frustration. In 1991 he had his last good overall ride at the Tour, coming sixth behind Miguel Indurain, but one place ahead of his old rival Greg LeMond.

'In 1984, during the Tour de France, I wasn't far from perfection,' he said. 'In 1989 I had some extraordinary moments. But I did the maximum that I was capable of doing. I'm not someone who does nostalgia.'

When he died of cancer, just after his 50th birthday in 2010, the Tour lost one of its great characters. In the end, Fignon is both the man who lost the Tour and won it twice.

6

Greg LeMond
1986, 1989, 1990

When you choose to become professional, you have to be young and either naïve or a megalomaniac.

Marc Madiot

On 20 January 1981, Ronald Reagan was sworn in as President of the United States of America. Fifteen days later, Greg LeMond rode his first race as a professional cyclist, the Étoile de Bessèges. The 1980s had begun – cycling's equivalent of the *belle époque*. It was an era of optimism, technological progress, innovation and growth – innocent times before darker, more cynical events made us less idealistic. Cycling was never so exciting and colourful as it was in the 1980s. The racing photography from the era has the bright jewel-tones of stained-glass windows, and there was a run of Tours, from 1983 to 1990, of which only one (1988) was less than a classic. During the eighties, a golden generation of stage racers – Bernard Hinault, Greg LeMond, Laurent Fignon, Stephen Roche and Pedro Delgado – were at their peak, or came to maturity. On top of being talented and athletic, they were interesting, outspoken, controversial, chaotic and complicated – all the things that modern athletes are trained not to be.

Greg LeMond was the golden boy of the golden generation. It was an accident of perfect timing that the first American cyclist to make a name for himself in professional road racing also happened to be the best: a genetic freak whose body processed oxygen like a mainframe computer crunches numbers; a study in how immaculately a body and a bicycle can tessellate. With his windblown blond quiff, electric-blue eyes, laughter lines and toothpaste-advert smile, LeMond looked like he'd been improbably confected in the creative suite of a Hollywood movie studio. 'In my next life I want to come back as LeMond. I want to be born in California with legs like Eddy Merckx and looks like Robert Redford,' wrote journalist and ex-professional cyclist Paul Kimmage.

LeMond's career looked equally scripted. He was the Bobby Fischer-style outsider, coming in from America to beat the established countries at their own game. He was involved in a fratricidal battle to win the Tour de France against his own teammate. He was shot in a hunting accident, coming within half an hour of bleeding to death, then bounced back to win the Tour de France by eight seconds. He was the innovator who brought or helped to bring higher wages, Oakley sunglasses, tri-bars, full-length zips on cycling jerseys, carbon-fibre frames, hard-shell helmets, power meters, race radios and single-peak seasons to cycling. He was a rare voice in American cycling speaking out against Lance Armstrong, years before it became fashionable to do so. LeMond's biography reads like a series of movie scripts, with goodies, bad guys and cliffhangers. Happy endings? We'll get to that.

Greg LeMond won three Tours, in 1986, 1989 and 1990, plus a couple of world championship road races. It's obligatory to add, as many of his fans do, that he should have won the Tour in 1985, if only he'd not been ordered to sacrifice his chances for his faltering team leader Hinault, and that he'd probably have won in 1987 and 1988 if he hadn't been shot. He's correctly seen as one of the greatest Tour riders in history.

This is impressive, because Greg LeMond wasn't actually very good at winning. Fignon, who might have eaten his words a few years later when LeMond narrowly beat him in the 1989 Tour, had this to say about the American: 'He isn't a leader. He's an excellent second, but not a winner.'

Of course, LeMond won a respectable number of high-quality races. He was a prolific winner as a junior, and the junior and senior World Road Race Champion. He picked up a few Tour stages along the way, plus the Critérium du Dauphiné Libéré, a Coors Classic, a Tour DuPont and Tour de l'Avenir. But he also came second and third a lot – he got top fives in Milan–San Remo, Liège–Bastogne–Liège, Paris–Roubaix and the Tour of Lombardy. Before he won the Tour he came third and second. He also came third and fourth at the Giro d'Italia.

LeMond was so prodigiously and precociously talented that winning as a teenager and young amateur seemed to come quite easily and naturally. But maybe as a consequence, he never needed to develop much of a mean streak. Exhibit A: the 1985 Tour de France.

History has boiled the 1985 Tour down into two moments: race leader Hinault's crash in St-Étienne, in which he broke his nose, and his La Vie Claire teammate LeMond's thwarted desire to attack in the Luz Ardiden stage, which was the penultimate day in the Pyrenees. Hinault, holding a 3-38 lead over LeMond, was suffering badly from his injuries, and LeMond, ahead on the road with third-placed Stephen Roche, sensed opportunity. So, it has to be said, did Roche.

Roche was a further 2-36 behind LeMond, and he urged LeMond to press on. The management of La Vie Claire dithered, then told LeMond that he could only go for it if he dropped Roche, which he didn't, or couldn't do, especially as Roche could hear the instructions being relayed to LeMond over the radio. LeMond toed the line, and the moment was lost. He also claims he was told Hinault was only a short distance behind him, and suspects the truth was somewhat different.

At the finish line, LeMond was briefly furious. 'I had my chance to win today,' he said. 'They lost me the Tour because they told me to stop working, when I was strong enough to attack.' Later he relented. 'I got a little carried away,' he said.

It's only natural to take sides when the opposing arguments seem so clear cut. On the one hand, LeMond was stronger than Hinault and should have been given his opportunity. On the other, Hinault was the race leader, and LeMond's job as a team-mate was to protect him. The irony is that LeMond had joined La Vie Claire from Renault over the previous winter, feeling that their team leader, 1984 Tour winner Fignon, would cramp his style. Fignon missed most of the 1985 season following an injury and an operation. The other interesting thing about La Vie Claire's recruitment of LeMond is that the American wasn't the only rider they'd gone after at the end of 1984 – they'd also tapped up Fignon and Roche as possible co-leaders with Hinault but both had already committed for 1985, and so they settled on LeMond.

You can understand the caution of La Vie Claire's management at Luz Ardiden. Apart from the fact that attacking one's own leader is generally disapproved of in cycling, the team was owned by French businessman Bernard Tapie, Hinault was French, and he was on the verge of taking a record-equalling fifth Tour de France victory. Furthermore, as things stood, La Vie Claire's closest rival was Roche, 6-14 behind Hinault. If LeMond had attacked and pulled Roche closer to the lead, the team would theoretically have been in a less strong position – say LeMond had finished with Roche, four minutes clear of Hinault (which is how much time stage winner Pedro Delgado gained on him), LeMond would be in yellow, Hinault second at 20 seconds or so, and Roche third at two and a quarter minutes. Given that Roche won alone on the Col d'Aubisque by over a minute the next morning, albeit with LeMond waiting for Hinault, you can see why Roche would be so keen for LeMond to indulge his ambition.

Or maybe, as LeMond thinks, he could have dropped Roche and won the Tour. LeMond believes that Hinault was minutes behind, not seconds, as he was informed by the team car. What's certain is that at the top of the Col du Tourmalet, the penultimate climb, LeMond and Roche were 1-16 clear of Hinault. One mountain later, at the finish line, LeMond was 1-13 ahead of his leader, having reduced his effort considerably.

And that's the 1985 Tour – LeMond versus Hinault in the Pyrenees. Depending on your world view, either the right man won the Tour, or the strongest man was denied his chance. But there's more to it than that. There are two facts about the 1985 Tour that are often forgotten – first, that until his crash at St-Étienne, Hinault had been by far the best rider in the race and, second, that there wasn't much to choose between Roche and LeMond.

Hinault was dominant until the finishing straight in St-Étienne. He'd won the prologue, then the long time trial in Strasbourg by two and a half minutes. During the first mountain stage to Avoriaz, he went on a long attack with Colombian rider Luis Herrera and gained another minute and a half. It might have been more, save for a late counterattack and chase by LeMond. On the morning of the St-Étienne stage, he led LeMond by 5-23 and Roche by 6-08. Interestingly, LeMond had been assiduously gathering bonus seconds in the hot spot sprints through the 1985 Tour – by St-Étienne he'd gained 36 seconds this way, and by the finish in Paris, he'd gained 70 seconds, against Hinault's 19. Did he recognize earlier than the Pyrenees that his best chance of gaining time was to do so covertly, rather than by open attacking?

Hinault crashing wasn't the only significant thing that happened on the St-Étienne stage. That day, LeMond had attacked, gaining almost two minutes on the main group of favourites, and Hinault diligently marked Roche all the way to the finishing straight, and that fateful crash. That LeMond was close enough to threaten Hinault's lead on Luz Ardiden was partly down to Hinault's benevolence.

In the end, Hinault beat LeMond by 1-42 in Paris. Take out the time bonuses and add the two minutes that Hinault gifted LeMond in St-Étienne, and maybe the strongest rider won after all.

As Hinault took the plaudits following his fifth Tour win, we'd learned two things about Greg LeMond: he was exceptionally strong, and he'd revealed a streak of timidity unusual in an elite cyclist. Their teammate Bernard Vallet summed it up: 'Greg doesn't have Bernard's destructive rage. He's a lovely boy but certainly too kind.'

Three years previously, at the 1982 world championships in Goodwood, LeMond's compatriot Jock Boyer was dangling 50 metres off the front of the lead group into the final kilometre. With LeMond right near the front of the chase group, normal team tactics would dictate that one of the other favourites should make the effort to close the gap. If they did, LeMond could sit on them, then jump around them once they tired; if they didn't, Boyer would win.

Instead, it was LeMond who closed the gap. It was suicidal, because his move was more of a steady acceleration than a jump, so it wasn't strong enough to shed the riders on his wheel, Giuseppe Saronni and Sean Kelly. It guaranteed two things: first, that LeMond wasn't going to win. But he wasn't concerned about that. LeMond rode for the second reason – to stop Boyer from winning.

The Americans were a team in name only. There weren't enough professional riders in the US to justify holding a national championships race, so the US Cycling Federation used the world championships as a way of deciding the national champion. That meant any American riders would have to ride against each other in the race, rather than as a team, and LeMond disagreed with this. Also, the worst possible thing for LeMond's burgeoning career as a major star would be for another American to win the world championships. LeMond was clear in his self-perception, right from the start – he was an athlete, but he was a businessman too. Furthermore, and this may have given LeMond's final acceleration just a bit of extra zip, LeMond and Boyer didn't really like each other.

Saronni won the gold, and LeMond held on for silver ahead of Kelly. Boyer faded badly to 10th. LeMond needn't have worried – Boyer had nowhere near enough of a lead, nor was he good enough a rider to win from that position, but LeMond's desire to make sure of it overrode any need for him to be seen to do the right thing. According to LeMond, Boyer had spent the entire race following him anyway.

The Goodwood world championships and 1985 Tour de France are interesting landmarks in LeMond's career. He came second in both races, but in one he was happy to chase down his teammate; in the other he rejected the temptation to attack his teammate through a combination of loyalty and tactics. However, only one of these races has caused him lifelong regret.

Twenty-seven minutes into my interview with Greg LeMond for this book, I asked my seventh question. I didn't open my mouth again for another 39 minutes: when I transcribed, his answer ran for five pages. This is not uncommon with LeMond. He has a stereotypically West Coast tendency to analyse and emote; a conversation with him is a mazy succession of entertaining tangents and non-sequiturs. LeMond's junior racing contemporary and lifelong friend Kent Gordis says of him, 'He's really bright, and he's an autodidact. But his mind moves so fast that it's hard for him to complete a sentence before he's on to the next point.'

LeMond thinks he can explain why he didn't win so prolifically once he'd turned professional for the Renault team in 1981, when he was 19. 'My personality changed when I turned pro,' LeMond tells me. 'I was definitely intimidated. Being on a team with Hinault was good, but it changed my personality a little bit. I became more reserved and less who I used to be.'

LeMond aspirates the 'H' in 'Hinault' – he rode for a succession of French teams, and lived in France for two years, but he never quite lost the American accent. 'Hinault was a hero to me. He was a strong character, and very popular, and I got a little more timid, a little more passive than I would have done on a US team,' he continues.

But it's not just that. With Greg LeMond, something always seemed to go wrong. It was the story of his life. In 1981, he'd listened too diligently to a Belgian friend who advised him to take it easy over the winter because it would be the last break he'd get for years – and duly showed up for his first season out of condition. In 1982 he broke his collarbone. In 1983 he thought he was too young to go to the Tour as a contender and decided to sit out what turned out to be a winnable race. He'd always told himself he'd try to win the Tour at his first attempt, and he'd planned on that happening in 1984. That year he got bronchitis during the Tour. There was always something.

'I think I was a well-rounded rider. In 1985 I was trying to win everything. I was good from February to September, and always fell short: second, second, third, second. But it was physiological, too. I was overtrained because of the volume of racing I was doing. I helped Hinault win his fifth Tour in 1985, but it was understood that we were co-leaders and if he had a bad day I could take over. In 1986 I decided to focus on the Tour.'

In October 1978, when he was 17, Greg LeMond wrote down a list of goals on a piece of paper. 'I wanted to accomplish something by the time I was 24 or 25. What I didn't want was to be the kind of cyclist who just stuck it out and stayed in the sport for 10 years without being successful,' he told American cycling journalist Sam Abt.

'I wrote that in 1979 I wanted to win the junior worlds. The following year I wanted to win the Olympic road race. By the time I was 22 or 23 I wanted to win the professional world championships, and by the time I was 24 or 25 I wanted to win the Tour de France.'

In the 1970s, it wasn't easy for Americans to get into cycling. There was little or no media coverage, and only tiny pockets of activity. It was lucky for the teenage LeMond that his home in Nevada wasn't far from Berkeley, California, where one of those pockets, in the form of the Velo Club Berkeley, had formed. Kent Gordis was one of the members, and he remembers his first encounter with the future Tour winner at LeMond's second ever race. 'I met him at a race on the outskirts of San Francisco in March 1976,' Gordis tells me. 'It was point-to-point, 25 miles for the intermediates, and just four or five kids. One was too fat, one was too skinny, they were all misfits, and in the middle of the misfits was a goofy-looking kid with a canary-yellow jersey and a Kucharik helmet, which made anyone who wore it look like a complete idiot. I dismissed him. The race started, he broke away right away and I could barely stay in his wheel. He beat me in the sprint and I was crushed. That was Greg. The third-placed rider was 10 minutes behind us.'

LeMond is often portrayed as an outsider in European cycling culture. The myth was propagated when he signed his first professional contract, with the Renault team, and Cyrille Guimard, the manager, and Bernard Hinault, then Renault's leader, flew to Nevada for a photo opportunity, complete with horses, cowboy hats and ranch fences. The story is a compelling one – the wide-eyed, outrageously talented *ingénu*, dropped blinking and surprised into the European peloton, where he impresses the locals with his incredible powers. A modern-day sporting equivalent of the Connecticut Yankee in King Arthur's Court.

But LeMond had more bike culture and experience of European racing at that point than the story allows for. Gordis's father lived in Geneva, and Gordis himself had lived there until he was 10, speaking both English and French, before moving to California. 'For me, bike racing has two functions: sport and culture,' Gordis says. 'There was a subculture of people into the culture of Euro cycling, and Greg was part of that.'

Gordis used to visit the French bookshop in San Francisco, where he'd find six-month-old copies of *Miroir du Cyclisme*, and pore over the contents with LeMond. LeMond also started to hang out at a workshop in Reno owned by Roland Della Santa, who built LeMond's frames for years and sponsored him as a junior. Della Santa's workshop was full of old Italian cycling posters and magazines, and LeMond was spellbound by Della Santa's stories of the Tour de France and Giro d'Italia. 'Roland had years of *Miroirs du Cyclisme*,' LeMond says. 'I used to go to his house and read them. They were in French, but the photographs caught my imagination.'

In 1978, LeMond went to Europe with Gordis and his parents – he raced in Switzerland, Belgium and France, pitching up at races in Gordis's father's Buick, and immediately winning. 'In Belgium I could barely finish the races, they were so difficult,' recalls Gordis. 'But Greg made a splash because he was winning.

He was a force of nature – he never ran out of power or breath.'

'Belgium was like a dream,' says LeMond. 'I could choose from 20 different races in a day and bike to them.'

LeMond wasn't out of his depth in Europe, and he'd long since outgrown the competition in the United States. 'People think I'm quite spontaneous, but I'm very analytical and think strategically. My training was planned out a year in advance even as a junior. I had two months in Europe where I won virtually every race I rode.'

LeMond won six out of eight races in Belgium, coming second in the other two. He won twice in Switzerland and twice in France. 'I was winning with ease, so I said to myself, "There's no reason I can't think of winning the Tour." Why wouldn't I make that a goal?'

Which brings us back to the list. He won the 1979 world championships in Buenos Aires. He was unable to win Olympic gold in Moscow in 1980, thanks to the American boycott of the event. This led to a minor rift with the coaches of the national cycling team, who wanted him to stay amateur until the 1984 Olympics. He won the professional world championships in 1983, aged 22, and won his first Tour de France in 1986, aged 25. He'd hit all but one of his very ambitious targets.

'It's funny, because I was 17 at the time, looking at what Merckx had done, seeing that he'd won the world champion-ships by 21, and giving myself just one extra year, because I was American,' says LeMond.

The list is a huge part of the LeMond mythology. He's still got it, a creased sheet of paper with faint blue lines, his name earnestly written at the top, along with the date 10/18/78, com-plete with a continental-style strikethrough on the seven, a habit he'd picked up in Europe. The list has been imbued with causative meaning, as if the act of writing down the targets made them LeMond's destiny. But the list may be an example of what's known in the financial world as 'survival bias'. Survival bias is a logical error where conclusions are drawn from successful results, but failures are ignored. It's entirely possible that many teenage cyclists around the world drew up similar lists of targets, it's just that none of the others managed to achieve them; their lists were quietly tossed into waste-paper baskets. We don't hear about the other lists because they don't support the narrative.

Bernard Hinault and Greg LeMond share little more than a genetic predisposition to ride bikes extremely fast. Life looks pretty easy and straightforward for Hinault – he doesn't think, he just does. He hasn't knowingly regretted anything in his life, never admits that he was wrong, and probably sleeps like a baby. For LeMond, you get the impression that cycling came a lot easier than life did. LeMond is frank, open, honest and reflective, with a tendency to think the best of people. The result is occasional disappointment when the real world doesn't quite measure up to the idealistic outlook.

Following the 1985 Tour, Bernard Hinault had promised to help LeMond win in 1986. But at some point, the gamekeeper turned poacher. Hinault couldn't help himself, attacking on the first Pyrenean stage, to Pau, with a teammate, Jean-François Bernard, and Pedro Delgado, and leaving the rest of the race minutes behind. It was the perfect break – Bernard was strong and committed, and contributed a lot of the pace-setting, while Delgado worked hard, knowing that in return for his effort he'd get the stage win, just over the border from his homeland. And Hinault? He was about to move into the yellow jersey, 5-25 clear of LeMond, a gap almost identical to the one he'd held midway through the 1985 Tour. He'd managed to defend that lead with a broken nose.

The next group on the road in Pau, LeMond's, contained only 10 riders, three of whom rode for La Vie Claire and therefore couldn't chase. Hinault had taken the initiative, while it hadn't even occurred to LeMond to attack that early. LeMond's racing style was always conservative. He was a stayer in a Grand Tour, a strong finisher, which bred in him a reluctance to attack early. It was a tactic which suited his physical and mental abilities, but it might also have reinforced the perception that he was not a natural leader. In the three Tours that LeMond won, his most significant effort came well into the second half of each race. It wasn't until the 1991 Tour that he seized the initiative early.

Unfortunately for Hinault, the success went to his head, because he attacked again the next day, on the hardest Pyrenean stage. This time, however, La Vie Claire's rivals were organized, and Hinault didn't have breakaway companions to share the work. He was caught on the descent of the third mountain out of four, the Col de Peyresourde. To win the Tour, all he would have had to do is sit tight and watch his rivals for the next week and a half; instead, hubris was his downfall. LeMond, who was livid with Hinault, attacked on the final climb to Superbagnères, and took back four minutes, 39 seconds, two seconds more than he'd lost the previous day.

Even after this, Hinault kept up the psychological pressure. He joined an attack on the stage to Gap, along with third-placed Urs Zimmermann, and LeMond was only rescued by the fact he was able to persuade the Panasonic team to chase, otherwise he could have lost minutes. Even now, LeMond wouldn't openly attack Hinault. The next day, on the Col du Granon, with Hinault in trouble with knee pain, LeMond followed an attack by Zimmermann, but wouldn't work with him. It didn't matter – the Swiss rider was going so well that he pulled LeMond over three minutes clear of Hinault and into the yellow jersey for the first time in his career.

And still Hinault wouldn't leave LeMond alone. He attacked early on the next stage, which finished at Alpe d'Huez, but this time LeMond was awake enough to chase him down. Their combined efforts destroyed their rivals – Hinault and LeMond climbed the Alpe together, five minutes clear of the next rider, and they crossed the line hand in hand. LeMond says he rode within himself, in order to allow Hinault a swansong stage win. It was a naïve thing to do – Hinault announced on television that evening, as he and LeMond were interviewed, that the Tour was not yet over. Theoretically he was right – LeMond could have crashed, or punctured, or got injured – but it was a provocation too far. LeMond doesn't have the ability to hide his emotions, and his facial expression went from happy, through incredulous, to angry in the space of just a few seconds. Hinault did win the final time trial, after LeMond took a corner too fast and crashed, but LeMond's final margin of victory was a comfortable three minutes, 10 seconds.

Hinault claims to this day that he kept his promise to help LeMond win the Tour. 'I spent all my time attacking his rivals to make it easy for him,' he wrote in his autobiography. However, the truth seems pretty clear, that Hinault's pride simultaneously almost won him, then lost him the 1986 Tour, and it was little to do with helping LeMond.

Hinault's claims are provocative, although LeMond seems not to lose any sleep over them. When I suggest he won't find closure about the 1986 Tour until Hinault admits he was riding to win, he laughs. 'No, I'm fine with it,' he says. 'This is all stories you journalists make! I have closure – it happened on the race. I'm done! I met Hinault at Alpe d'Huez last year and we took a picture together.'

One of Hinault's racing contemporaries, who spoke to me on condition of anonymity, suggests that the truth is a little more complicated: 'Bernard is a strong character. He's very sure of what he believes in, but he is not a big thinker. He's not lying about 1986 – he actually believes it. He believes he gave LeMond the race.'

Greg LeMond never did quite fit in. Professional cycling in the 1980s was a conservative environment, with certain cultural and behavioural norms, and a strictly observed hierarchy. LeMond did things differently, not because he was a natural rebel, but because he was used to the way things were done in America, and he carried on doing things that he thought were completely normal.

He didn't just bring his wife to the Tour de France (an unusual thing in itself), he built up an entourage. In his book about the 1994 racing year, *A Season in Turmoil*, Sam Abt lists the LeMond party who followed the 1991 Tour: Kathy LeMond, son Geoffrey, his parents Bob and Bertha and Greg's granddad Art LeMond. Abt continues: 'Randy Rupracht, the Nevada teenager with cystic fibrosis who was Greg's guest on the Tour for the second year. Kathy's parents, Sacia and Dr David Morris . . . Dick and Frieda Lauer, the couple who sold Greg and Kathy their home in Minnesota and then became close friends . . . Lisa and Tim Morris, Kathy's brother and sister-in-law . . . Fred Mengoni, Greg's longtime friend and adviser . . . There were more. Pat and Joyce Morrisey, the senior LeMond's friends.' LeMond's entourage needed four cars, and nine to 12 hotel rooms, although not all of them were on the whole race. Nobody batted an eyelid, because Greg was Greg.

At team dinners, French teammates tutted as LeMond got out a book to read. There is a well-known energy-saving rule in cycling: never stand if you can sit, never sit if you can lie down. For LeMond, the rule was never sit if you can play golf instead. So when LeMond was shot in a terrible and unlikely hunting accident in early 1987 – which would have been comedic if it hadn't been so serious (his brother-in-law mistook him for a wild turkey) – the wise heads of the European cycling press nodded sagely, as if LeMond had brought calamity on himself, by having hobbies and interests outside cycling.

LeMond was never the same again after his hunting accident, even though he won two more Tours. He could have called it quits – his insurance company offered him one million dollars to retire after the accident, 1987 was a write-off and he raced infrequently with little success in 1988. 'It was a major trauma,' LeMond says. 'I was completely rewired after it. UC Davis [where he was operated on to save his life] is a trauma centre so, for them, me surviving was all that mattered. I was struggling in 1988, digging myself into a hole of chronic overtraining.'

Halfway through 1989, he barely finished with the back-markers in the Giro d'Italia, until his *soigneur* noticed that he was looking unusually pale and grey and prescribed iron shots. The turnaround was immediate – he came second in the final time trial of the race, and started the Tour de France with renewed confidence.

The 1989 Tour was the closest in the history of the race. I think it is the most exciting edition ever, simply for the way the advantage swung back and forth between LeMond and Fignon, who was himself coming back after four lean years. Neither was the strongest rider in the race – defending champion Pedro Delgado was on scintillating form in the mountains, and was very strong in the first long time trial. But he'd had to spend that form on pulling back a deficit of seven and a half minutes, incurred when he arrived late for his start in the prologue, made a panicky, wasteful attack on the next morning's stage, then got dropped by his team in the afternoon team time trial, where they nursed him round in last place again. 'People always say the Tour takes years off your life. Well, just Luxembourg took away a few months,' Delgado said of his opening weekend disaster.

LeMond disagrees that Delgado was the strongest. 'It was Fignon,' he says. 'The Tour is raced upon where people are at that point, and when Delgado was making time up, he was not a contender. A lot of leeway gets given to people in that position. He was riding incredibly well, but I think Fignon was the strongest rider.'

Delgado's comeback over the course of the Tour was only the backdrop to the main battle between LeMond and Fignon. Fignon's Super-U team won the team time trial, then LeMond won the long time trial at Rennes. Fignon dropped LeMond at Superbagnères. LeMond gained time on Fignon in the mountain time trial at Orcières Merlette, and in Briançon the next day. Fignon dropped LeMond at Alpe d'Huez, then gained more time with a solo attack in Villard-de-Lans. And LeMond overturned Fignon's 50-second lead with a win in the final time trial, to win the Tour by eight seconds. The lead swapped between them no fewer than five times.

LeMond would never have got away with it now. He used tribars, which were a new development, in the three time trials (although not in the prologue), and his net time gain over Fignon in these stages was two minutes, 41 seconds. The 7-Eleven team had quietly used them at the Tour de Trump that spring, the first time they'd been used in a professional bike race, and when LeMond (and 7-Eleven again) used them at the Tour, the officials let it pass. New equipment is strictly controlled these days, but LeMond had timed his innovation well – tribars were the first modification to the rider's position in decades, and race officials simply didn't have the experience to understand whether they were legal or not. Fignon and his manager Guimard complained bitterly about LeMond using the bars, but history has shown them to be on the losing side of that argument.

'I won that Tour on willpower, some luck, and

determination,' says LeMond. It was a win that earned him a million-dollar-a-year contract with the Z team, and the *Sports Illustrated* Sportsman of the Year award. He'd achieved the recognition and the rewards which he felt were his due. It's curious, however, that LeMond never tried to form an American team, especially once he had the clout within the sport to attract sponsors. He'd made a small impact on the consciousness of the American public, but he'd spent most of his career with French teams, plus a year each on a Dutch and Belgian team. Perhaps his impact would have been bigger had he signed for 7-Eleven, but on the other hand their budget was much smaller, so LeMond had to choose between his own salary and the greater good of US cycling. There were enough good North American riders by the late 1980s to form a team – Andy Hampsten had come fourth in the 1986 Tour, Canadian Steve Bauer had worn the yellow jersey and come fourth in 1988, Davis Phinney won a stage in both 1986 and 1987, while Alex Stieda had worn yellow in 1986 – and LeMond, plus these four, plus a handful of French or north European *domestiques*, could have made a very strong Tour team, but it never quite happened.

With his new Z outfit, LeMond won the 1990 Tour. It was neither as politically exciting as 1986, nor as finely balanced as 1989, but it was by far LeMond's most complete Tour win.

It was also the last true chaotic Tour. From 1991 onwards, as team tactics evolved (and also thanks in no small part to the advent of EPO), the race became more controlled in general. The lack of control by any single team in 1990 was given tangible form by a break of four riders on stage one which gained 10 minutes. That in itself wasn't unusual – similar things happened in 1984, 1987 and as recently as 2001 – but the 1990 quartet consisted of some extremely threatening riders: Steve Bauer, Ronan Pensec, who was LeMond's teammate and had twice finished in the top 10 of the Tour, plus Claudio Chiappucci and

Frans Maassen. Maassen was no danger overall, but 1990 was Chiappucci's coming-out party as a Grand Tour contender – the rest of the race completely underestimated him.

When the four riders went away, the peloton chased, but relented – with a team time trial in the afternoon, nobody wanted to sacrifice their strength. Tactically, it suited LeMond's Z team – with a man in the break, they didn't have to chase. But the other general classification contenders – PDM's Erik Breukink and Raúl Alcalá, and Banesto's Pedro Delgado – had made a serious error.

The presence of the four riders so far ahead of the rest of the field had a chilling effect on the general classification for a long time. At the first long time trial, Pensec rode out of his skin, dropping only 15 seconds to LeMond, who was fifth, two minutes behind Alcalá and six seconds behind Delgado. Then, on the first mountain stage at Mont Blanc, Pensec again finished with LeMond, taking over the yellow jersey.

Not for the first time in his career, LeMond found himself with a Breton teammate in the yellow jersey, preventing him from attacking. On Alpe d'Huez, LeMond held back, following the attacks but not committing to them himself, while Pensec again dropped minimal time. The top three overall at Alpe d'Huez were Pensec, then Chiappucci, one minute 28 behind, then LeMond in third at a whopping nine minutes. It looked as if Pensec was quite capable of riding a defensive race, Chiappucci would carry on losing small chunks of time, and LeMond would be trapped.

But liberation arrived the very next day, in the mountain time trial at Villard-de-Lans. Pensec cracked, losing almost four minutes, and the way was clear for LeMond to start working his way towards the yellow jersey. In his favour, he was now the sole leader of Z, although he was running out of territory to gain time. Furthermore, Chiappucci had only dropped nine seconds to him at Villard-de-Lans and was the new yellow jersey, while Breukink had won the test and now led LeMond overall.

In his autobiography, *The Agony and the Ecstasy*, Stephen Roche wrote of Jean-François Bernard taking the yellow jersey in 1987, 'Bernard could not be permitted one easy day in yellow.' His point was that the longer a rider holds the yellow jersey, the more his confidence grows, and Chiappucci, who'd never figured in a Grand Tour before, was suddenly looking like a genuine contender.

There were now two races in one. LeMond, Breukink and Delgado were the three strongest climbers in the Tour, and they were still dangerously close to each other overall. However, all three needed to find enough common cause to put Chiappucci out of the running as well.

The next day, LeMond and Z took Chiappucci and his Carrera team apart. On a hilly, grippy, kiln-hot day through the Massif Central to St-Étienne, they sent Pensec on the attack, forcing Carrera to chase. The situation was so threatening that Chiappucci had to join in the pace-setting. Pensec was caught, but that meant that Chiappucci was tired as the race approached the Col de la Croix de Chaubouret, a hard climb, but not with the same degree of difficulty as the Alps or Pyrenees. LeMond might have noticed that it was the same climb that had been used in the 1985 Tour, when he'd put two minutes into Hinault before the Badger had crashed at the finish.

LeMond and Breukink attacked with a small handful of stage hunters, while Delgado initially sat tight, waiting for Chiappucci to react. But the Italian was suffering, and Delgado's teammate Miguel Indurain had to drop back and pace him up the climb, about 30 seconds behind the LeMond group. By the finish in St-Étienne, LeMond had gained almost five minutes on Chiappucci, whose lead was down to two minutes over Breukink, and two and a half minutes to LeMond.

LeMond's performance on Luz Ardiden, three stages later, crystallized everything you need to know about him as a rider. It summed up both his extraordinary physical powers, and his reluctance to attack until the last minute. Chiappucci, who'd settled comfortably into the persona he'd occupy for the rest of his career – the cheeky, antagonizing, tactically inept gadfly – had attacked early in the stage while LeMond hung back. Even when Chiappucci was caught, at the foot of Luz Ardiden, LeMond held back. But when he finally went, halfway up, it was the race-winning move. Luz Ardiden, 1990, was the last time we saw LeMond at his best – he motored up the climb, eventual stage winner Miguel Indurain hanging on to his wheel, and took all but five seconds out of Chiappucci's lead.

The Tour was LeMond's. He survived a brief scare the next day when he punctured midway through the stage, and Chiappucci and Delgado broke with race etiquette by gently forcing up the pace. But in the final time trial, which Chiappucci inexplicably rode without tri-bars, making an unlikely event – hanging on to yellow – an impossibility, LeMond easily took back the time he needed.

'Compared to 1986 and 1989, 1990 didn't seem like hard work,' says LeMond. 'It was a bizarre race because of the 10-minute deficit, but it was purely a strategic decision to find the right days to take the time back. I never thought I wouldn't win it.'

His third win, however, blinded us and him to the reality of his career: that its decline was about to begin.

Unlike his contemporaries – Stephen Roche, Sean Kelly and Laurent Fignon – Greg LeMond retired unhappy. He'd had comparatively poor form for the second half of the 1991 Tour, then he was a shadow of himself for the next three seasons. He struggled to find high-level fitness, and looked bulky and unfit, in spite of his insistence that he'd trained hard in the off-seasons. He swore by doing a lot of cross-country skiing over the winter, but the upper body muscle this discipline develops can't have helped with his climbing. Since his shooting accident, he'd never been on form in the early season, but the funk extended into and beyond the summer every season after 1992. He proposed various causes in interviews – allergies, low-level lead poisoning from the shot still in his body – but while he had an idea about the problems affecting him, he didn't have a solution.

LeMond knew his body well, and through his career, he'd trusted it. In an interview with *Cycle Sport* magazine in 1995, he reflected on his victory in the 1989 world championships: 'I remember feeling so bad that day. All day I was looking at where the car was parked and thinking each time, "I'll do one more lap and if I feel worse I'm going to quit." I didn't feel good that day. With two laps to go I almost crashed . . . That gave me an adrenalin rush and from that point on I felt good.'

LeMond was also an incurable optimist. He even looked on the bright side when he was suffering the terrible after-effects of his shooting accident, telling Sam Abt that 'the shooting gave me a break that left me enthusiastic about cycling again'. But LeMond's decline wore away at that optimism, and he cut a frustrated figure at the end of his career. It looked like LeMond's self-esteem had been so wrapped up in winning and being physically powerful that, when he couldn't rely on those things any more, it hit him hard. His dwindling powers were put into starker relief by the growing usage of EPO in the peloton through the 1990s.

It had happened suddenly. In 1991, he'd hit the Tour de France like a whirlwind, attacking on the first stage with Erik Breukink and a handful of non-general classification riders, and putting almost two minutes into every other contender. It looked like LeMond was bored with winning the Tour conservatively and was going to try to do so with panache. 'I called Kathy and said I was going to win this breathing through my nose,' he says. In the long time trial at the end of the first week he was pipped by Miguel Indurain, but nobody else was close, and he went to the Pyrenees with a minute's lead over Breukink, and two over everybody else. And then, during two days in the Pyrenees, LeMond became ordinary.

It's a shame LeMond didn't win more often, because few cyclists before or since have looked as happy in victory as he did – at the 1989 world championships, or after the 1989 Tour de France. But there's a paradox at the heart of his career – he's seen as one of the greatest Tour riders of all time, but one who could or should have won far more, *and* one whose three wins were all in doubt at some point along the way.

Greg LeMond: should have won six Tours; could have won none. Three seems a good compromise.

7

Stephen Roche
1987

Why, I can smile, and murder whiles I smile.
Richard of Gloucester, *Henry VI Part 3*, William Shakespeare

Stephen Roche is the nicest guy who'll ever stab you in the back.

He's a journalist's and fan's dream, Roche. He's a people person, who talks openly and enthusiastically, with a habit of calling you by your first name. His teammate at Histor in 1990, Brian Holm, told me that they were habitually the last team to leave the finishing area of races to get to the hotel because Roche would be out talking to the press, the fans and anybody else who fancied a chat.

The Irish rider is more famous for having won the 'Triple Crown' – the Tour de France, Giro d'Italia and world championships in 1987 – than Eddy Merckx, the first and only other rider to do so, in 1974. He's as famous for sandwiching that one extraordinary season between a dozen more seasons (six before and six afterwards) in which more seemed to go wrong than right. Like Bernard Thévenet (his one-time team manager) a decade before, Roche started out alternating good seasons and bad, and also like Thévenet his good years seemed to come in odd-numbered years: 1981, 1983, 1985 and 1987 saw a crescendo of good results, culminating in the Triple Crown. Then the bad seasons seemed to stack up.

When Roche won the Tour de France, I was 14 years old and I thought he was great. The fact that an Irishman had gone over to France and won the Tour in a crazy, unpredictable see-saw battle which included one of the most exciting single moments in the history of the sport, his comeback on La Plagne, made for a fascinating story. Roche beat Pedro Delgado by 40 seconds – 1987 might have been overshadowed by the 1989 race in terms of the closeness of the final result but in many ways 1987 was even more open and unpredictable. It was one of the all-time great Tours.

Roche had bright cornflower-blue eyes and chubby cheeks, framed by dark choppy curls. The downturn at the corner of his eyes made him look a little bit sad, but the impression was banished by an easy smile. My experience of professional cyclists up until that point had mainly been of exotic bronzed continental types, but Roche looked like he'd get sunburn if he spent too long out on his bike. He never really had the face of an elite athlete, although that was just an innocent front for a calculating, tactical brain.

Later, I started to wonder whether I was confusing his cherubic appearance, emotional intelligence and people skills with his character. Contractual problems and spectacular fallings-out seemed to follow him around like plot twists in a soap opera. *L'Équipe* once called him '*ange et démon*' – angel and devil. The more I looked at his career, the more I thought that the friendly, compelling personality concealed a streak of ambition that was at least as wide as his smile. I had a nagging impression that behind the genial exterior hid a right bastard. But then I read about Allan Peiper's last race, Paris–Tours, 1992.

Peiper was a contemporary of Roche at the Peugeot team in

the early 1980s – both were outsiders in the conservative world of professional cycling at the time, Roche from Ireland, Peiper from Australia. Peiper spent the '92 Paris–Tours going around the peloton saying goodbye to the various friends he'd made over the years, which was not as easy a task as it sounds. 'I said goodbye to Olaf Ludwig in a side-wind echelon,' he told *Cycle Sport* magazine. 'Then I was riding next to Roche and said to him, "See you later, Steve." He said, "Hang on, I don't want to say goodbye to you just like this in the middle of the race."'

They initially agreed to meet in the changing rooms after the race, but were worried about missing each other in the chaos, so they decided whoever finished first would wait after the finish line for the other. Peiper got dropped on the final hill, so Roche waited a few minutes on the line for his ex-teammate. 'We gave each other a hug, and that was it,' said Peiper. 'He was basically the only person I said goodbye to properly. It was a pretty touching moment.'

That's Roche. On the one hand, Roberto Visentini, the team-mate who Roche divested of the pink jersey in the 1987 Giro d'Italia, still won't talk about it, he's so upset by Roche. On the other, Peiper's memory is that of all the couple of hundred riders in the Paris–Tours peloton, only Roche was thoughtful enough to stop and say goodbye properly.

Roche's ability to charm people, either consciously or not, either with the best intentions or the worst, also explains Stephen Roche the cyclist. As he works people, so he could also bend a race to his will, manipulate it to further his chances. Of all the Tour winners I've ever met or read about, he appears the least likely champion on the surface. If you could make any generalization about Tour winners it would be that they are tough, physically robust types. Bernard Hinault looked like he was carved out of the same granite as the bedrock of his home region Brittany; Cadel Evans looked as tough as old leather;

Jan Janssen, Eddy Merckx and Bernard Thévenet seemed indestructible at their best; while Miguel Indurain was so physically and mentally imposing that hardly anybody dared attack him for five years. Even the skinny, spiky types like Bradley Wiggins, Chris Froome or Alberto Contador look fast. Roche, however, was physically fragile and prone to injuries. His power lay elsewhere: in a supple and bewitching pedalling style, and an instinctive politician's understanding of bike racing. And, it must be acknowledged, an ability to silently slip an assassin's stiletto into his rivals' ambitions.

You had Roberto Visentini for breakfast at the 1987 Giro, didn't you, Stephen?, I suggest when we talk on the telephone. 'Yeah,' he answers. Then says, 'Yeah' again, just to confirm. 'I knew I was being cheeky,' he says. 'I couldn't attack him, but I thought, when I sense an opportunity, I'm going to take it.'

When Roche says 'I couldn't attack him' he's being slightly disingenuous, because that's exactly what he did, on stage 15, to Sappada. 'I went down the descent very fast. Extremely fast,' he continues. 'I thought, he *could* be with me, but then again, he could *not* be with me. I got to the bottom, he wasn't with me, and I linked up with the group in front.' It was soon after this that he found out his own team, Carrera, were chasing him down.

From Roche's perspective going into the 1987 Tour of Italy, he felt he should be at least joint leader of Carrera. Visentini felt that he, and not the Irishman, should be the team leader. He was the reigning champion, but hadn't done much in the intervening 12 months. A knee injury had ruined 1986 for Roche, but he was the form rider in 1987, having already won the Tour of Romandy and Tour of Valencia, and been the strongest rider but come second in both Paris–Nice and Liège–Bastogne–Liège. All of which put the Carrera team management in a delicate situation, which they didn't handle brilliantly. Before the Giro, they'd weighed up Visentini's position as defending champion against Roche's position as the better rider, and used Visentini's nationality to tip the balance in his favour – Visentini would be the nominal leader in the Giro, while Roche could lead at the Tour. To be fair to Carrera, most teams will back the established leader in almost every situation and, going into 1987, Visentini had won a Grand Tour, while Roche's best was third in the 1985 Tour de France. But Roche never bought it. He told *Winning* magazine in their preview article that 'the legs will decide' who the team leader would be. You can interpret that as meaning that his head had already decided it should be him.

Roche had the edge for the first two weeks of the race, chiselling out a small advantage on Visentini by the point they reached the long and hilly San Marino time trial, and wearing the pink jersey. Herbie Sykes, in his book *Maglia Rosa*, reports, in an interview with the Carrera manager Davide Boifava, of a team meeting held on the eve of the time trial. 'It was agreed by all that, should one or the other lead the race at the conclusion, the rest of the team would work for him, without exception,' said Boifava.

Visentini put almost three minutes into Roche in the time trial. Roche blamed a lack of concentration, exacerbated by fatigue from leading the race for 10 days, and poor recovery from a crash a few days previously. He also admitted that Visentini had mentally cracked him – while Roche tried to follow his normal focused build-up to the start, the Italian had been puncturing the bubble of his concentration with jokes, questions and chatter. After the stage, while Boifava probably breathed a sigh of relief at the newly reinforced hierarchy, Roche decided that the pre-time trial agreement didn't apply.

Sappada was two days later. As Roche rode in the front group, which initially consisted of just three riders, Visentini panicked and put his Carrera teammates on the front of the bunch to pull Roche back. It was one of the worst decisions he could have made. With a rider of Roche's calibre off the front, Carrera's rivals would have had no choice but to have chased, but they were saved the effort by Carrera suddenly descending into civil war.

Boifava, in a later interview, said, 'I asked [Roche] his reason for what he was doing. He told me that he only wanted to win the stage. I told him that if this was his objective, he should just sit and stay in the wheels. Instead he continued to pull, to keep the pace very high.'

Basic cycling tactics would say that Roche had no business riding hard in the front group, and Carrera had no business chasing him down. It was a shambles.

Roche's side of the story has tended to naturally receive more coverage in the English-language cycling press than Visentini's. But look back over his career, and there's a pattern of putting his own ambitions above those of his teammates. This is not necessarily a criticism – you don't become a team leader without personal ambition, and, in many cases, Roche's tactics could usually be construed as good for the team. In his first autobiography, *The Agony and the Ecstasy*, Roche tells the story of an amateur race in the 1980 season, where one of his teammates, Loubé Blagojevic, had been earmarked for the win. Blagojevic and Roche had been part of a three-man break. 'I reckoned that either Blagojevic or I would win and I told myself it would be me,' wrote Roche. Blagojevic jumped away and looked set for the win, but Roche started to chase him down. The riders' manager, Paul Wiégant, drove up and told Roche to stop riding, before giving him a rudimentary and uncompromising lesson in adhering to the team hierarchy. 'As I thought about it, he just ran me off the road and into the ditch,' said Roche.

In the 1981 Paris–Nice, Roche joined an attack that ended up taking nine minutes out of the bunch, which contained his team leader and 1979 winner Michel Laurent, who also happened to be leading the race. When Greg LeMond was undergoing a minor crisis on the Col du Tourmalet during the 1985 Tour about whether it was right to attack his injured team leader and yellow jersey holder Bernard Hinault or not, it was Roche on his shoulder, urging him to take the initiative. In the 1988 Tour of Britain, Roche's Fagor teammate Malcolm Elliott was in the yellow jersey, but Roche joined an attack on the stage to Liverpool and forced the pace, almost taking the race lead. In every one of these situations, there was enough plausible deniability to disguise attacking ambition as effective team tactics.

Roche tells me now, 'I wasn't attacking Visentini. I was following the groups. I never attacked.' But looking at Roche's previous form in gently manoeuvring himself in front of his teammates, I feel that one of his greatest skills is his ability to believably cover his backside. His denials remind me a little bit of Bill Clinton.

Visentini cracked terribly on the Sappada stage, and Roche was chased down, but when the counterattacks started going, Roche just had the strength to follow and Visentini didn't, nor did he have any teammates to help pace him to the finish and limit his losses. He lost six minutes.

Initially, it looked like bad, or at best risky tactics from Roche. Before the Sappada stage, Visentini led overall, with Roche in second by 2-42 and Tony Rominger third at 3-12. After it Roche was in pink, with Rominger in second by five seconds. Carrera had gone from a position of extreme strength – leading their closest rival by over three minutes with two contenders – to one of potential weakness (with only one contender and their closest rival five seconds behind). Roche's confidence in himself wasn't misplaced, however. He emerged as the strongest rider in the final week and won the race, in the face of howling derision from the partisan Italian fans.

Visentini is collateral damage in the Stephen Roche story. Roche might have gambled Carrera's position of strength in the Giro against his own ambition, but he won the bet by holding on to the pink jersey. Visentini, on the other hand, was never the same again, and he retired a few seasons later. Roche had broken him.

Irish cycling's run of success in the 1980s was a statistical outlier. In Sean Kelly and Stephen Roche Ireland had two of the best four or five cyclists in the world. The apparent contrast in their characters and backgrounds, and their slightly differing skill sets, meant that fans didn't necessarily have to choose between one or the other – although there was some overlap in their ambitions, most overtly at Paris–Nice, where they got caught up in a bad-tempered battle for victory in 1987. Kelly was the Classics specialist and sprinter who once won a Grand Tour (the 1988 Vuelta a España), and Roche was the Grand Tour and stage-race specialist who once won a major one-day race (the 1987 world championships). Kelly was the hard bastard from the countryside, while Roche was the city boy from Dublin. To a certain extent, the stereotype of Roche was true, but he was a hard bastard too, a self-made man. When he was a boy, he did a paper round and got paid a penny per newspaper delivered, which was enough to give him a bit of pocket money. But unlike most other paperboys, Roche would go back to the houses at the end of the week, pick up the papers and sell them on to the paper mill.

Perhaps being a city boy made for a different kind of hard. Roche went on his own to France at the age of 20, living in the Parisian *banlieue* and racing for the Athletic Club de Boulogne-Billancourt, the ACBB. That took a certain amount of resilience.

On the day of his arrival, his flight was delayed and he missed his ride to the team's headquarters. No panic; he made his own way there and found it was deserted, then hunkered down in the porch with as many clothes on as possible to protect against the freezing February night. A city boy he may have been, but Roche was never soft.

Roche was also an outlier in terms of his talent. He turned professional in 1981 and won Paris–Nice just a couple of months later – no other first-year professional has won that race. He was 13th in his first Tour de France in 1983, then third in 1985, behind Hinault and LeMond. In between, poor form in 1982, a Tour crash in 1984 and an end-of-year crash in 1985, prevented Roche from getting consistent results.

He was neither climber nor time triallist, although he developed enough in both disciplines for them to be significant parts of his armoury. He didn't waste energy, however – he had a smooth and efficient pedalling style. This, combined with the physiological equivalent of a diesel engine, made him good in stage races and Grand Tours. While his rivals muscled the pedals around with their strength, Roche's power was delivered in a much more fluid style, and the longer a race went on, the more energy he'd save.

'A lot of Tour contenders are very powerful and can put out the big watts,' he tells me. 'I could put out the watts, but I was very supple. I'd ride small gears, although in a time trial I could use a big gear. I wasn't really capable of using big gears on climbs so I'd use small ones. If I wanted to climb with the first guys, I had to use my pedalling.'

Roche's other main asset was that he was a racer. In cycling, the strongest man or woman sometimes wins – but as often it's the rider with the best understanding of the dynamics of bike racing. When a rider is the best time triallist or climber in the world, the Tour de France is much more of a personal battle, and winning the yellow jersey boils down to expressing those talents, then riding defensively for the rest of the race.

For Roche, though, bike races were him against his rivals. 'I raced to win, no matter what the odds were,' he says. 'It didn't matter whether it was the Tour de France or the tour of my back garden, I wanted to win it. It didn't matter whether it was uphill or downhill. It wasn't just about the hardness of the stage, it was about looking at the weather, yourself, your team, your form. When I was racing I had one eye and one ear on talking to my neighbour, and one eye and one ear on what was going on around me. So when breaks were going, I didn't have to have my teammates come over and tell me who was in it – I knew who was in it, roughly. If I missed a break, I'd know if there needed to be a chase, or a second group. I tried to analyse everyone around me – who could win, what team was doing what, what the ongoing strategy of other teams was, seeing who could help me, who wanted to win, who could win. Knowing who was going to be my ally, who the favourites were. One of my big things was feeling the race. My advantage was to have a nose for the break and what was going to happen. I was always one for knowing the climbs, knowing where I could make the difference and where I could afford to lose time. I did my homework.'

Roche is a born storyteller, who speaks as fast as he used to ride. The thing about storytellers, however, is that sometimes the narrative takes control. I've interviewed him a couple of times, and the stories pour out, sometimes almost word for word the same as when he's been interviewed by others. Occasionally there are discrepancies – he's written two autobiographies (one at the end of 1987, the other in 2012), and the anecdotes don't always chime perfectly. In *The Agony and the Ecstasy* he states that he could see the Charly Mottet-inspired echelon attack on the Blagnac stage of the 1987 Tour happening at close quarters; in *Born to Ride* he says that Mottet's team rode away when he'd gone back to the car for a rain jacket. No matter, it's easy for memories to merge and change under the pressure of time, or for specific details to morph into different times and places. But there's a strong impression that his stories have been told before, which suggests to me a certain disengagement from them on his part.

One of the striking features of his books is that there is not much in the way of introspection, and he is at pains to emphasize that he doesn't do regret. This is a function of his personality – he's a can-do, optimistic type. But this leads to the central paradox of Stephen Roche: he's an open book – in fact, he feels his honesty has sometimes been a fault – yet I feel like he's extremely difficult to know.

Regarding those falling-outs with almost every team he rode for: he had prolonged contractual difficulties with Peugeot, which took years of legal action to settle – in his favour; Carrera didn't go well the first time round, although ironically he finished his career with them on good terms; Fagor, between 1988 and 1989, was a shambles of a team, with the problems exacerbated by his injury; Histor, in 1990, went OK, although he fell out with his mechanic-turned-team manager Patrick Valcke during this period; Tonton Tapis in 1991 was disastrous – a horrendous failure in communication led to Roche missing the start of the Tour's team time trial and he was eliminated ignominiously from the race, and he admitted that he and the manager, Roger De Vlaeminck, couldn't get on; and going back to Carrera for his last two seasons might have seemed impossible after the 1987 Giro, but in comparison to that race, the seasons between 1988 and 1991 had been almost as chaotic. It was as if the knee, and subsequently back injuries that intermittently left his form in ruins were just a physical manifestation of a deeper malaise in his career.

And, of course, there's one more issue. Doping runs through the history of the Tour de France like the word 'Blackpool' in a stick of rock. It's not fair to single out Roche – EPO abuse didn't become endemic in the peloton until the 1990s, which coincided with a poor period for him, and it almost certainly wasn't even around in the peloton in 1987, when he was at his best – but he had a brief late flowering in 1992 and 1993, winning a Tour stage in La Bourboule in 1992 and coming 13th overall in his final Tour the next year, just as he had in his first. His name was linked to an official judicial investigation by Judge Franca Oliva in Italy into Professor Francesco Conconi, in which it was concluded that some riders from Carrera in 1993 were administered EPO, but Roche firmly denied involvement, and he never tested positive during his career.

There was an awkward appearance for Roche, along with his former friend and ghostwriter, and now doping-inquisitor-in-chief David Walsh, on the Irish *Late Late Show* in 2002, where Roche's body language appeared to me full of the small tells – the pursed lips, the briefly protruding tongue, the rapid blinking – that indicate stress. Roche asserted that he was not involved, and he repeated those assertions in *Born to Ride*.

Revolution, or more likely its distant cousin anarchy, was in the air at the 1987 Tour de France. The former *patron* of the Tour, Bernard Hinault, had retired, the reigning champion Greg LeMond was recovering from his shooting accident, and two-time winner Laurent Fignon was mired in erratic form – there was simply nobody with the authority or aura of a Tour champion in the field. And behind the scenes, long-time joint director of the Tour, Félix Lévitan, had been fired amid accusations, albeit unproven, of financial impropriety. It seemed fitting with so much in the way of background politics that the Tour would start behind the Iron Curtain, in West Berlin. The racing was wild, uncontrolled and unpredictable. Eight different riders wore the yellow jersey. *L'Equipe* called the race 'The Waltz of the Yellow Jerseys'. It was incredibly exciting to watch. The riders hated it – the incessant attacking and stress wore them down.

Roche's 1987 Tour win was brilliant, in the academic or artistic sense of the word. It may be the best example of a Tour won by tactics and willpower, by brain against brawn, in the last half-century. It may not have quite reached the gold standard of excitement that was 1989, but consider 1987: in 15 separate stages, one of the eventual top two, Roche and Pedro Delgado, put time into the other – Delgado put time into Roche on eight occasions, while Roche put time into Delgado seven times. (Whereas in 1989, Fignon and LeMond only put time into each other nine times in total – and there were four more stages in 1987 than in 1989.) What's more, 1987 was a four-way battle, with Jean-François Bernard and Charly Mottet also heavily involved in the general classification. Of these four riders, Delgado was the strongest climber and Bernard was probably the strongest time triallist, although Roche beat him in the long early time trial in Futuroscope. Mottet was the luckiest – he gained five minutes on his three main rivals in a soft break on stage three, but he was a strong time triallist as well.

Roche had the strongest flatland team in the race – Carrera won the team time trial (putting a minute into Delgado's PDM team when the final difference between them was 40 seconds), but he wasn't really the best at anything. He even made a good number of tactical blunders through the race, but he did one thing better than his three rivals: he kept his hopes of victory alive. If you could identify one single reason Roche won the Tour de France, it would be that he did so by not losing it.

Tactically, each of the four main protagonists had their moments. Mottet's soft break, followed up with second place to

Roche in the Futuroscope time trial, meant that he went into the Pyrenees in second overall, but 3-23 ahead of Roche, 5-31 ahead of Bernard and 7-26 ahead of Delgado. He also engineered the crosswind split in the transition stage to Blagnac, covered from different angles in Roche's two books, where he and Delgado gained over a minute on Roche and Bernard.

Bernard, for his part, gained over three minutes on Roche, Delgado and Mottet with a clever break on the first Pyrenean stage to Pau, where he combined with Luis Herrera, attacking late and picking up Erik Breukink and Pablo Wilches from the early break, in an echo of the escape his former leader Hinault had made with Herrera to Avoriaz in the 1985 Tour (or the break Hinault, Bernard and Delgado had made to Pau a year later). Bernard was often presented as a naïve tactician because of what happened later in the 1987 Tour, but he had a talent for spotting openings and acting on them. Bernard then handed out a walloping on the Mont Ventoux time trial, winning the stage by some distance. Into the Alps, with only seven stages left, he led the Tour with Roche and Mottet two and a half minutes behind, and Delgado at five minutes. More importantly, at that point he had momentum.

Delgado had the luxury of being the strongest climber in a backloaded Tour. He made a slow start to the race, but on the three major summit finishes – Luz Ardiden, Alpe d'Huez and La Plagne – and in Villard-de-Lans in the Alps, he finished first of the four main contenders.

Roche rode his Tour around racing and beating each of these three riders in turn, treating the race as a series of problems to be solved. The first problem was Mottet. He was probably the easiest problem for Roche, in spite of the fact that he was very tactically astute and therefore a dangerous rival. Roche wrote in *The Agony and the Ecstasy*, 'I did not regard Mottet as a likely Tour winner. Each time there was an acceleration on the climbs, he was left behind and I did not see him getting through the Alps without losing time.' It took a defensive ride by Roche on Luz Ardiden, then the Mont Ventoux time trial, to overtake Mottet. Once his early advantage had been eaten away, it was unlikely Mottet would make any more significant gains.

Solving the Jean-François Bernard problem, following the Ventoux time trial, was much more difficult. Roche couldn't rely on Bernard getting dropped in the mountains. After all, he'd just put over two minutes into Roche in a single climb. What's more, he'd outwitted his rivals with his equipment choice – instead of riding the whole time trial on a single bike, he'd ridden the flat first half on his time-trial bike, then changed to a light climbing bike for the Ventoux. At that point, Bernard looked like the cleverest rider in the race.

Bernard had a weak spot, however. He wasn't well liked, and Roche was prepared to harness the general anti-Bernard feeling among the other riders, especially the French, against him. In Paris–Nice earlier in the year, Bernard and his Toshiba team manager Paul Köchli had concocted an unpopular stage win on Mont Faron. Roche alleges that Bernard had told everybody he was just heading up the road for a toilet break, but that he'd carried on going and built up a substantial lead before anybody realized what was up. There was also a report that Köchli had told Roche's Carrera teammate Erich Mächler, in their native Swiss-German dialect, that Mächler's team car had broken down, but that manager Davide Boifava had told Köchli to tell Carrera not to chase (which he obviously had not done). Bernard's subsequent win was hugely unpopular, and he was badly worked over the next day, by Roche, Kelly and a few other senior riders, and lost the Paris–Nice race lead.

Back in Provence, 'He'd basically felt he'd won the Tour on Ventoux,' says Roche. 'He was on television saying he were the strongest in the race. Who did he think he was? There was still the Alps to go.' The Tour ganged up on Bernard the next day, a grippy middle-mountain stage to Villard-de-Lans. Mottet came from the region, and he knew the roads well – he plotted with Roche to take advantage of the position of the feed station, on a narrow road through the village of Léoncel, which was followed by a climb. Köchli had sent three of Bernard's teammates into the break, leaving Bernard potentially isolated. He punctured just before Léoncel, then his chain came off.

Attacking through feed zones and attacking rivals when they've had a mechanical are both ethical grey areas in cycling, but Roche and Mottet didn't care – they went for it anyway. Nobody else much cared either, and Bernard was hung out to dry. If he'd had as many friends in the bunch as Roche, for example, he might have got a helping hand, but as the smoothly rotating and co-operating group at the front, containing Roche, Mottet and Delgado, hammered clear, Bernard had to chase alone, with a large group sitting behind him, front-row spectators to his misery.

Bernard told me when I interviewed him a few years ago that he felt the peloton was also putting Köchli in his place. 'Tactically, it was very badly played on Köchli's part. I found myself with a single teammate, while we had three riders in an escape up the road,' he said. 'I had the impression that I was being made to pay for the actions of others. I could have bought the services of other riders or teams, but the management said no. Köchli didn't have a good reputation among the other team managers. He was a bit of an outsider.'

The final problem, the most difficult of all, was Delgado. At Alpe d'Huez, Delgado put almost two minutes into Roche, taking the yellow jersey by 25 seconds. If he'd done the same at La Plagne the next day, the Tour would have been over.

It was on this stage, which crossed the Col du Galibier, Col du Télégraphe and Col de la Madeleine *en route* to La Plagne, that

Roche's nose for a break caused him to become overconfident, or at least over-optimistic. At this point, a defensive ride would have been quite justifiable, with the final time trial at Dijon to come. Instead, Roche got carried away and joined a break just off the descent of the Galibier, when he noticed Delgado was looking isolated from his PDM team. Really, it was suicidal – with a long valley road to the foot of the Madeleine, and the Madeleine itself, PDM had plenty of time to get organized, and they cut Roche's lead from 1-40 at the bottom of the Madeleine to 40 seconds at the top, then caught him by the start of the climb to La Plagne.

What happened next sealed Roche's place in cycling history. Delgado attacked him at the bottom of the climb and built a lead of a minute and a half. But Roche gathered himself for an all-out effort in the last five kilometres, which he hoped would pull back enough time to keep his hopes alive. Delgado had slowed in the final few kilometres of Alpe d'Huez the day before and Roche suspected he'd do the same at La Plagne.

Modern television coverage would have taken the surprise out of Roche's comeback. These days, there would be a camera on each rider, and regular GPS time checks, and we'd have been given a slow reveal, rather than the sudden shock of a wasted Roche coming within four seconds of Delgado by the finish. In 1987, there were only two camera bikes – one had been with Delgado, the other with eventual stage winner Fignon – so Roche was able to creep up stealthily, almost invisibly. The first time television viewers saw Roche was when he burst around the final corner, just behind Delgado. The moment was immortalized for English-language fans by Phil Liggett's astonished commentary for Channel 4; I've since watched the Spanish coverage, and it's fair to say the Spanish commentator was less overwhelmed by Roche's appearance.

Roche blacked out after the finish line and had to be given

oxygen. But his comeback also seemed to kill Delgado's hopes of winning. There was still a major mountain stage to come, with a downhill finish, but this time Roche was able to put a handful of seconds back into Delgado. With the time trial to come, and only 21 seconds to make up on the Spaniard, Roche, who had spent the whole Tour not losing the race, finally was in a position to win it.

Delgado himself best summed up Roche's strengths as a competitor, paying tribute to his tactical instincts. 'He was very astute. A tough rival, a real old fox,' Delgado said. 'He was an able rider, capable of worming his way through the peloton and sneaking off the front when you didn't expect him to. That made him very difficult to handle. I would be watching him and he'd disappear.'

When summing up Roche's career, it's hard to work out whether 1987 was a lucky aberration, or whether the bad years, of which there were a number, were a more realistic reflection of his talent. Roche suffered more than his fair share of bad luck, but he had an impressive list of wins. It's just that they mostly happened in the space of one season, while other riders spread them out over entire careers.

8

Pedro Delgado
1988

Delgado was very popular with the team, even if everybody says, 'We don't really know him.' He doesn't show his emotions. He smiles a lot, but you never know it's really meant.

Harrie Jansen, PDM team manager

Pedro Delgado was the cyclist you liked if you preferred Jimmy White to Steve Davis, or Graeme Obree to Chris Boardman: compellingly chaotic, capable of world-beating feats, but generally second or third, behind more organized riders. As Delgado himself said, you couldn't risk leaving the room with the television on when he was racing – in the time it took to go and make yourself a cup of coffee, he'd have blown and lost five minutes, or attacked and won the race.

We'll get to Delgado's 1988 Tour win, which ironically was comprehensive, well organized and by far the least interesting race he ever participated in. Because Delgado was living proof that sometimes losing spectacularly is a lot more memorable than winning straightforwardly. Unfortunately for Delgado, he'll be remembered more for his unsuccessful title defence than for winning it in the first place.

It took two minutes and 40 seconds for Delgado's Tour challenge in 1989 to collapse into a shambolic heap. Tours have been lost in many ways – crashes, misjudgement of form, bad tactics, bad luck, illness, or simply coming up against better opposition. But Delgado is the only reigning Tour champion to have turned up late for his prologue.

The sensation must have been like being woken from a dream. Delgado, just finishing his warm-up, slowly became conscious that his mechanic, Carlos Vidales, was shouting at him. So was his manager, José Miguel Echávarri. He'd made a mistake about his start time, and he was already supposed to be on the road. An argument with the Tour organizers ate up further time – 'I had quite a bit of a tussle with them,' he said. 'They said I was late and wouldn't let me start.' Finally allowed to start, Delgado rode the course 14 seconds slower than the winner, Erik Breukink, which was better than he'd managed in any other prologue during his peak years – he'd conceded 19 seconds in 1986 and 1987, and 24 in 1990 (there wasn't a prologue in 1988). Added to the time lost in missing the start, however, he was a distant last, almost three minutes behind most of his rivals.

You had to laugh, because Delgado did – he always had an easy smile anyway; he looked good company. In an interview with Paul Sherwen shown on Channel 4 the evening after the prologue, Delgado looked relaxed, and finished each answer with a natural-looking smile. Yes, he'd just made a mistake about the timing. No, his chances to win the Tour weren't over. Yes, his morale was fine. There was only one hint of the frustration he must have been feeling – at the end of the interview, as he thanked Sherwen, the smile slowly disappeared, and there was just the briefest flash of Delgado's tongue as he poked it through his lips. At the same time, when he talked positively, his head was actually shaking slightly, rather than nodding.

These are what body-language experts call 'tells', and they are a popular trope with television psychologists, because they provide the kind of footage that can be zoomed in on and replayed in slow motion, and used to present a dramatic open-or-shut case of what people are really thinking. The shake of the head is an obvious one – while he's talking positively, his body language is negative. The reason given for the tongue protrusion is that people do it when they are talking about an idea they find unpleasant or distasteful – it's a hangover from infancy which is linked to the physical act of food rejection. Delgado was trying to be positive, but the reality was that he knew he'd probably blown it, and brave words and smiles couldn't cover up the fact he knew it.

What the situation probably needed, with the long time trial and mountain stages a way off, was a cool head. Better to regroup, hide away and identify the days on which he could start to chip away some of his deficit. Instead, Delgado attacked in the closing moments of the first stage, with just over three kilometres to go. He was chased down, and now he'd wasted a bit of physical energy to add to the emotional and mental energy he'd already lost. 'I knew I couldn't get the time back, but I went for it anyway,' he said. 'It didn't work – I just got more knackered.' Then, the same afternoon, he was dropped by his Reynolds team during the team time trial – to make things worse, initially nobody had noticed, or heard his shouts, and a desperate Delgado was tailed off, before his teammate Julián Gorospe dropped back to rescue him. Reynolds came last, and Delgado conceded another four and a half minutes to Laurent Fignon, whose Super-U team had won, and three and a half minutes to Greg LeMond and his ADR team. His deficit coming out of the opening weekend was seven minutes. Laurent Fignon approached him on a stage later in the week and asked him why he was still bothering.

From that moment on, however, Delgado was the rider who gained the most time in the race. His early start in the long individual time trial to Rennes in stage five meant that he missed the terrible weather which slowed down most of the favourites, and he came second behind LeMond. His deficit also meant that when he went for a long-range attack in the Pyrenean stage to Superbagnères, he was left to more or less get on with it – that was another three and a half minutes, to add to 30 seconds he'd nipped from the others at the end of the first Pyrenean stage. He'd actually moved up to fourth overall, just 2-53 behind Fignon: one second less than he'd conceded in total in the prologue. If anything, his rivals had probably been a bit too generous with him.

But he couldn't do any better than that. As Fignon and LeMond battled it out in the Alps, Delgado wasn't allowed to gain any more time, and though he moved up to third, he was stuck, 3-34 behind. It's fair to say that while he might not have lost the race in the opening weekend, it confirmed the impression that while he was a talented climber and stage racer, disaster was never far away.

In 2003, as part of their series of interviews with the living winners of the Tour, *L'Équipe* went to Segovia in Spain to meet Delgado. He came across as one of the most well adjusted of all of them. Typically, and perhaps fittingly, Delgado showed up an hour late, and *L'Équipe* described their impression: 'There is no anger. Only the permanent smile, and a pleasant disposition.'

Delgado does come across as a very friendly individual. He grew up in Segovia as part of a close-knit family. Like most cyclists, Delgado was a rider before he became a racer. 'I got my first bicycle when I helped my brother Julio on his paper round for the local paper, *El Adelantado de Segovia*,' he says. 'After saving for three months, I convinced him to buy our first bike. It was an Orbea, the brand that later formed a team, for whom I rode in 1985 and won the Tour of Spain. It was blue, and actually it was a girl's bicycle because it didn't have a top tube. It cost us 3,000 pesetas. But I wanted a racing bike and, after saving for a few more months, I was able to buy my first racing bike, which cost me 5,000 pesetas. It was made of iron, but it was marvellous.

'I had a friend at school called Frutos Arenal, who competed in bicycle races, and sometimes I would visit his house to see the trophies and medals he'd won.'

As a young boy, Delgado didn't fit the mould you might expect of a Tour winner. Bjarne Riis might have followed a strict training programme since the age of seven, while Bernard Hinault describes the fights he had at school, with the adrenalin rush of excitement at the memory. But Delgado, on the other hand, was a bit of a crybaby. His sister Marisa once said, 'You should have known him as a little boy. Pedro was always crying. I had to protect him all the time against the other boys in his class. They were teasing him all the time, he was so small, so timid. He's always been very sensitive.'

While his sister protected him, Delgado also had a very close relationship with his mother. Perhaps the female influence in his family made him less of a stereotypical alpha-male athlete. His mother died during the 1986 Tour, which upset him so much that he withdrew from the race. 'The hardest thing about losing my mother was not being able to say goodbye,' he said. 'My love for my mother was a profound and personal sentiment. Cycling was only a job, a game. I never got the two confused.'

But don't be fooled by the emotional intelligence. Delgado could also be hard-edged, when necessary. He won the Vuelta a España twice, in 1985 and 1989, and each time there were questions about the sportsmanship he had demonstrated.

In the 1985 event, Scotsman Robert Millar was safely in the lead with two stages to go, one middle-mountain stage and one flat stage. Millar should have been on his guard – the middle-mountain stage finished in Segovia, Delgado's home city. Delgado was actually languishing over six minutes down, but a conspiracy of events led to one of the most dramatic changes of lead ever seen in a Grand Tour. Delgado escaped to follow an attack by Spanish rider José Recio, during foul weather. He was wearing his rain cape, which might have meant Millar missed him going – it wasn't until 26 kilometres to go that Millar was told Delgado was four minutes up the road. Millar, meanwhile, was isolated from his teammates and Delgado and Recio were riding with incredible speed. Millar was left to chase on his own, with a peloton of Spanish riders unwilling to contribute, preferring to see a local victory rather than a Scottish one.

Rumours of a conspiracy gained hold. Delgado didn't engineer anything untoward himself, but he benefited from circumstances such as a level crossing being closed (despite no sign of a train) which prevented Millar's teammates Ronan Pensec and Pascal Simon from rejoining his group and adding crucial firepower to the chase. The Spanish riders were overt in their glee at having put Delgado into the lead, even though many rode for rival teams. In fact, Delgado himself said the original intention of his attack was to try to soften up Millar so that third-placed Pello Ruiz Cabestany might still be able to attack him. In the end, Delgado took enough time to win the race overall.

Four years later in the Vuelta, Delgado was wearing the yellow jersey and coincidentally the penultimate stage was mountainous, and finished in Segovia. This time, however, it was him who was under pressure, from Fabio Parra, the Colombian rider. Parra attacked on the Navacerrada climb, where Delgado had trained as a teenager, and gained 50 seconds by the top. Seven more, and he would take the overall lead. However, Delgado was aided in the pursuit by Russian rider Ivan Ivanov, and the gap was closed to 35 seconds at the finish. A Colombian television crew reported that on the morning of the final stage, they'd seen Delgado passing an envelope to Ivanov, which they alleged, admittedly without much in the way of evidence, was stuffed with cash. Delgado insisted that they'd become friends and he'd written his address down for Ivanov. Whenever Delgado won a race, there seemed to be some kind of question about it.

There was no question, initially, about Delgado's dominant form in the 1988 Tour. He'd been beaten by 40 seconds by Stephen Roche in 1987, after having been the strongest climber in the race, and he showed up to the 1988 event in even better shape. Just as importantly, his rivals were falling by the wayside – LeMond was still recovering from the injuries suffered in his hunting accident of 1987, Roche's damaged knee kept him from starting, Fignon was still not at his Tour-winning best, Charly Mottet was erratic in the mountains anyway, and Jean-François Bernard had won three stages and led the Giro but crashed out, injuring his back, and wasn't recovered in time for the Tour. For once, the only rider avoiding bad luck was Delgado.

There was no single display of dominance that won Delgado the Tour – he was so superior that he didn't have to pick his moment. Instead, as he gained in confidence, he'd wait for the final climb of the mountain stages, and surge away from his rivals in the last few kilometres. He bided his time until the 12th stage to Alpe d'Huez, which was the hardest stage of the race – he was in sixth place overall, but less than two minutes down on the yellow jersey, Steve Bauer, with none of the riders ahead of him likely to keep pace with him in the mountains.

With the damage having been limited on the flat stages, Delgado set about winning the race. He attacked on the Col du Glandon, the last climb before Alpe d'Huez, and was followed by eventual runner-up Steven Rooks. The pair were caught on Alpe d'Huez by Rooks's teammate Gert-Jan Theunisse, and Fabio Parra, and they finished a minute clear of the next rider. Delgado went into the yellow jersey, then increased his lead by winning the mountain time trial at Villard-de-Lans the next day. 'Alpe d'Huez was the key to winning the Tour,' Delgado says. 'I didn't mind not winning the stage, as the thing I was looking for was eliminating my possible rivals. I expected to keep the jersey after that, although I didn't expect to win in Villard-de-Lans. That was a pleasant surprise.'

There were three more summit finishes spread over the next six days – two in the Pyrenees and one at the Puy de Dôme in the Massif Central. Delgado launched late attacks in all three, gaining 41 seconds, 38 seconds and 52 seconds respectively. The attacks seemed almost gratuitous – he was safely in the lead, and in each case the stage winner was five or more minutes ahead. 'You constantly think that the time you have over your rivals is too little,' says Delgado. 'I felt in better form in comparison to my rivals, but victory is never easy.'

Fourth place in the final time trial at Santenay gave him the yellow jersey by seven minutes. On a sporting level, it had been a straightforward, even bland Tour in terms of the battle for the yellow jersey.

But Delgado's inability to win a stage race without attracting some kind of criticism was also true in the 1988 Tour. In Bordeaux, where the Tour's 17th stage finished, the French television channel Antenne 2 broke the story that Delgado had tested positive, for probenecid, after the Villard-de-Lans time trial. Probenecid is a diuretic, primarily used in the treatment of gout, but it can also be used as a masking agent for other drugs. The issue was already complicated by the fact that probenecid had been added to the International Olympic Committee's banned list, but that the UCI wouldn't be banning it until the start of 1989, which meant that Delgado wasn't penalized. 'The case should never have existed,' Delgado says now.

It was the first real doping scandal of the modern television age, and perhaps in the absence of any real intrigue in the race, the story quickly took hold. The rumour was that somebody high up in the race organization had leaked the information to Antenne 2 in order to flush the story out into the open, rather than risk looking like the positive test would be covered up. However, the Tour and UCI didn't help things by refusing to comment officially on the matter, while the press room and Tour entourage seethed with rumours and speculation. Delgado, for his part, adopted the normal tactic for positive riders – deny, express mystification over how such a mistake could have been made, then go off and gain more time the next day, which he did on the Puy de Dôme. He was backed up by his fellow riders – Rooks announced that if Delgado were penalized time or disqualified, he would travel to Spain the day after the Tour finished to go and give Delgado his yellow jersey back, which is the kind of suggestion somebody might make if they had been up to exactly the same kind of tricks that Delgado had been accused of. (Rooks admitted in 2009 that he'd doped for more or less his entire career, and his teammate Theunisse tested positive in 1988, for testosterone, and was docked 10 minutes.) In the end, the affair blew over – Delgado had escaped on a technicality, and cycling wasn't yet ready for the kind of searching self-examination that it would undergo at the turn of the century.

Was the real Pedro Delgado the dominant and imperious 1988 Tour winner, the tactically vulnerable runner-up of 1987, or the chaotic and hapless third-placer of 1989? Delgado is probably right when he admits it's probably a bit of each. 'The real Delgado is all of those three years,' he says. 'Especially 1989, when a silly mistake deprived me of my second Tour de France, and which I think was my best year as a professional cyclist.' Delgado holds a mirror up to us as fans of cycling, helping us to answer the question of ourselves. Which do we prefer? Winning ugly, or losing pretty?

9

Miguel Indurain
1991, 1992, 1993, 1994, 1995

Whether or not he ends up in the top ten and a name anybody will know, Michael Joyce will remain a paradox. The restrictions on his life have been, in my opinion, grotesque; and in certain ways Joyce himself is a grotesque. But the radical compression of his attention and sense of himself have allowed him to become a transcendent practitioner of an art – something few of us get to be. They've allowed him to visit and test parts of his psychic reserves most of us do not even know for sure we have. Joyce is, in other words, a complete man, though in a grotesquely limited way.

David Foster Wallace, 'The String Theory'

Miguel Indurain's team manager José Miguel Echávarri used to say that Miguel Indurain spoke with his silences. If that's true, it might still be tempting to conclude that he didn't have much to say. 'Do his still waters run deep?' asked Sam Abt rhetorically of Indurain in his account of the 1994 season, *A Season in Turmoil*. 'Do they run at all?' he followed up, crushingly.

Boring, boring Indurain. He won five consecutive Tours, with nary an interesting post-stage quote, nor much variety in the way of tactics, nor any doubt in his total superiority. After several years of unpredictable and compelling Tours (with the exception of 1988, won by Indurain's teammate Pedro Delgado), the early 1990s were less riveting, from about midway through the 1991 race. Indurain was the anti-tactician – he built up a huge lead in the time trials, then kept pace with his rivals in the mountains, which was impressive, given his weight of just under 80 kilogrammes. His Banesto team was strong enough to control the race, especially in the mountain stages.

And that was that. Indurain was invincible in the Tour de France from 1991 to 1995 – in the middle three races, his time trialling was so astonishingly dominant that he didn't need or want to attack. In the first and last, there was a bit more tactical subtlety, but only in comparison to the rest of his wins – he still won in the time trials, and was still all but undroppable in the mountains. Indurain was living evidence that in cycling, as in life, imperfection is what makes things interesting.

His performance in the Luxembourg time trial midway through the 1992 Tour de France summed up everything you need to know about Miguel Indurain. He'd already won the Tour de France the previous year, and he'd started the 1992 race as the favourite, but not by much. Three-time winner Greg LeMond was expected to figure, having blamed his seventh place in 1991 on illness. Indurain's contemporary Gianni Bugno, runner-up in 1991, had centered his entire season on the Tour, missing his home race, the Giro d'Italia (which Indurain had won), in order to be ready. And there was anticipation that Claudio Chiappucci, second and third in the last two Tours, could counteract Indurain's time trialling with attacks in the mountains.

How hollow and naïve these prognostications appeared after the time trial. In Luxembourg, Indurain demolished everybody, to an extent rarely seen in Tour history. Bugno was never the same again. Nor was LeMond. Bugno was patient zero in a paralysing psychological illness that afflicted a lot of Grand Tour contenders over the next few years: the Indurain Complex.

Until the very last moment, the television coverage of the Luxembourg time trial failed to really convey Indurain's speed. Instead, it's the still photographs of the day which tell the story most effectively – the background is a blur of panning movement, Indurain's face is half-covered by his helmet and visor so that only the lopsided grimace of his mouth, and the Desperate Dan square chin, are visible. His legs look huge – sculpted and perfectly proportioned, the Platonic Form of *rouleurs*' legs. Compared to a lot of cyclists, especially modern ones, moulded into streamlined contortions in wind tunnels, Indurain doesn't look particularly elegant or aerodynamic on his time-trial bike, but there's no doubting the raw power and speed with which he is propelling it. He was compellingly photogenic anyway, but the Luxembourg pictures still convey a sense of a once-in-a-decade cycling exploit.

There's just one moment in the television coverage which demonstrates the shock and awe of Indurain's time trial, right at the very end: the look on Laurent Fignon's face as he sprints to the finish line in Indurain's wake. The Frenchman, a former winner of the yellow jersey, the winner of four Tour time trials, and two days away from a stage win in Mulhouse, had started the time trial six minutes in front of Indurain. Fignon described the experience as a humiliation. 'I was wounded to the quick,' he said.

Indurain won by three minutes in Luxembourg, ahead of his teammate Armand De Las Cuevas. Third-placed Bugno, the closest of Indurain's supposed rivals, was another 41 seconds behind. LeMond conceded over four minutes. 'How is it possible?' asked the American. Indurain's *directeur sportif*

Eusebio Unzué later said that Indurain had been under-geared, and could have gone faster.

The margin of victory wasn't exactly unprecedented, but it had been a long time since any rider had dominated a time trial to the extent that Indurain had in Luxembourg. Jacques Anquetil won a couple of time trials by just under three minutes in the 1960s, but you had to go back to the early 1950s, and the days of 100-kilometre time trials, to find a larger margin of victory. (Jan Ullrich won a time trial in the 1997 Tour by 3-04.) It's fair to say that Indurain won the 1992 Tour in that one stage. You could argue that he won 1993 and 1994 on that stage too, such was the aura of invincibility he created.

Indurain was invincible, but not obnoxiously so. Unlike Merckx, Hinault or Armstrong, for example, he felt no need to compete for stage wins outside the time trials – he didn't win a single road stage in his five Tour victories. Whatever non-negotiable urge or need to get into a fight with rivals existed in riders like Merckx and Hinault, Indurain didn't have it. He had a politician's understanding of the Tour and the peloton which was far more subtle than theirs, yet it made his domination of his rivals every bit as complete. He allowed others to scrabble for stage wins, bartering that brief moment of glory against the understanding that they'd be better off not wasting energy trying to take time off him. Merckx and Hinault needed to remind themselves of their superiority by winning head-to-head fights – in the case of Hinault, he actually drew motivation from it. Indurain was more certain of himself. Unlike Hinault, he didn't need the reassurance.

It's hard to know which was more intimidating: the physical strength, or the intractable refusal or inability to show any emotion, weakness or pressure. In fact, these two aspects of Indurain were inseparable, and an entire mythology was built up about them. The Indurain mythology was based on a few guesstimated quantifications of his physical prowess, combined with anecdotes of his legendarily laid-back persona. There was Luxembourg, of course, and the three-minute margin of victory. But two years later he won a time trial at Bergerac, two minutes ahead of Tony Rominger, while in third Armand De Las Cuevas was 4-22 behind – and this was possibly an even more impressive time trial than Luxembourg. In Bergerac Indurain was almost six per cent faster than the rider in third, who was himself a strong time triallist.

In a sport where the margins between elite riders are necessarily fine, six per cent is a staggering difference. Magazines printed Indurain's physical stats: the resting heart rate of 28, the VO_2 max of 88, the sustained power output of 550 watts, and the 7.8-litre lungs. Tales leaked out of his extraordinary capacity to recover from hard efforts. Unzué reported that during the Luxembourg time trial, Indurain's heart rate had hit 190; a minute after he finished, it was already down to 58. There was the story of how he'd had a resting pulse-rate test, and he'd fallen asleep during it. And the one about the wattbike he broke during a physical test at Navarre University. And his old team-mate Gérard Rué's story of being on a plane above Brittany during a terrible storm: 'It was the fright of my life,' said Rué, before adding that Indurain had barely noticed the turbulence. Furthermore, Indurain was widely reported to conduct himself with gentlemanly modesty.

Indurain seemed curiously indifferent to his talent. This was often explained with reference to his rural upbringing. Pedro Delgado once said, 'I never know what is going on in Miguel's head. He gives the impression that he treats racing the same way he would treat working on his father's farm.' He came across as shy, but at the same time, he had rock-solid self-esteem. He wasn't egotistical in victory, nor in defeat when it finally came in 1996 – he didn't take his loss that year to Bjarne Riis personally, he just realized his Tour-winning years were over and seemed to lose interest, retiring at the end of the year. He was mentally strong, and stubborn. He was coached by José Miguel Echávarri for his entire professional cycling career, from 1984 to 1996, but when they fell out over his sponsor's insistence that he ride the 1996 Vuelta a España, Indurain didn't speak to Echávarri for years.

My perception at the time of Indurain's Tour wins was that apart from the Spanish, for whom he was an unimpeachable role model and hero, the people who liked Indurain didn't like cycling, they liked winning. What Indurain achieved was incredible, of course – of all the Tour winners in history, I think only Anquetil and Merckx were capable of similar physical feats. On the other hand, he wasn't at all emotionally engaging. Unpredictability, one of the most important aspects of a race for neutrals, was more or less stripped out of the Tour between 1991 and 1995. But while Indurain's Tour wins lacked suspense, he remained popular, both among his peers and among fans. He was impossible to dislike, like magnolia paint. And there was something aesthetically compelling and classy about him. The yellow of the Tour's *maillot jaune* and the pink of the Giro's *maglia rosa* seemed to suit him perfectly.

In *Indurain: A Tempered Passion*, the biography written in what seemed to me to be a hagiographical style by Javier García Sánchez, there's a story about a brief flicker of irritation the Spaniard had over criticism (by an unnamed rider) of his defensive riding style. According to García Sánchez, Indurain complained to *Miroir du Cyclisme* magazine about it. 'I know a champion said in your pages that he didn't like the way I won,' Indurain said to them. 'That's his right. But it's also my right to believe that winning is the only thing that counts, and that in 10 or 20 years' time they'll only be speaking about my *palmarès*, and not about the manner of the victories.'

Unfortunately for Indurain, people have been speaking about the manner of his victories since the very beginning.

There's a photograph of Miguel Indurain in the November 1986 edition of *Winning* magazine, taken during the Tour de l'Avenir that year. He's only 22, but everything else is familiar: he looks no younger than he did at 27 or 32; he is wearing the yellow jersey; and in spite of the stories that Indurain was several kilos heavier in the first few years of his professional career than later, he looks fairly fit – although he's got big shoulders. The only thing that really dates the photograph is the old-fashioned leather crash hat. The Tour de l'Avenir is a race for young riders, but it should be pointed out that Indurain had started five Grand Tours by this point in his career, and finished two. He'd even led the Vuelta a España briefly, in 1985.

Indurain's Tour de l'Avenir race lead was under threat in the stage to Briançon, which crossed the Col d'Izoard. RMO's American rider Alexi Grewal was climbing more strongly than Indurain and attacked on the Izoard, quickly moving ahead. With a 1-20 gap between them overall, it looked like Grewal might be able to take enough time to win the race. But that was before Colombian rider Abelardo Rondón, representing a different team, Café de Colombia, moved in front of Indurain and paced him all the way to the summit. Fittingly, Rondón would later do the same for Delgado in 1989 and 1990, and Indurain in 1991, after he signed for their team. Rondón's efforts pulled Indurain to the top of the climb 1-19 behind Grewal, but the Spanish rider was much faster on the downhill and he closed the gap to 26 seconds by the finish. Had there been a deal between Rondón, who had no obvious interest in working for the Spanish rider, and Indurain? 'Rondón and I are just good friends,' explained Indurain.

Even five years before he won the Tour, Indurain was

demonstrating two things that would remain true throughout his career. First, that he understood the value of making allies in the peloton. 'One of Indurain's strong points is that he's friends with everyone,' said Stephen Roche. Secondly, every now and again, behind the laconic exterior, there was a hint of the depth of his ambition. For somebody who seemed to take great care to be respected by his peers, Indurain didn't mind putting noses out of joint if a race win was at stake. There was nothing wrong in Rondón riding in a way that helped Indurain, but it might well have cost Grewal victory, and neutrals might have felt a twinge of sympathy for the American.

Before winning the Tour de France, Indurain won Paris–Nice twice, in 1989 and 1990, both times at the expense of Roche, who was runner-up on each occasion. There was the impression the second time round that Roche wasn't impressed with Indurain's tactics. 'He's the strongest on any one hill, of course,' he said of Indurain after the race. 'But he only put his nose in front the day before yesterday. I've been riding on the front all week and so have the other lads. He's been riding in the bunch and that's his way.' Roche warned: 'It's good, until the day he gets flicked and left behind.'

In 1990, the careers of Roche and Indurain were following opposite trajectories: one was a former Tour winner whose realistic ambitions were beginning to shrink, the other was a future Tour winner whose ambitions were quietly growing. Paris–Nice just happened to be the point where their careers crossed. Roche, unable to physically challenge Indurain afterwards, did get to live his ambitions to thwart Indurain vicariously through his Carrera teammate Chiappucci. 'I know Indurain well,' said Roche. 'I saw him under pressure one day in the Giro and said to Claudio he should go, and I was right. I know how he moved, when he's not going well, he's not as smooth. When he's going well he twirls a little gear and just bridges the gaps.'

Roche and Indurain had one last contretemps, on the final stage of Roche's last Tour, in 1993. Roche had accelerated to the front of the peloton to cross the finishing line first on the opening lap of the Champs-Élysées circuit, by way of a personal farewell to the race. Indurain's Banesto teammates had felt it was an honour reserved for the yellow jersey's team, and Indurain leaned on Roche further up the circuit. Roche relays, 'I said to him, "Miguel, you're only *un petit champion*. If you were *un grand champion* you'd have more respect for me." Then I pushed his bars away.'

There's a small postscript to the mini-rivalry between Roche and Indurain. Roche was co-commentating for Eurosport during the 1996 Tour when Indurain cracked on the stage to Les Arcs at the end of the first week. Roche could barely conceal the glee in his voice when commentator David Duffield asked him if there was some kind of problem with Indurain. 'No. Legs. He's blown,' Roche said. Then, shortly afterwards, spotting the lead group starting to realize what was happening and accelerating away, he had some helpful advice for them. 'They *must* ride as hard as they can,' Roche urged. His warning, spoken at the end of the 1990 Paris–Nice, had finally come true.

Miguel Indurain wasn't typical. The stereotypical Spanish cyclist is the climber, and while Indurain could ride up mountains as fast as, or even faster than, most climbers, his body type was that of the *rouleur*. Indurain's predecessors as Tour winners, Federico Bahamontes, Luis Ocaña and Pedro Delgado, were unpredictable and unreliable in comparison. Each won a single Tour, but couldn't maintain a consistent challenge in the way that Indurain could. His successors, Carlos Sastre and Alberto Contador, are also climbers, although Contador has managed to harness the psychological discipline necessary to win more than one Tour.

Early 1990s Spain was a country with one foot mired in the political and cultural shame of the Franco era, and one foot trying to stride ahead into the modern world. The Franco era ended in 1978, and Spain joined the European Community in 1986. Cultural commentators describe the country as having suffered from an inferiority complex in the post-Franco years, born from the perception that they were struggling to modernize and catch up with the rest of western Europe. Indurain's Tour wins were a source of pride, and a rare international sporting triumph for Spain at the time. Spanish cycling writer Carlos Arribas was interviewed in *Procycling* magazine in 2013, and he said that it was the fact Indurain *wasn't* seen as typically Spanish that made Spanish people so proud. 'For decades we saw great French and Italian champions and the great races – and racers – were elsewhere,' he said. 'Historically we had talented climbers, people like José Manuel Fuente, Pedro Delgado and Luis Ocaña, but they were always irascible characters and always prone to collapse.'

Indurain, on the other hand, was perfect and reliable. An international role model for a society that wanted to move on from a complex past.

Indurain was taking part in his sixth Tour de France, in 1990, before he even looked like a potential winner. Between 1985 and 1989 his record read: DNF, DNF, 97th, 47th, 17th. Of all the Tour winners in post-war history, only Bjarne Riis (107th in 1991) and Bradley Wiggins (121st in 2006) have finished lower in a Tour than Indurain's 97th in 1987.

He'd been an able *domestique* for Reynolds team leader Pedro Delgado during these years, but he'd mainly been break fodder in his first few Tours. In 1987 he was sixth in the final time trial, one place ahead of Delgado, who was in the process of losing the yellow jersey. In 1989 he won a Pyrenean stage, but the curious thing was that he showed few signs of his future dominance in the time trials, rarely breaking into the top 10 in the flat ones, with third in the mountain time trial at Orcières Merlette in 1989 the highlight.

However, in 1990, he was one of the strongest riders in the race, and would have finished a lot higher than 10th overall if he hadn't consistently sacrificed his chances for those of Delgado, who'd not been on form and suffered from illness in the second half of the Tour. Indurain won another mountain stage, at Luz Ardiden, following Greg LeMond's race-defining attack, dropping him easily at the finish. It was apparent that given a clear run, he could realistically hope to at least finish on the podium at the Tour. His ambitions came at the expense of his attacking instincts, however – like many riders, he rode a lot more interestingly before he became a general classification contender.

Indurain won the 1991 Tour, but first LeMond had to lose it. The American, aiming for his fourth win in the race, had out-witted and outridden Indurain in the first week. The Spaniard had missed out when LeMond infiltrated a break on the first road stage, gaining a minute. Indurain won the first long time trial, by eight seconds ahead of LeMond, but as the race approached the Pyrenees, LeMond was in the yellow jersey. Indurain was third, 2-17 behind.

Indurain was always more at home in the Pyrenees than the Alps. He won stages there in 1989 and 1990, and made race-shaping attacks in 1991 and 1994. But even on the first Pyrenean stage of 1991, to Jaca over the border in Spain, he still looked reluctant to trust himself to try to win the yellow jersey. While LeMond was in the process of losing the race lead to a long break by Luc Leblanc, Indurain bided his time. He was clearly strong, and the Banesto team was far outnumbering the isolated LeMond, but all Indurain had the nerve to do was make an attack on the run-in to the finish, gaining six seconds on a handful of rivals and eight on LeMond.

LeMond was teetering, however. One more push, Indurain sensed, and he'd fall.

It happened on the Col du Tourmalet the next day. As Indurain and Chiappucci pushed the pace at the front, towards the summit, LeMond started rolling his shoulders and pedalling in slow motion. An era had come to an end, just like that.

Indurain and Chiappucci made good their escape on the descent of the Tourmalet, and rode together over the Col d'Aspin and up the final climb of Val-Louron. Their co-operation, and LeMond's visible disintegration, hid the rest of the carnage they inflicted until the clock started ticking after they crossed the finish line, Chiappucci first, Indurain second. Bugno, late to realize that Indurain was in the process of riding away with the Tour, limited his losses to 1-29. The next riders in, Fignon and Charly Mottet, were three and four minutes behind, respectively. Andy Hampsten and Eduardo Chozas conceded six minutes. Ninth place might not have sounded disastrous for LeMond, but he was a whopping seven minutes behind. At Val-Louron, what had until that day been an open, attacking Tour was shut down. The Indurain era had begun.

LeMond was in denial about it. He attacked on the stage to Gap, gaining only 30 seconds. One day later he conceded two minutes to Indurain at Alpe d'Huez. Indurain, so aggressive at Val-Louron, was now in defensive mode. In that single climb to Alpe d'Huez, he not only killed Bugno's hopes of winning the 1991 race, he visibly broke any ambition the Italian had of ever beating him in the Tour. Bugno attacked four times on the ascent, but each time Indurain's teammate Jean-François Bernard brought him back. Towards the top, with Bernard spent, there was only Indurain, Bugno and Leblanc. As the trio rode up the final ramps of the climb through the town of Alpe d'Huez, Bugno turned and said something to Indurain. It looked like the age-old cycling compromise: 'You have the yellow jersey, I'll take the stage.' Indurain had safely contained Bugno. The Spaniard casually added a further 30 seconds to his lead over Bugno in the final time trial of the race. After all the excitement of the first week, it looked like a straightforward victory.

In 1992, it was even more straightforward, following Luxembourg. Eventual runner-up Chiappucci did chisel some time out of Indurain at a couple of points during the race – a lot is made of his long escape on the mountainous Sestrière stage, where he gained 1-45 on Indurain, but Chiappucci gained as much time on the stage to Brussels, where he and LeMond escaped with two others to contest the stage win well ahead of the peloton. The three and a half minutes Chiappucci did gain over these two stages on Indurain were more than accounted for in Luxembourg – the Italian conceded five and a half minutes there, then another three minutes for good measure in the final time trial. As for Bugno, he'd slipped down to third place without ever looking like he could provide a coherent challenge to Indurain.

The following two years, Swiss rider Tony Rominger was touted as Indurain's most realistic challenger. He was a strong time triallist and a stayer in the mountains, but Indurain contained him in just two stages in 1993. At the Lac de Madine time trial, Indurain won by over two minutes, then he stayed with Rominger during the two days in the Alps, allowing the Swiss rider to take the stage, with the unspoken agreement that second overall was the highest he could hope for. Rominger actually beat Indurain in the final time trial that year – Indurain had been suffering from toothache and a fever. But Rominger's challenge faded under pressure the following year. Indurain identified him as the main threat, and spent the Bergerac time trial, then the Pyrenean stage to Hautacam, putting him out of the race, while the rest of the field was collateral damage. By the time the race left the Pyrenees, Indurain's lead over Rominger in second was just under eight minutes. Even a three-stage assault by Latvian rider Piotr Ugrumov in the Alps, during which Indurain conceded eight minutes, including three minutes in the mountain time trial to Avoriaz, was nowhere near enough to overturn Indurain's lead. He won the Tour, with Ugrumov in second, by almost six minutes.

Was Miguel Indurain ever vulnerable? He was extraordinarily consistent over the five years he won the Tour, and while he had bad days, nobody was capable of identifying them at the time. It's not really surprising that a man who shows as little of himself as Indurain does in his human interactions would have no trouble covering up his suffering in the Tour.

He also seemed to be able to put the hex on his rivals. There were five different runners-up between 1991 and 1995, and nobody seemed capable of sustaining anything approaching a realistic rivalry with him. It helped that three of his runners-up – Bugno, Rominger and Alex Zülle – were very similar riders to him, but inferior, both physically and psychologically. None tried to tactically outwit him in any way, they generally just did the same as him, which was time-trial well and ride defensively in the mountains, only a bit slower. (Zülle did gain time on Indurain in a long-range mountain attack at La Plagne in 1995, but he'd already conceded five minutes by then.) Indurain's other two runners-up, Chiappucci and Ugrumov, were attacking climbers, both of whom conceded significant time in the flat time trials.

In short, Indurain's rivals tried to beat him in a physical contest, which was a hopeless enterprise. It was only in 1995 that a team – the Spanish ONCE outfit – tried to undermine him tactically, and, coincidentally, this was the same year that Indurain had chosen a less predictable method of gaining time on his rivals. 1995 was the only one of Indurain's wins that didn't feel like an outright procession, even if the final result was pretty similar.

Everybody expected Indurain to seize the initiative in the long time trial between Huy and Seraing at the end of the first week of the 1995 Tour. Instead, he went on the attack on a hilly stage the day before, with 25 kilometres to go, pulling Belgian rider Johan Bruyneel clear and gaining 50 seconds on his rivals. Bruyneel, riding for Zülle's ONCE team, would not contribute to the pace-setting, and *L'Équipe* described the Spaniard's escape as 'Indurain, alone against everybody.'

Then, for good measure, he won the time trial the next day anyway. Not by his usual massive margins, but enough so that only one rider, Bjarne Riis, was within two minutes of him going into the Alps. At La Plagne, Zülle won alone, but Indurain was second, two minutes ahead of the next rider, and it looked like the race had settled into its normal pattern.

However, on Bastille Day, where stage 12 finished at Mende, in the Massif Central, ONCE almost cracked Indurain tactically. They put three riders off the front of the race in a series of attacks, including sixth-placed Laurent Jalabert and eighth-placed Melcior Mauri. With three more riders from other teams, the group built a lead of 10 minutes while Indurain panicked. As ONCE leader Zülle sat on Indurain, only a late chase by Indurain's Banesto team brought the gap to a manageable level. Jalabert still put almost six minutes into Indurain.

In the end, ONCE's attempted coup was unsuccessful, but it was the only stage in five whole Tours that Indurain's final victory was actually in question. It makes you wonder why Indurain's rivals didn't try to subvert his physical supremacy by using these kind of tactics more often.

*

There's one more thing that a lot of Indurain's defeated rivals have in common: they were involved in doping, positive drug tests, blood manipulation or ethical grey areas in cycling.

Bugno received a suspended sentence and a fine for involvement in the shipping of a package of amphetamines, while Italian judge Franca Oliva found that Bugno had worked with Professor Francesco Conconi, who was found 'morally guilty' of promoting doping. Chiappucci was withdrawn from racing twice in 1997 following blood tests in which his haematocrit (red blood cell concentration) was above 50 per cent. He also told an Italian prosecutor the same year that he had used EPO since 1993, although he later retracted this statement. Rominger tested positive for salbutamol, which was banned under French rules but not UCI rules, at the 1994 Tour. He was also linked by Judge Oliva to Professor Conconi. Ugrumov was reported to have registered a haematocrit level of 60 per cent in a test in 1995. Zülle confessed to doping in 1998 when he was involved in the Festina scandal.

These five riders are not the only professional cyclists from the 1990s to have been involved in doping scandals. It is widely reported that EPO was introduced into the peloton in 1990 or 1991, becoming more common through 1992, 1993 and 1994, and endemic in 1995, until Festina put the brakes on, temporarily, three years later.

With the background knowledge we now have, it seems reasonable to ask if Miguel Indurain, the dominant rider during what are now acknowledged to be the first of the EPO years, was ever involved in doping. Indurain did not have a typical body shape for a Tour winner – he was taller and heavier than most climbers, yet he still managed to climb the high mountains of the Tour at the same speed or faster than most of his rivals, many of whom had boosted their performance artificially. He was reported in *Winning* magazine in January 1992 to have been tested by Professor Conconi at the University of Ferrara. Conconi's opinion at the time was that Indurain was 'too heavy'.

In an interview with *Marca* in 2007, Indurain was asked if he'd doped. 'I would say, "No,"' he replied. 'I passed all the controls, thousands of them, so many I lost count. It's something normal. You win, you pass controls and there's no problem.' That said, Indurain did test positive for salbutamol, which is an asthma medicine, at the Tour de l'Oise. Salbutamol was permitted if a rider suffering from asthma had applied for an exemption, but there was a complete ban on it in France. Indurain was cleared by the UCI after his explanation that he was suffering from asthma was accepted by the cycling authorities.

Does it matter in 2015 if a rider was one of dozens or hundreds to cheat, during what is acknowledged to be a dark period for the sport? I would say, 'Yes,' but the more important thing is what we do with that information.

10

Bjarne Riis

1996

Taciturn, silent, insensible to the new breath of vitality that was shaking the house, Colonel Aureliano Buendía could understand only that the secret of a good old age is simply an honourable pact with solitude.

Gabriel García Márquez, *One Hundred Years of Solitude*

We'll start with Hautacam, because an entire cycling life and an entire cycling era, in all their complexity, variety and imperfection, have been boiled down into the 34 minutes and 38 seconds that one man spent riding up its slopes in the 1996 Tour de France. Think of Hautacam, and you immediately see the image of Bjarne Riis in the yellow jersey, thrashing his way to the top, mouth agape, his broad shoulders and long arms making his bike look a size too small, a corona of gingery hair around his balding head. If you were playing a word association game, it might go Hautacam – Bjarne Riis – doping.

Hautacam, where the Tour finishes, sits on a shoulder of the mountain of the same name whose actual peak is a couple of kilometres to the north. Hautacam is not really a place in the way that most locations for a Tour stage finish are places

– there's no community, no church, no *mairie*, no schools, no café. It's just a car park around which a limited range of cross-country skiing trails and downhill red runs are arranged. Even the car park is just a widening of the road, and the only infra-structure is an *auberge* another 500 metres on. The road peters out about a kilometre further up the mountain, just over the Col de Tramassel – beyond that, it's a hiking trail, heading down the other side of the pass in the direction of the Pic du Midi de Bigorre and the Col du Tourmalet. Hautacam looms physically over a valley along whose floor the Gave de Pau river flows from south to north before joining the Adour on its journey to the sea at Bayonne. It also looms, a convenient metaphor, over the cycling career of Bjarne Riis.

There are two important narratives from the Hautacam stage of the 1996 Tour. The first is that it is where Riis committed regicide. Reigning Tour champion Miguel Indurain had already been grievously wounded over the previous two weeks by the stabs of Luc Leblanc, Evgeni Berzin, an inexplicable attack of average form and the terrible weather in the Alps. On Hautacam, Riis struck the mortal blow, on Indurain's 32nd birthday, of all days. *Et tu*, Bjarne? Then fall Indurain. All that was left to deal with was Indurain's funeral cortège – a 262-kilometre stage to the Spaniard's home city of Pamplona the next day, where Riis finished so far ahead of Indurain that the tomatoes some of the locals threw at him in their pique had dried in the sun before their hero came in.

The second narrative is that Riis's ascent of Hautacam was as clear a demonstration of the transformative powers of EPO and blood doping as there has ever been, a red flag fluttering its warning to a cycling world that was not yet ready to take any notice, a direct contradiction of the saying that a doped ass will never win the Derby. In his autobiography, *Stages of Light and Dark*, Riis admits that he used EPO, which ensured he was on superhuman form for the race. He was already in the yellow jersey before Hautacam. By the day's end he would be almost three minutes clear of second place.

It's easy to forget how ridiculous the 1996 Tour de France was. Conceptually it was no more ridiculous than any other Tour in the 1990s or the first half of the 2000s, but it still resonated. Riis has attracted more opprobrium than any other tarnished Tour winner except Lance Armstrong. There are reasons for this, including the fact that Armstrong and Riis aren't the easiest of individuals for fans to empathize with, but there was something about Riis's rise to the yellow jersey. It just seemed more blatant than anybody else's had been in that era.

On Hautacam, the favourites hit the bottom of the climb fast, and just kept going, bobbing out of their saddles as if performing dips on parallel bars. Through the village of Artalens-Souin on the lower slopes, Alex Zülle attacked, chased down by Indurain, two also-rans still under the illusion that they mattered in this race. Then Jan Ullrich went to the front under his teammate Riis's instructions, stretching the group into a single line, 15 riders long.

As they emerged from the village, Riis dropped back down the line, being passed by Richard Virenque, fourth in line, just as they both rode over the Frenchman's name written on the road. Riis slotted in a few more riders back beside Leblanc, who'd won at Hautacam two years previously, and just sat there. Ninety seconds later, he breezed back up to the front of the group as if they'd suddenly slowed, and carried on past everybody, off the front. It wasn't a real attack, more a statement to his rivals that he was finding the pace easy, even though it caused some damage. Indurain latched on to Riis's wheel, and Riis continued on the front, looking back every now and again, even freewheeling. The group, momentarily split into two, reformed behind him, but then he went again. The accelerations were invisible – Riis didn't need to make a perceptible effort, he had enough strength to vary his pace at will, but the effects could be seen in the way the group of riders behind compressed and coiled, like a spring, then stretched out again, to breaking point, at each fresh increase in speed.

The second attack was a short one, 10 seconds or so in duration, but it was immediately followed by a third, longer surge. The fourth attack got rid of everybody except Leblanc, Virenque and Laurent Dufaux, and the fifth attack wasn't even an attack. Riis just carried on pedalling, while his three rivals simultaneously went backwards.

Riis was riding on his big chainring, on a much higher gear, an unimaginable thing to do on such a difficult climb. Years later, Riis stated that he'd fitted a smaller chainring, which actually gave a lower gear, while giving his rivals the perception that he was finding the climb easy. The effect was to crack them physically and mentally.

Watching the footage on YouTube, his gear still looks pretty big – the unofficial time for his ascent, 34-38, was almost three minutes faster than 2014 Tour winner Vincenzo Nibali managed.

It's fitting that Hautacam is not far from the pilgrimage town of Lourdes. Lourdes is the site of an alleged miracle, but the reality is hokey tourist tat: kitsch, flesh-coloured Christs that glow in the dark, bad hotels, industrial quantities of holy water and cynicism dressed up as hope and sold for a margin. Riis couldn't have chosen a more apt place for his miracle.

'Some would say Riis is a complex character but really, it's probably more complicated than that,' Danish journalist Lars Jørgensen, who covers cycling for the *BT* newspaper, tells me. 'He's not a great talker, and he's kind of emotionally restrained.

Maybe elite athletes can often be emotionally restrained, but some of them mature as they grow up; they become more round and more reflective. I don't think that's the case with Riis.'

Riis is not an easy person to understand, and he comes across as very intense. He doesn't smile easily, is uncomfortable around the media and is given to long silences when answering questions. It can be unnerving, until you remind yourself that for Riis, silence is his default mode, his comfort zone. It means he's thinking, although I've had the impression that he's not necessarily thinking up an eloquent response to help with my enquiry, he could just be building a wall between us as a defensive strategy.

You could argue that it comes with the territory. Brian Holm, Riis's compatriot and former teammate at Roland in 1986 and Telekom 10 years later, told me that at the level of performance Riis reached, it's unusual to find anybody who's particularly normal. 'Everybody who's won the Tour is quite complex. You have to be slightly different. Take them one by one, none are normal, are they?' he said.

You can take your pick of reasons for Riis's unusual and distant personality. He was brought up partly by his father, Preben, from whom Riis inherited his taciturn nature. There was a documentary shown on Danish television in 2014, called *Riis Reset*, directed by Danish Broadcasting Corporation journalist Niels Christian Jung, which showed footage of a young Bjarne Riis eating a meal with his father before going out training. The long, empty silences in their non-conversations were excruciating and uncomfortable to watch.

Preben Riis was a restless, unsettled soul, who worked long hours in different jobs and seemed unable to commit emotionally to people for a long time. In *Stages of Light and Dark*, Riis recalls a constantly changing childhood landscape of different girlfriends – the regular upheaval of moving in with them, then inevitably moving out some time later – and his father's working patterns, which meant that Riis's grandma Anne did the majority of his upbringing. Preben and Bjarne once did a runner from a soon-to-be-ex-girlfriend's house on Christmas Day.

Riis's mother Bodil, after divorcing Preben, went to live in a commune with Riis's brother Flemming, and Riis rarely visited. 'Perhaps subconsciously I saw her choice to live in the commune as a sign that she didn't really want to spend time with me,' wrote Riis in *Stages of Light and Dark*. It was a dysfunctional family, touched by tragedy – Riis came to realize over the course of his childhood that he'd had an older brother, Michael, who'd suffered brain damage in a drowning accident when he was a toddler, and died. Preben being Preben, he didn't talk about it.

Preben and the young Bjarne bonded over one activity: cycling. Preben was a coach with the local cycling club, and Riis trained obsessively, even from the age of seven. For Riis, cycling was how he tried to get his father's attention. 'Dad tried to compensate for the lack of real quality time at home with me by being there as my cycling coach,' said Riis. 'I needed more from him than that – not just a dad who helped me train. I wanted him to be there for me on a daily basis.' Riis recalls riding home from their training sessions with tears streaming down his face as his father went back to work, or to his latest girlfriend's house, while Riis was sent back to his grandma's.

You don't have to be a psychologist to see the damage done by Riis's relationship with his family. It's obvious that the working relationship Riis and his father developed as rider and coach over his teenage years was a substitute for a more normal relationship. But at the same time, it was a close relationship, but one in which neither communicated much with the other.

In *Riis Reset*, Riis talks more about his father, whose recent death had hit him hard. 'I don't think he knew what to say. I don't think he ever learned how, so he couldn't teach me. I never learned how either,' he said. 'I've never learned how to share, I've never learned how to solve problems by sharing them. I've always kept them to myself. I've been like that all my life. It's been very inhibiting – learning at the age of 50 isn't easy.'

Some Tour winners seemed to be naturals, born to win the yellow jersey. Others had to graft their way to the top. Riis belongs to the latter group. Obviously, his willingness to take part in the doping arms race contributed to his success, too. Morally, Riis has rarely given the impression that he questioned the rightness or wrongness of it – in the chapter of his book called 'EPO in the Fridge', the main worry seems to be making sure his children don't get into his packets of drugs, or the hiding of them when guests come round. For Riis, his willingness to embrace unusually hard work was one of his strongest assets, and taking drugs, in his eyes, was part of that hard work.

It took Riis a long time and no small amount of stubbornness to get himself into the Danish national team when he was young, then into the twilight world of semi-professional *kermesse* teams in Belgium before, finally, a professional team. And even then, his first manager, Yves Hézard at Toshiba, told him in 1988 that he'd never make it as a cyclist. 'You no longer have a place in this team and I'm going to give you some advice – go back home to Denmark, you'll never do anything as a bike rider,' he said. Hézard wasn't the only coach not to have had faith in Riis's potential. The Danish national coach Otto Olsen gave Riis some unsolicited advice at an impromptu meeting in a car park in 1984, when Riis was 20, 'Bjarne Riis, I think you should go home, hang your bike on a hook and give up riding.'

Riis's willingness to persevere was illustrated when he turned professional for the small Belgian Roland–Van de Ven team in 1986. He'd asked his amateur team manager Marcel Gilles, who had good contacts with the professional teams, to see if anybody was interested that year. Gilles told him the teams were mostly full. As Riis wrote in *Stages of Light and Dark*: '"What's left?" I asked him. "Only crap teams," he told me. "One of those will do me," I said.'

According to Brian Holm, others might have doubted Riis, but self-doubt was not an issue, and that was clear in the way Riis approached life, as well as cycling. 'There were a lot of guys more talented than him, but he was stubborn. And he was always working out how to do things better. He was organized,' says Holm. 'I remember him at training camps. I'd see him sitting there in the evening, cleaning his chain with pipe cleaners. He was a perfectionist even then. When we turned pro – me, him and Jesper Skibby – we signed for the equivalent of 10,000 euros a year. A few years later he bought a new house in Luxembourg, a really nice house, three or four floors. It was beautiful. Me and Skibby thought, "What the fuck? How did he do that?" He was out of contract the next year, but Bjarne was confident that he'd make it, and he did.'

Things didn't go brilliantly at Roland, which focused mainly on *kermesse* races in Belgium. Riis described it as a 'school of hard knocks'. He managed to sign for a small pay rise the next year with the Lucas team, although salary payments were frequently late, or non-existent. One month, after he'd complained, he was paid in furniture instead of money. It was a chaotic and precarious existence, yet Riis still got a good opening the following year when he signed with Toshiba, thanks to their rider Kim Andersen, a Dane, putting in a good word for him.

After years of bad luck, however, he got one break at the end of 1988, when he rode the Tour of the EEC (the rebranded Tour de l'Avenir) for a composite Danish north European team. Toshiba had more or less stopped selecting him for races by this point. At the Tour of the EEC, Riis and his teammates chipped in to help Laurent Fignon and his Système-U team defend Fignon's lead, and Fignon was impressed enough to offer Riis a place on the team for 1989, just when the Dane was considering giving it all up and moving back to Denmark.

Paradoxically, it was at this moment in his career that Riis stopped trying to win races, temporarily at least. 'I was convinced that if I couldn't win races, then I would make myself indispensable in the team,' he said.

Fignon always had a soft spot for Riis, and the feeling was mutual. When I spoke to Riis before writing this chapter, I'd asked him for his memories of a few of the other Tour winners he'd worked with. His quotes about Jan Ullrich, Carlos Sastre and even Alberto Contador, the team leader of Riis's Tinkoff–Saxo Bank team, were pretty functional, even distant. But he was noticeably warmer about Fignon. 'There was confidence between us when we rode in the peloton. He'd sit on my wheel, not speaking, and he'd follow me wherever. He trusted me 100 per cent. When you have that connection, it's fantastic,' said Riis. 'It's like when you are so connected with your wife that when you are thinking about her and she calls, you know what she is thinking.'

There was some overlap in Riis and Fignon's personalities. Fignon was more demonstrative in his emotions than Riis, but they were both prickly, private characters. 'He was a very quiet guy and very private,' said Riis. 'What I liked with him was that he could be like I was. We didn't have to talk a lot.'

Fignon wrote about Riis in his autobiography *We Were Young and Carefree*: 'Bjarne was happy to get stuck in. Riding on his wheel was a total joy, because he could do anything: go fast when he had to and go through a gap with perfect timing. I never had to tell him anything, never had to say, "Come on," or "Slow down." I glued myself to his wheel and didn't have to do anything else.'

The Frenchman was brutally honest about Riis's capabilities as a rider, however. 'This has to be made clear: he was a good rider but not capable of winning a Tour de France in normal circumstances.'

Fignon told me in an interview years ago that one of the things which had instigated his retirement was the effect of EPO in the peloton. By 1993 Fignon simply couldn't keep up. 'I was riding with people who should not in a million years have been able to ride with me in the mountains,' he told me.

Riis wrote of the 1993 Tour too: 'The EPO I was taking had begun to take effect, and started to give me the results that people told me it would.' The Dane finished fifth overall, his breakthrough Grand Tour result. It's not hard to imagine that Fignon would have noticed Riis's transformation that year. By this point their career trajectories were following very different directions.

The character trait that makes Riis such a frustrating person to deal with on a journalistic level, his stubbornness, saw him survive, find a niche, then develop into a team leader, Tour contender and winner. At virtually every level he's ridden at, and in his subsequent career as a manager, people have doubted Riis, and he's generally proven them wrong. Interestingly, there's little evidence of satisfaction on his part at proving doubters wrong, and he doesn't seem to need to find people to pick fights with in the same way Bernard Hinault and Lance Armstrong do. Bjarne Riis's primary antagonist is himself – he wouldn't even have been a professional cyclist, let alone a Tour winner, if he hadn't been so driven. Then again, the battle to beat other riders in a professional race is nothing compared to the battle of a 10-year-old boy trying to gain the approval of a distant father.

Is Bjarne Riis happy? It's a difficult question to answer. When he won bike races, his face didn't relax into a smile – he carried the intensity and the effort of the race beyond the finish line. His defensive body language and evasiveness when faced with questions from the media made him look like he'd rather be anywhere else than at the centre of attention. Furthermore, Riis has experienced episodes of depression, and he describes coming close to a nervous breakdown in the very first chapter of his book. Unhappy? Possibly. Serious? Very. But the earnestness and defensiveness don't mean that he's not sensitive.

'Sometimes you might see that I look very serious, and you think that I'm not happy, but that's just my face,' says Riis. 'You have to remember where I come from – Jutland, where people are very serious.'

Riis is on good form when we speak. He's not exactly forward, and the conversation is punctuated with the usual long silences, but there are several moments in the conversation where he laughs out loud, generally when he's just poked fun at himself, which I find surprising, initially. Riis tells a story about a cruise he went on with his first wife, Mette, in the Caribbean. They'd share a dinner table with guests from other countries in the evenings, and his travelling companions would express concern that he wasn't having fun. 'They were Americans, and you went round the table to say what you'd been doing, and how your day was,' Riis says. 'I'd say, "My day was OK." In my world, where I come from, OK is not too bad. Pretty good! They'd ask me, "Is something wrong?" "No! It's fine!"'

Riis has attracted a lot of criticism from cycling fans for using EPO to win the Tour, which he finally confessed to in 2007, but also for not going public about what he has seen or known about as a team manager since the early 2000s. Tyler Hamilton, in his book *The Secret Race*, describes Riis as the best team manager he ever had, but makes it quite clear that Riis knew about Hamilton's doping, both at US Postal and at Riis's CSC team. Riis is a distant enough individual anyway, without his silence on this matter adding even more distance between him and cycling fans.

'I think I'm a pretty honest person,' Riis tells me. 'Although a lot of people don't think that. Just because I haven't told my story from the beginning doesn't mean I can't be an honest person. Some people can't understand that, and I'm sorry I can't help them. Sometimes it's nice to be me. Other times it's tough to be me. I am a pleaser; I love to please other people. But sometimes you have to say, "OK, I can't do it, I'm sorry."'

The perception I've always had of Riis is that he's hard, level-headed and organized. Not necessarily your first choice as someone to hang around with, but good at his job. The vulnerability and depression he experienced in 2013 show that it's more complex than that. I ask him how he manages it.

'My family and friends take care of me,' he says. There is a long silence; he doesn't want to say more. Later he'll tell me that his position in society doesn't help. 'It's a private matter, a very personal one,' he says. 'The problem is that I'm a very public person.'

It says something about Bjarne Riis's psychological make-up that he was the only Tour contender in the mid-1990s who didn't develop the Indurain Complex. I thought at the time he was over-competitive, but not in a way that made him likeable. Some riders, like Thomas Voeckler, Mark Cavendish or Robbie

McEwen, have a scrappy attitude to racing that means they never give up, and that's as much an asset to them as strong legs, or an efficient cardiovascular system. Riis, on the other hand, exuded icy menace. The day after Fabio Casartelli died in the 1995 Tour, when Riis was third overall, the peloton was too shocked to race, and turned the stage, through the Pyrenees, into a procession. Racing was the last thing on anybody's mind. Except Riis. He was interviewed on French television and bemoaned the lost opportunity to attack and gain time on race leader Indurain.

But Riis was unique among his competitors in that he thought he could realistically beat Indurain. In 1996, he moved to the Telekom team and set about winning the Tour.

The first week of the race was notable for atrocious weather and not much happening among the favourites – most of the stages finished in bunch sprints apart from a small group staying away on stage four. The rain and the cold seemed to affect Indurain's form, and the Spanish rider cracked terribly on the climb to Les Arcs during stage seven, and behind stage winner Luc Leblanc 10 riders finished over three minutes clear of Indurain, including Riis. The Dane moved to fourth overall, while just over a minute covered the whole top 10 behind yellow jersey Evgeni Berzin. The next day was a mountain time trial at Val-d'Isère, which Berzin won, ahead of Riis, with Abraham Olano third and Tony Rominger fourth. These four riders also occupied the top four overall.

At this point, Riis was probably not the favourite, but that changed the next day at Sestrière. The stage was considerably shortened in the continuing bad weather, with two mountains cut out owing to blizzards. Riis put in a lung-bursting attack almost from the beginning of the truncated stage, immediately carving out a 30-second lead. Behind him, Berzin, who was rumoured to be less than popular among his peers, was forced to lead the chase alone – with Riis not seen as a real threat, the half-minute they conceded to him was a worthwhile payoff at forcing Berzin to ride himself out of the yellow jersey. The race then settled into an uneasy week-long truce through the Massif Central. Riis wore yellow, with five more riders within two and a half minutes. Pundits even optimistically talked up Indurain's chances of a comeback – the Spanish rider was in eighth, four and a half minutes down.

But then came Hautacam, in which Riis demonstrated that he was the strongest rider in the race. The next day, a multiple mountain stage to Pamplona held in scorching weather, saw eight riders, the eventual top eight overall, put eight and a half minutes into the next rider on the road. Indurain, second-placed Olano and third-placed Rominger were the main casualties, unable to keep pace with Riis and his breakaway companions. Riis couldn't win the final time trial – that honour fell to his young teammate Ullrich, who took two minutes out of Riis's four-minute overall lead in one day and came second overall. But Riis had finally won the Tour.

Does it matter that Riis doped in order to win the yellow jersey? Yes, it does. If the peloton had been clean, Riis would not have had the physiology of a Tour winner. He responded extremely well to EPO, although that isn't to say that he wasn't also training or working hard in order to maximize his chances. Tyler Hamilton tells a story about some advice Riis gave him about losing weight in order to get into top form which says a lot about Riis's obsessive nature. Riis, Hamilton said, would finish a hard training ride, guzzle a bottle of fizzy water, take two or three sleeping tablets, then sleep the rest of the day, or even right through to the next morning, in order not to eat.

But it matters just as much, if not more, that in 1996 almost everybody was cheating. The organizers of the Tour made a half-hearted effort to strip Riis of his win following his admission, but with the statute of limitations having run out, his name remains on the official list of Tour winners. Riis didn't win the Tour fairly, he won it unfairly, in an unfair era.

Riis's relationship with the public has been a complicated one. The reaction to his win in Denmark was huge, with thousands of people turning up to the Tivoli Gardens in Copenhagen to his victory parade. Here, Riis looked far happier than normal, a wide grin on his face, his skinny body disappearing in a new-looking bright white shirt that was a size too big and accentuated the sunburn on his face and head.

Lars Jørgensen explains that Riis was one of the first internationally famous Danish sports stars, following on from the success of the national football team in the 1992 European Championships: 'It was enormous. He was welcomed home in the manner of a US president coming. He was escorted from the airport to central Copenhagen, and the Prime Minister was there. Denmark embraced this mute, strange, sometimes stubborn, sometimes uncommunicative, sometimes not charming, but very admirable person. People liked the tale of the underdog coming up from nowhere. It was a tale of the ugly duckling, by Hans Christian Andersen.'

Riis was fêted by the Danish public, but he quickly moved from object of idolization to object of fascination when his marriage ran into trouble towards the end of 1996. Riis had started an affair with a national team handball player and Olympic gold medallist, Anne Dorthe Tanderup, who he went on to marry, following his divorce from Mette. The affair of the yellow jersey and the gold medallist was too good a story for the gossip columnists to ignore, and Riis's reputation with the public suffered. The fairytale of the quiet, shy country boy who'd been married to his childhood sweetheart Mette had been changed into the modern morality tale of the celebrity sportsman acting scandalously. (On a side note, one of the interesting things about Riis is that while his own family had been spectacularly dysfunctional, he's maintained his second marriage, has had six children – two with Mette, four with Anne Dorthe – and in interviews the elder children come across as well balanced, open, intelligent, positive and communicative. 'That might be due to their mum,' jokes Jørgensen.)

'I've often wondered how so many people can like such an unlikeable person,' says Jørgensen. 'I don't have the answer, but I think that to both men and women, this grumpy, grunting, emotionally restrained man is not actually so uncommon in modern society. He is something a lot of us can relate to. He's maybe not yourself, but your father, your uncle or grandpa. That kind of male character is all over the place. He's not easy to like but you have to accept that he is there anyway, that he is achieving something despite his awkwardness. And he can be charming. We did an interview some years ago in his mansion in Jutland. He came and picked me up at the station, he was relaxed and smiling, and suddenly it felt like he put down his suspicions. It's not often you see him like that, but when you do, you think maybe he's not that bad after all.'

In the end, Riis seems incapable of having an uncomplicated relationship with anything or anybody, and the contradictions in his character will not easily resolve themselves. For every journalist who has experienced the monosyllabic, uncommunicative Riis, you'll find a current or ex-rider from one of his teams who extols his abilities as a communicator and leader. For every critic who feels that Riis's willingness to cheat has been the foundation of his success and prosperity, there's somebody to point out that he was one of several hundred doing exactly the same thing.

'You are not what you are today if you haven't been through the past. And you don't have the experience at 25 that you do when you are 50,' Riis tells me. 'As the Indians say, "You have to be smart and clever to be old."'

11

Jan Ullrich
1997

Jan waits until the water is up to his nose. Then he starts to swim.

Walter Godefroot

Jan Ullrich beat his rivals so easily in the 1997 Tour de France that you have to go back to the 1984 race to find a bigger margin of victory. But his rivals weren't ever really the problem. Ullrich's most formidable enemy was himself.

Laziness, procrastination, poor discipline, weight gain, injuries, bad luck, a tendency to go off the rails and a general atmosphere of chaos followed Ullrich around like wheelsuckers on a club run for all but the first three years of his 11-and-a-half-year career. When he won the Tour at the age of 23, one year after coming a shock second to his teammate Bjarne Riis, it was hard to see how he wasn't going to win multiple Tours for years to come. Just what fans of suspense and surprise in sport needed – only two years after Miguel Indurain's run of five predictable, crushing victories had come to an end, we were set fair for another five, or six, or seven. If anything, Ullrich looked even better than Indurain – he could drop the best climbers in the high mountains, and his time trialling was as dominant. When Indurain was 23, he was barely scraping into the top 100 in Grand Tours.

It's easy to forget how striking Ullrich's emergence was, and how phenomenal seemed his talent (although there were reasons, obvious in retrospect, for that). His backstory was not dissimilar to Lance Armstrong's – absent, alcoholic father, raised by a single mother – although a lot less was made of it than with Armstrong, perhaps because Ullrich wasn't so visibly psychologically affected by it. The more compelling narrative, for a Western audience still getting used to the fall of the Berlin Wall, was about the freckly wunderkind from the East German *Kinder- und Jugendsportschulen* system, with the chiselled legs, square jaw, red hair and nineties goatee. Tyler Hamilton, in his book *The Secret Race*, recalled his awe at Ullrich's physical presence. 'Ullrich's body was unlike any other rider's I'd ever seen,' he wrote. 'I'd sometimes try to ride next to him just so I could watch: you could actually see the muscle fibres moving. He was the only rider I've ever seen whose veins were visible under the Lycra.'

Riders from the former Eastern bloc had done well in professional cycling up to that point, but Ullrich was the first to really capture the imagination in the Tour de France. It helped that he was young, good-looking, photogenic on the bike and frighteningly strong – three years prior to Ullrich's win, Latvian Piotr Ugrumov had come second in the Tour, but there was something about Ugrumov, perhaps his taciturn nature or laboured style on the bike, that didn't quite resonate with fans. Russian rider and 1994 Giro winner Evgeni Berzin used to refer to Ugrumov as 'the old communist'.

But if Ugrumov was the old communist, Ullrich wasn't quite the young capitalist – he had one foot in the old system of state-run sports schools, and one foot in the gaudy world of professional cycling. This might or might not explain the trouble he had with self-discipline – after years of being institutionalized, it would be easy to suggest that he couldn't deal with the freedom. He'd spent most of his life in the hermetically sealed bubble of the old East German sports-school system, then had to live his life in the full glare of the German tabloid newspaper spotlight. He was also Germany's first Tour winner, and there had been no gradual build-up of good results by other riders to protect him from instant celebrity. Ullrich also rode for the *de facto* German team, Telekom. He didn't have time to adjust.

After the 1997 Tour, the only question was, how many Tours will Ullrich win? But instead, Ullrich's career had already peaked. He would never win the Tour again, although four more second places, between 1998 and 2003, plus a Vuelta a España title in 1999 and the Olympic road race gold medal in 2000, demonstrated that raw talent still goes a long way in sport, even in the face of Ullrich's best efforts at sabotaging it. The career of Laurent Fignon, his predecessor as a young Tour prodigy, was almost too similar. Fignon had won the Tour at 22, then again at 23 by a huge margin. Yet the remaining nine years of his career were underwhelming in comparison – with the exception of 1989, and even then he didn't win the Tour again.

Ullrich was second overall at 22, then winner at 23. But his ambitions from 2000 onwards bumped up against those of Lance Armstrong, whose organization, competitiveness and alpha-male posturing were in stark contrast to Ullrich's easygoing, herbivorous nature and chaotic form. Despite very rare flashes of world-beating excellence, the general consensus was that Ullrich had wasted his talent. At the end of each season, he'd promise it would be different next year, but the only real uncertainty was over exactly how Ullrich would cock up his preparation, and how many kilogrammes he'd put on – one

winter, 1997–1998, his weight gain was reported to be somewhere between 15 and 17 kilos. In the end, he was sacked, by
fax, after he became embroiled in the *Operación Puerto* doping
scandal which erupted in the run-up to the 2006 Tour. Ullrich's
biggest rival – himself – had finally won.

Let's not beat about the bush: the 1997 Tour was probably as
bad as it got with regard to EPO abuse in cycling. The sport
was still a year from the Festina scandal of 1998, during which
riders still doped, but at least some had the decency, according
to several accounts, to ditch their stash in the face of police raids
and general public disgust at the goings-on. In 1997, there were
no such fears in the peloton, and you only have to look at the
riders in the top 10 and below who would later test positive, or
confess to doping, to know that the race was irredeemably
tarnished.

It wasn't a vintage Tour in terms of intrigue or excitement,
partly for the above reasons. Human fallibility is one of the
most emotionally engaging parts of sport, and the riders
were more or less infallible when EPO abuse was rife. Of course,
some riders rode faster than others, but fewer riders cracked,
and there was little in the way of tactics or drama, just stage
after stage of Ullrich bludgeoning his rivals into submission.
The flat stages were moribund, too – seven out of the first eight
road stages finished in bunch sprints.

Riis, the defending champion, was nominally the Telekom
team's leader, but priorities in the team were divided, both by
Ullrich's form and momentum, and by trying to put the team's
sprinter Erik Zabel into a position to win stages and contend
for the green jersey. It took only two days for Riis to start feeling
that a successful defence of his Tour title was not the main focus
within the team. Before the race had started, Brian Holm had
told him that while general manager Walter Godefroot was

supportive of Riis's ambitions, the team manager Rudy Pévenage was much more involved with Ullrich. 'Rudy's only interested in Jan, so watch him,' warned Holm.

The problem for Riis, and the advantage for Ullrich, was that Telekom was a German team, and Ullrich was a young German contender for the yellow jersey. Telekom had evolved from a lower-division team sponsored by the city of Stuttgart and, until Riis joined in 1996, it was anything but the model of stereotypical Teutonic efficiency that it later became. Even as late as 1995, Telekom's Tour berth depended on forming a composite team with Italian outfit ZG–Selle Italia. The resulting squad consisted of two-thirds Telekom riders, one-third ZG riders, and it's fair to say the experiment wasn't a satisfactory one, although Zabel won two stages. But by 1997, despite having won the Tour with a Danish rider the previous year, the team was becoming a big story back home in Germany, all the bigger for Ullrich's presence.

In the prologue, Ullrich came second behind Britain's Chris Boardman, but 13 seconds ahead of Riis. The next day, a late crash split the field into three main pieces and Riis was marooned in the second group, 58 seconds behind the first group, which contained 64 riders. To inflame Riis's ire, he could see the first group, led by a magenta-coloured echelon of Telekom riders, riding away, working to set Zabel up for the sprint, while nobody waited for him. Riis had time to answer one question to journalists after the stage, before he was ushered away by a team official: 'There was sod-all support from [my team] today,' he said.

Meanwhile, Ullrich was riding the perfect Tour. He marked an attack by Richard Virenque and Marco Pantani on the first, minor, Pyrenean stage, at a point where Riis was simply incapable of following. That gained him another 27 seconds on Riis. The Tour was more or less over for the defending champion. One day later, it was over for everybody else. Ullrich, given the green light to abandon Riis by the Telekom management, put in a career-defining attack on the stage to Arcalís, in Andorra.

On the final climb, Ullrich put over a minute into Pantani and Virenque, who were supposedly the best climbers in the world, and who would both run into trouble with the anti-doping authorities within a couple of years. Italian rider Francesco Casagrande was another minute behind – he tested positive in 1998. Next were Riis, who admitted doping during this period in 2007, and Dufaux, who was embroiled in the Festina affair of 1998. It doesn't pay to run your finger down the list of results on many of the key stages of the 1997 Tour to try to find the best clean rider. It was a dirty race, even by the standards of the 1990s.

Ullrich's ride looked exhilarating at the time – a dominating, snarling, Tour-winning performance. Even now, watching it on replay, there is something compelling about how the young German powered up the climb. He simply rode away from the lead group, and when he turned around to see Virenque and Pantani struggling to make inroads on his lead, he sat down, held on to the handlebar drops, and went even faster. Fans tried to run alongside him as he climbed, but they couldn't keep up, even though some were *sprinting*. Through the white side panels of his shorts, the shape of his hip bones were clearly visible; his muscles bulged and flexed. Ullrich's barrel chest was accentuated by the stripes of his German champion's jersey. Meanwhile, his face still looked like that of a young boy – his curly red hair and freckles belied the demonstration of physical power he was engaged in.

And Arcalís wasn't even the most impressive ride of the Tour. Ullrich's win two stages later in the St-Étienne time trial, which passed over a second-category climb, the Col de la Croix de

Chaubouret, was even more dominant than any of Miguel Indurain's time-trial performances. Second-placed Virenque conceded 3-04. In the Alps, Ullrich could afford to let Pantani win two stages and Virenque one, although Virenque gave him a brief scare on the stage to Courchevel by isolating him from the other Telekom riders and gaining an advantage before the race settled down again. With a long time trial on the penultimate day giving him one last chance to gain time, Ullrich's Tour win looked impressive: Virenque was nine minutes behind in second, Pantani another five behind in third. But just as the 1997 Tour, and especially Arcalís, define Ullrich's racing career, so they also define the era. It might have been entertaining, but unfortunately it wasn't sport.

'Jan has been professional since he was 10 years old. He grew up as a sportsman, in an academy away from his parents, he was committed to cycling and he didn't know anything else,' Ullrich's teammate and friend (and, since 2006, brother-in-law) Tobias Steinhauser, told *Cycle Sport* magazine in 2005. 'The human body and mind can adapt to anything, but perhaps now it is not a surprise that he is not a machine. He was made into a machine as a child. Now as an adult he has realized there is more to life, and he wants to explore it.'

Ullrich drove his fans up the wall with his inability to focus on his training from one season to the next. He showed up overweight every year from 1998 onwards, sometimes by several kilos, sometimes by 15 or more. His fellow German rider Marcel Wüst once told a story about Ullrich putting a jar of Nutella in the microwave, then drinking it with a straw. 'He lived to the max, then trained to the max,' said Wüst.

As the seasons passed, so the excuses piled up. In 1998, he almost won the Tour again, wearing the yellow jersey through the Pyrenees and into the Alps, but was undone by Pantani on the soaking stage to Les Deux Alpes. Riis wrote in his auto-biography *Stages of Light and Dark* that he'd tried to make Telekom send team staff to wait at the top of the Col du Galibier, where Pantani had attacked and Ullrich had chased, with dry and warm jackets to give to the riders for the freezing descent. He'd also told Ullrich not to chase Pantani, and to save his effort for the long descent instead, even if it meant conceding just a couple of minutes. Riis was ignored both times, and Ullrich lost nine minutes and the Tour.

In 1999, Ullrich got injured. In 2000 and 2001 he'd been overweight in the early season, and couldn't match Lance Armstrong's form at the Tour. In 2002 he was injured, then tested positive for amphetamines which he claimed he'd taken in a nightclub, crashed his car and fled the scene, and gave a very good impression of a young man crying for help under the pressure of fame and frustration. A change of teams in 2003 might have provided a confidence boost and a new beginning, but the Coast team for which he signed ran out of money before the summer. Bianchi stepped in and wrote the cheques, and Ullrich miraculously ran Armstrong very close in the Tour. It looked like he'd turned his career around, against the odds.

But in 2004, and 2005, he fell into the same bad habits. There was a return to Telekom, now called T-Mobile, more early-season travails and a fourth and a final third place in the Tour (now annulled after the Court of Arbitration for Sport ruled that Ullrich had been involved in blood doping). Each time it was the same: Armstrong would make his habitual attack on the first summit finish of the race, and the television cameras would pan back to a puffing Ullrich, pedalling a suffocating gear. In 2005, the ignominy had been complete – Ullrich was caught by Armstrong in the opening short time trial of the race. Ullrich was suffering from injuries caused by having crashed into his pacing car on a training ride just a couple of days before. It could only happen to Jan.

The latter part of Ullrich's career took place against the backdrop of a spectacularly dysfunctional relationship between his personal coach, Rudy Pévenage, and T-Mobile's manager, Walter Godefroot. 'Pévenage is a person with whom I have no problems because I don't talk to him,' said Godefroot. All that was left was for Ullrich to be pulled out of the 2006 Tour when *Operación Puerto* blew up, and the fall of Jan Ullrich, spread out in slow motion over nine seasons, was complete.

In 2013 he finally confessed to doping, but there was something unsatisfactory about it, even if his apology seemed sincere. 'I didn't take anything which the others were not taking,' he said. 'For me, betrayal only begins when I gain an advantage, but that was not the case. I just wanted to ensure equal opportunities.' It's an illustration of the skewed moral compass of professional cycling, where the cheating wasn't held to be a problem so long as it didn't involve getting some kind of unfair advantage compared to the other riders. Not cheating fellow competitors isn't the main point – they were still cheating their fans.

Why couldn't Jan Ullrich focus? Godefroot once observed that if you'd combined Erik Zabel's diligent attitude to training and preparation with Ullrich's talent, the result would be another Eddy Merckx. He also observed, as many have, that Ullrich was too nice to be a successful professional cyclist. It's true that there's a human side to Ullrich that isn't shared by many other members of the yellow jersey club. His fallibility made him much easier to identify with, even if many sports fans prefer successful athletes to well-rounded personalities. What made him win only one Tour, despite physical gifts which should have won him multiple yellow jerseys, ironically probably made him a better human being.

The pressure of bike racing was too much for Ullrich. He'd been hothoused since the age of 10, become the amateur world champion at the age of 19, was introduced to performance-enhancing drugs at some point along the way, and become an international superstar before he was psychologically equipped to deal with it. According to Steinhauser, Ullrich needed to have a life away from cycling, even to the point that it caused real problems with his career, but Telekom, and Germany, expected him to win the Tour.

The German cycling journalist Sebastian Moll compared Ullrich to the 1970s German cyclist Dietrich Thurau, and more modern stars like Boris Becker and national team goalkeeper Oliver Kahn. Thurau had worn the yellow jersey for 15 days during the 1977 Tour at the age of 22, but had never lived up to his promise. Becker and Kahn were constantly in the tabloid headlines for their private lives. 'It seems that once athletes have become stars in Germany they have a very hard time coping with that status,' said Moll. 'They effectively become public property, and the urge to break away from the constant surveillance by the media, not to mention the expectations regarding their behaviour as role models – as well as their athletic performance – seems to grow unbearably.'

Perhaps the question shouldn't be: why couldn't Jan Ullrich focus? It might be more enlightening to ask, with him having lived the life he had, how *could* he have focused?

'I'm not disappointed with Jan Ullrich's career,' Godefroot tells me. 'The general perception of Jan Ullrich is that he could have done better, but that's because we sometimes fall into the trap of thinking sport is binary, divided into winning and losing, success and failure. The five second places tend to outshine the single win at the Tour, but the problem is that we compare him to riders like Lance Armstrong, or Miguel Indurain, between whose eras Ullrich's win fell. It would be better to compare

Ullrich to ourselves because, really, he was one of us. Jan was a nice boy, and very talented. But in Flanders we say of someone like that that 'the sun shines for everybody'. That means that he's happy, whatever. When Jan was second in the Tour de France, he wasn't disappointed. He didn't have the spirit of the great champions, who needed to be killers, and I mean it as a compliment to him.

'I'm like that as well. In fact, most people are.'

Godefroot was ubiquitous throughout Ullrich's career. He met him in a restaurant when he was still a young amateur, and they agreed that Ullrich would sign for Telekom in 1995. The contract was completed after Ullrich won the 1994 World Amateur Road Race Championships. Godefroot was his team manager from then until the end, with the exception of Ullrich's year at Coast and Bianchi.

'I didn't know then that he was going to win the Tour. You never know, even with good amateurs. You can find a good amateur who can ride well in the middle mountains, but even then you have no real idea of how he's going to cross the high mountains in the Tour. You can find a rider like Sean Kelly, who can cross the middle mountains, and win a race like the Tour of Switzerland, but he can't ride the high mountains with the best. We were very surprised with how Jan climbed in his first Tour,' says Godefroot.

But Ullrich's talent was not matched by his commitment to living like an athlete. 'Jan couldn't live for sport 12 months a year,' says Godefroot. 'He just wanted to relax at home, eat what he wanted and live how he wanted. The pressure of sport was too much for him, and he didn't have the mentality of a star, he didn't need to have a private plane. In the winter, he lived like a normal man, and he put on weight like a normal man. Jan loved cycling and he loved sport. But he didn't love being the centre of attention. He once told Rudy Pévenage that he was happiest when he was at the Olympic Games. He thought that was true sport – he was in the village with the other athletes, no journalists, no press, no publicity. That shows what kind of man he was – a nice guy, well balanced.

'All the great champions of cycling have special characters. Jan is not a special man, he's a normal man.'

12

Marco Pantani

1998

For Sonny Liston, it was easy being a superman. It was being a man that was often difficult.

Boxing Yearbook, 1964

What explanation is there for the fact that millions of pilgrims flock to view the Turin shroud whenever the Cathedral of St John the Baptist in Turin puts it on public display, other than that people have a profound need to believe in incredible things? It was believed by the faithful that the shroud was stained with the image of Jesus, miraculously formed when he was wrapped in it after falling from the cross – until 1988, when a carbon-dating test run by Oxford University found that the shroud was a medieval creation, just over 700 years old. Yet on the three occasions the shroud has been put on display since, millions more still made the pilgrimage to Turin to see the image of Jesus.

Cycling fans are still worshipping at the church of Marco Pantani. He is the personification of romance in the sport – his climbing verve, bold attacks and psychological fragility appealed to a common and significant tendency in sports fans, that of imbuing human achievements with superhuman status. It's either a natural thing to do, or so culturally ingrained that it might as well be – and why not? What better way of dealing with the daily grind than to enjoy a few fleeting moments of escapism, via the exploits of great athletes, or great musicians, or great actors?

Pantani was easy to idolize. He won the 1998 Tour de France in spectacular circumstances, with a long-range attack in atrocious weather in the Alps. It was a throwback to the old days of cycling myth, when eyewitnesses and coverage were so scarce that creative newspaper journalists could essentially invent the narrative in purple prose. His unpredictable, organic, harrying tactics were a refreshing contrast to the metronomic, implacable, bullying strength of Jan Ullrich, his main rival that year. The 1998 Tour was a clash of cultures, stereotypes and cycling ideologies: the Latin versus the Teutonic, the climber versus the *rouleur*, the attacker versus the defender, romanticism versus classicism, the underdog versus the favourite, fire versus ice. Cycling fans loved Pantani. He was capable of riding at great speeds uphill, despite looking inelegant on his bike – his riding style and attacks resembled a persistent wasp spoiling a picnic. He looked quirky – he'd covered up his premature baldness by shaving his head, cultivating a goatee beard and wearing a bandana, earrings and a nose stud (he might not have stood out now, but in 1998, not many professional cyclists wore facial jewellery). His sticky-out ears and crooked smile made him seem accessible, normal and likeable. He wasn't good-looking, although when he was off the bike, his neutral facial expression was unusually placid – or maybe that was just in comparison to the grimace he wore when cycling. There was also a vulnerability about him, which appealed hugely to cycling fans.

However, as well as the glorious cyclist, there was also the depressive, the cheat, the drug addict, the fallen hero, the psychologically damaged victim and, ultimately, the unspeakably horrible, lonely death in a seedy hotel room in the eerie quiet of an off-season seaside town.

Would it ever have been possible to have one without the other? Is it possible to celebrate the cyclist, and enable his ascent to the emotional heights, without somehow playing a part in his descent to psychological obliteration? Pantani's psychological complexity and addictive personality got him hooked on the adulation, and the withdrawal symptoms eventually killed him. He made people happy, but he was not happy.

Pantani the cyclist and Pantani the person seemed inseparable from each other. In life, Pantani was given to profound and honest ruminations about his nature and thoughts. Consider his post-stage quote on the crucial stage of the 1998 Giro d'Italia (which he also won), when he'd attacked on the summit finish at Montecampione: 'I just thought, either it works, or I'm going to blow everything. I had no alternative. I had to see, to know who was the strongest,' he said. Then he continued: 'When I had my nose pierced on New Year's Eve, it was a symbol of my independence, that I didn't want to be told what to do by anybody. With three kilometres to go, just before I had to attack, something told me to throw it [the nose piercing] away.'

There's a depth to these words which is unusual in the run-of-the-mill quotes people expect to hear in the aftermath of a stage. The sense is less of a sporting competition to be won – with dispassionate tactics and superior strength – and more of a compulsion, and a degree of self-exploration that is frightening in its intensity. Pantani seemed to be harnessing not just physical and mental strength, but also emotional force. We loved it. But nobody realized that the adulation wasn't a by-product of the primary aim – winning races. Pantani actually needed it.

In Matt Rendell's book *The Death of Marco Pantani*, which is comprehensive on the subject, there are forensic accounts of blood values, doping and the races he won that leave little room for theorizing about Pantani's sporting ethics – there is no doubt he was taking EPO from at least early 1993. But there's also a psychiatric report on Pantani, undertaken in 2002 by Dr Mario Pissacroia, who was a specialist in substance abuse. Pissacroia diagnosed both depression and bipolar disorder in Pantani, along with narcissistic and obsessive elements. He also deduced that Pantani had been using crack cocaine. But the terrifying thing about the report is one of Pissacroia's conclusions, that Pantani experienced high stress from sporting competition. The point is that narcissism and obsessiveness are often seen as assets for an elite athlete – we celebrate the self-belief of someone who has become the best in the world at what they do, and admire their ability to organize every last detail in their lives in order to harness their talent. The conclusion Pissacroia came to was that involvement in competitive cycling didn't help Pantani, it actually made him worse. Pantani's life was a tragedy in the dramatic sense of the word: a worthy protagonist, weakened by character flaws, put into a difficult situation, whose fall is inevitable, and fatal.

If that wasn't enough, there's more bitter irony in Pantani's career. The 1998 Tour is defined by two things: Pantani's glorious victory, and the Festina scandal, which almost made the race grind to a halt. And while fans and the general public shared a sense of shock at the revelation that there was organized, endemic doping happening in cycling, they still cheered a winner whose blood records indicated career-long EPO usage. What's more, Pantani's 1998 Tour samples, when retested in 2004, demonstrated that while the race had been falling apart around him, while riders were arrested and detained for possession of doping products, he was taking EPO all the time.

The Festina scandal erupted in the run-up to the 1998 Tour.

A Festina team car, driven by their *soigneur* Willy Voet, was stopped as he crossed the border from Belgium into France on his way to the race. The car contained a staggering range and number of doping products, a mobile library of pharma-cological research from which riders could borrow at will. This went beyond individual riders testing positive – the realization that the team infrastructure was involved in the cheating eleve-ated matters to an entirely new and more serious level. France had also recently passed a law making doping a criminal offence. The shining of light into cycling's dark corners, still ongoing, had begun.

The Tour tried to tough it out – the prologue took place in Dublin, with Britain's Chris Boardman taking the yellow jersey (and Pantani finishing 181st out of 189 starters, 48 seconds behind). The show went on – commentators commentated, primarily on the action, and the riders kept racing, although an anonymous professional once told me that the opening weekend was enlivened by the sight of riders dumping their stash in advance of leaving Ireland, before the French police could start sniffing around once the race reached the mainland. The Festina riders got as far as the end of stage six before their situation became untenable and the Tour organization threw them off the race on the morning of the first long time trial.

This incident provided an interesting comparison between French idol Richard Virenque, Festina's leader and the runner-up to Jan Ullrich in 1997, and Pantani. Virenque was devastated at his exclusion from the Tour. He and the Festina riders called an impromptu press conference in which Virenque sobbed his denials. Virenque, like Pantani, was dependent on the adulation of the public. But after this episode, and eventu-ally confessing to doping, Virenque was back racing with no hint of self-doubt or regret and he retired happy in 2004, having won a total of seven King of the Mountains titles and three more Tour stages to add to the four he already had. Pantani's dependence on public adulation was rooted in insecurity and mental fragility; Virenque's was based in having a huge ego and an almost complete absence of self-awareness – he was as uncomplicated as Pantani was complex.

Ullrich won the long time trial, with Pantani another four minutes behind, but the Italian's fightback started in the Pyrenees. He squeezed 20 seconds out of Ullrich on the stage to Bagnères-de-Luchon, then a minute and a half at Plateau de Beille. Against the backdrop of more scandal – Rodolfo Massi of the Casino team would be arrested, the TVM team's hotel rooms raided – the riders collectively decided, with a demonstration of self-righteousness that would be staggering now, to protest against their treatment. The day after Plateau de Beille, they staged a sit-down protest while their self-appointed representatives, Laurent Jalabert and Bjarne Riis, bickered with each other and with the Tour's boss Jean-Marie Leblanc. Tour de Farce, wrote the headline-makers, shooting into an open goal.

As a sporting spectacle, the 1998 Tour had questionable worth. First, there were more important things going on. The Tour organization were set on the race finishing as planned – they simply didn't have the imagination to consider any other options – but the ongoing police raids and scandal made it clear that the problem was huge. Secondly, many of the riders, including the two main protagonists, were still taking EPO. It meant that the race, and the narrative that the organizers and many commentators and cycling media were writing, were essentially fiction. Entertaining fiction, but fiction nonetheless.

But why, then, is the Deux Alpes stage of the 1998 Tour still such a compelling spectacle? I can take or leave the rest of the race – as a sporting spectacle it was worthless. But watching video footage of that stage, or reading about it, is like picking at a scab – both painful and irresistible.

Ullrich wore the yellow jersey going into the stage. Bobby Julich was in second, just over a minute behind, while Pantani was fourth, three minutes in arrears. The weather was atrocious through the stage – chilly rain soaking the riders and huge, thick cloud blanketing the race – reflecting the rumbling thunder of doping scandals which followed the Tour from start to finish, and beyond. The terrain suited Pantani, to a point – while the Col du Galibier was perfect for his climbing skills, the long, draggy descent to the foot of Les Deux Alpes was less so. The summit finish itself was hard, but not at the same level of difficulty as Alpe d'Huez or Plateau de Beille.

Pantani attacked on the Galibier, his turquoise and yellow Mercatone Uno kit greyed and muddied by the rain and grit, but illuminated in the headlights of the following cars and motorbikes. He crossed the summit just over two minutes ahead of Ullrich. At this point, there was no danger in terms of time conceded by the German – he could expect to put minutes into Pantani in the final time trial, and his cushion was already three minutes. But the body language and presence of mind of both riders was telling. Pantani stopped to put on a rain jacket, his frozen hands and arms incapable of the dexterity needed to do it on the bike. Ullrich didn't put on a rain cape, and his cadence was sluggish. His face was swollen, as if he was absorbing the rainwater through his skin. 'He looked like a boxer,' said his teammate Bjarne Riis.

Ullrich suffered on the descent, but the gap was still only four minutes at the bottom of Les Deux Alpes. If he conceded only one more minute in the next 10 kilometres, he would still be in a strong position to win the race comfortably. Instead, Pantani put another five minutes into him.

The iconography of the stage was overtly religious. *L'Équipe*'s headline was '*Pantani au plus haut des cieux*', which translates as 'Pantani on high' or 'Pantani in heaven'. There is a French hymn called '*Gloire á Dieu au plus haut des cieux*' ('Glory to God on High'). *L'Équipe* also reported his victory salute: 'As he crossed the finishing line, he closed his eyes and spread his arms, like Christ on the cross. This man has forged himself in suffering.'

He took the yellow jersey by five minutes on Les Deux Alpes, then was the only rider strong enough to respond to Ullrich's attack the next day on the Col de la Madeleine. But sporting intrigue enjoyed only two days in the spotlight. The next day, the riders went on strike again, the Spanish teams pulled out, and the race limped on to Paris, not quite mortally wounded. The fact that Pantani only conceded two and a half minutes to Ullrich in the final time trial, coming third, underlined the distorting effect EPO had on bike racing. Pantani had won the yellow jersey, but the taint seems even now to be incompatible with the feeling of excitement generated by the Deux Alpes stage. Without EPO, there would be no Deux Alpes. We don't want EPO in the sport, so what does that say about our enjoyment of Les Deux Alpes?

Pantani grew up in Cesenatico, a small seaside town on the Adriatic Riviera. His father Paolo was a buttoned-up disciplinarian who occasionally administered corporal punishment to the young Marco. The psychological issues caused by this remained with Pantani for the rest of his life – when Pantani was withdrawn from the 1999 Giro after failing a health test, the moment at which the brittle foundations of his self-esteem definitively cracked for ever, he admitted that one of his first reactions on seeing his father was the combination of shame and fear he felt when he'd been in trouble as a child. Pantani's mother Tonina, on the other hand, was described by his manager Manuela Ronchi as an 'emotional volcano'. Tonina was a formidable woman, the very stereotype of the Italian mother, yet prone to personal crises – she attempted suicide when Pantani was a baby.

Pantani grew from hyperactive toddler, through introverted but headstrong child, to awkward adolescent, while his path into two-wheeled sport was the usual one for any Italian teenager – he couldn't play football, so he cycled. Cycling brought discipline to Pantani's life, and he was a born physical talent, but it also exposed a reckless, self-destructive streak which didn't help his mother's anxious temperament. Pantani, whether through bad luck or the ability to override sensible limits, was prone through his entire cycling career to bad crashes. He was hit by an oncoming car on a ride in 1986, which caused him a ruptured spleen, then hit a van during a sprint with his friends, which caused significant facial scarring. There would be more serious crashes, throughout his career, including the one in the 1995 Milan–Turin race in which a car had found its way on to the race route. Pantani rode into it on a fast descent, and suffered a serious fracture of his left leg – it would be a year and a half before he could race seriously again.

As a cyclist, Pantani was destined for greatness. His climbing talent was immediately clear, and he won the Baby Giro, the amateur version of the Tour of Italy. He turned professional in 1993, and emerged as a star in 1994. In the Giro d'Italia that year he was completely unknown internationally but, in winning two stages and contributing to the first defeat of Miguel Indurain in a Grand Tour since the Spaniard had won the 1991 Tour de France, he became the darling of the cycling world. Balding, still wearing a monk's halo of wispy blond hair, fresh-faced, big-eared and awkward, he beat Indurain and came second overall, behind Russian Evgeni Berzin.

He made his Tour de France debut the same year, and Indurain, now at the very top of his form, personally saw to it that Pantani wouldn't enjoy the same freedom to attack him as he had in Italy. Pantani conceded 11 minutes to Indurain in one time trial alone, but he still rose to third overall by the end of the race.

Injury kept him out of the 1995 Giro d'Italia, but in the Tour de France he won two stages. 1997 was almost the same again, following his comeback from the Milan–Turin crash. A crash caused by a black cat – what else? – running into the road during the team time trial forced his withdrawal from the Giro d'Italia, then he won two stages at the Tour, finishing third overall. At this point, cycling fans and the media were on Pantani's side – his attacking riding and time-trial defeats made him easy to support, in contrast to Indurain and Ullrich, whose defensive, negative Tour wins were impressive but too well planned, too cold to be emotionally engaging. So when he won the Giro d'Italia in 1998, followed by his Tour, it was a refreshing antidote to years of domination by time triallists.

But Pantani soon found out how fickle the media can be. When he raced through the 1999 Giro and dominated his rivals with insouciant ease, the voices of dissent were already starting to make themselves heard – Pantani winning every mountain stage turned out to be as dull and predictable as Indurain winning every time trial had been. Journalist Angelo Zomegnan's editorial in *La Gazzetta dello Sport* sniffed disapprovingly about Pantani leaving few crumbs for his competitors as he gorged himself on stage wins and time gains. While the public swooned at their hero's feats, journalists grumbled about the lack of variety. It put Pantani into a defensive, prickly mood, but that would soon develop into full-blown paranoia when, with two stages to go, he was given a morning blood test in the town of Madonna di Campiglio by the UCI. His haematocrit level was 53 per cent.

In 1999, the UCI's blood tests were branded as 'health checks' – a very blunt tool to keep rampant EPO use if not under control then at least within certain limits. EPO usage boosts the number of red blood cells in the body, thus improving oxygen-carrying capacity and therefore endurance. One of the side effects of taking too much EPO is death, from the blood thickening to the point that the heart can no longer pump it. In the mid-1990s, riders, including Pantani, were being measured with haematocrit levels of 60 per cent, a level impossible under normal circumstances. The UCI's limit of 50 per cent, if breached, wouldn't count as a positive test (EPO was still undetectable) but riders would be withdrawn from competition.

The irony is that the tests were a piece of cake to beat. It can only be surmised that Pantani's 53 per cent haematocrit level was down to a mistake by either him or the individuals who facilitated his doping. Either way, the mistake had cost him the Giro with only two days to go, but he would have been free to return to competition in two weeks, and defend his Tour de France title. But the Madonna di Campiglio blood test instead marked the point at which Marco Pantani's life arced gently beyond its apex and began a terrifyingly vertiginous descent via paranoia towards tragedy.

In *The Death of Marco Pantani*, Matt Rendell writes about *dietrologia*, a specifically Italian concept in which individuals are obsessed with hidden, conspiratorial reasons behind events. The travel writer Tim Parks describes in his book *Italian Ways* a similar paranoid streak in Italian society, known as *campanilismo*, which is an 'eternal rivalry that has every Italian town convinced its neighbours are conspiring against it'.

Pantani railed against the perceived injustice, citing a powerful, unnamed conspiracy against him. Pantani, in his pride, simply couldn't deal with the shame of the association with doping – he'd built his self-esteem and identity on success in bike racing to the point of denial about the methods he was using, and the blow to his ego was mortal. Many observers have stated that Pantani was never the same after Madonna di Campiglio, but actually he was exactly the same – only more so. Perhaps he realized that he'd been part of a collective hypocrisy in cycling – able to smile his way through the 1998 Tour de France and enjoy the spoils of victory while others were taking the blame for the doping – but didn't have the courage to admit it. Perhaps he'd thought that, as a sporting icon, he was untouchable. But rather than confront his problem, he hid behind his denial. It was not long after Madonna di Campiglio that Pantani started using cocaine. The cycle of self-destruction had begun.

Pantani came back and won two stages at the 2000 Tour de France, although stomach problems forced him to withdraw from the race before it ended. But his physical and psychological deterioration was starting to accelerate. His enablers in this were a motley collection of hangers-on and friends. And, in a small way, the cycling world, which continued to idolize his triumphs while trying to ignore the cognitive dissonance caused by thinking too hard about how he achieved them.

In February 2004, he checked into a hotel room in Rimini, where he accidentally overdosed on cocaine, a shocking, poor, shadow of the man who had won the Tour de France.

'Lord protect me from my friends; I can take care of my enemies,' wrote Voltaire.

Marco Pantani died a lonely, ugly death, caused in the end by a terrible alchemy between what he achieved, what he was, and the way the world viewed it.

13

Lance Armstrong
~~1999, 2000, 2001, 2002, 2003, 2004, 2005~~

Lance talks about how much he hates losing, but to me it's something deeper than hate. Losing short-circuits his brain: it's illogical; it's impossible. Like something in the universe is messed up and it needs correcting.

Tyler Hamilton, *The Secret Race*

'I'm just a regular guy,' wrote Lance Armstrong in his second autobiography, *Every Second Counts*, and we all knew that was bullshit, even before the real extent of his estrangement from conventional ethical norms became clear. It's the kind of self-deprecating humblebrag that celebrities and megalomaniacs whose life trajectories have taken them to a place diametrically opposed to regular guyhood come out with. But the more important bit comes two paragraphs later, when he warns, 'It may get wearying doing the work of interpreting me.' Knowing what we know about Armstrong, it's tempting to think that he speaks from experience. The impression from almost everything that he says and does is that the Texan doesn't apply the same level of scrutiny and analysis to his own character and behaviour as he did to winning the Tour de France. In *Tour de*

Lance, his book about Armstrong's comeback in 2009, the American cycling journalist Bill Strickland observed that asking questions of the Texan wasn't going to give him the answers he wanted. 'This was not only because of the reluctance of those close to Armstrong to fully and truthfully answer questions,' wrote Strickland. 'It was also, I thought, at least when it came to Lance himself, because of an inability to think too much about himself. One of the people closest to him in all the world had said to me something I'd heard about him before: when it came to asking Lance to elucidate who he was, "You might as well interview a shark about why it's biting you."'

Armstrong is a problematic inclusion in this book. He is not really in the yellow jersey club – when he was stripped of his seven wins for doping, he was blackballed, although a few other members have wisely kept their counsel on that subject.

He's not the only person to have been kicked out of the yellow jersey club. The first was Maurice Garin, in 1904, who'd taken illegal feeds, and was one of several riders to have taken a train instead of completing a stage. 1904 was a dirty Tour, even by modern standards: the first four riders were eventually disqualified, and the subsequent winner Henri Cornet had been warned about having had a lift in a car – I like to think Armstrong would appreciate the fact that Garin wasn't the only rider cheating in 1904. (And, technically, Garin was never in the yellow jersey club – the Tour organizers introduced the yellow jersey in 1919.) The only other rider to have been kicked out of the club is Floyd Landis. He lasted four days after his win in 2006, before his positive test for testosterone led to him being stripped of his win.

But the difference between Garin, Landis and Armstrong is that while Garin's and Landis's disqualifications handed victory to Cornet and Óscar Pereiro respectively, the cycling establishment knows better than to give Armstrong's equally ethically dubious runners-up the victories by default. Better to leave the whole period blank, an uncarved gravestone to mark the unmourned era of industrial-level cheating.

Armstrong's opinion is that he won those seven Tours. For a while after his sanction, he deleted the words 'seven-times Tour winner' from his Twitter biography, but they've been quietly reinstated since. His contention is that while he did cheat, so did nearly all of his rivals.

It's important to understand that this is true, but also that the drugs and blood-doping do not have the effect of improving everybody by the same amount. Armstrong gained enough from the drugs that he could convert himself from a good one-day rider into a Tour de France winner. Some naturally good Tour de France riders might not have received the same proportional benefit as Armstrong did, and the natural conclusion to draw is that if the whole field had been clean, Armstrong would not have won any Tours.

I think Armstrong was a talented bike racer who made up for a lack of top-end class with a very high level of competitiveness and aggression. If EPO and blood-boosting had never caught on in cycling, he might even have got as far as making the podium of the Tour, maybe getting a few second or third places at his peak if circumstances had been right, like an angrier, less likeable twenty-first-century version of Raymond Poulidor. It's actually one of the minor tragedies of Armstrong's story that if nobody in cycling had cheated, we might be talking now of one of the greatest one-day racers in cycling history – but we'll never know.

However, Armstrong does have a point in claiming that it's inconsistent to strip him of the yellow jersey and not, say, Marco Pantani or Jan Ullrich. He's not going to get his wins given back to him, but I do wonder what the relationship between Armstrong and the cycling world will be in another 20 years, when time has mellowed all of us, and we're not quite so angry about the whole thing. Will he still polarize opinion? Will he still be a golf-club bore, complaining about being victimized? Or will he accept it and move on? Will he be forgiven? Every now and again he re-emerges into the cycling world's consciousness, like Magwitch from the swamp, to state his case for a reduction in his life ban, or to opine on the state of the sport. And each time, the debate between critics and fans is sharply delineated.

Armstrong didn't apologize during his confessional interview in early 2013 with Oprah Winfrey, although he did seem to show genuine contrition on Twitter not long afterwards. But his position has ossified into one in which he appears to be more sorry to have been caught. 'Losing and dying: it's the same thing,' Armstrong told Alastair Campbell in an interview for *The Times* in 2004, but in the end, Armstrong can't win. You could see it as poetic justice.

Cycling expanded its horizons during Lance Armstrong's reign as Tour champion, and it's something he continues to take credit for. More fans became interested in the sport, especially from the United States. Armstrong was able to make Americans take notice of the Tour in a way that Greg LeMond couldn't quite manage – this could just be an accident of timing, and it's probably true that LeMond, and then the 7-Eleven team, prepared the ground for Armstrong, but it's more likely that the scale of the two men's ambition was different. LeMond was ambitious for himself, and was a major influence on the sport modernizing itself, but he still had to integrate himself into the culture of European cycling in order to succeed, and to change things. Armstrong, on the other hand, either deliberately or not, remained culturally American and was at pains to separate himself from his predecessor. 'I'm the first Lance Armstrong,' he replied when a journalist asked him if he was the new LeMond, early in his career.

As interest in Armstrong – the story of his comeback from cancer, and his dominance at the Tour – grew through the early 2000s, so more and more fans, more sponsors, and therefore more money came into cycling. And Armstrong brought a whole new subspecies of hanger-on into the sport. The old-fashioned shysters, small-time sponsors, pushers and low-level local politicians who'd congregated around bike racers since time immemorial were gradually moved aside for a new breed: polo-shirted, fit-looking individuals with MBAs, wrap-around shades and Trek bikes.

But while cycling's fan base broadened and grew, Armstrong highlighted the conflicts between what different people expect from the sport. For some of the newer fans from the United States, it's fair to say that they were interested primarily in Armstrong winning. His victories, which came against the background of swaggering American aggression on a geo-political level, reinforced a certain narrative. And who doesn't enjoy watching their team, or man, or woman win?

However, for fans who considered themselves first and fore-most fans of cycling as a sport, Armstrong was less attractive. His seven wins, with one exception in 2003, were crushing and predictable, lacking sporting intrigue. It's a generalization, rooted in some truth, that French sports fans especially appreciate the aesthetic value of sport, and are extremely susceptible to the idea of glorious defeat. It's why they politely clapped Jacques Anquetil, but cheered Raymond Poulidor to the rafters. Armstrong never really won over the French, nor the people who were suspicious of his methods, nor the fans who appreciated the nuance in bike racing and didn't like Armstrong's brashness and dominance. There was no point criticizing him, however – he thrived on criticism, and he was addicted to picking fights, either physical or otherwise. 'It's as though he's allergic to calm,' said Tyler Hamilton.

Armstrong was more comfortable in the role of outsider. He was the American doing well in a European sport, the elite triathlete who'd converted to cycling. Look further back in his life, and he was the misfit at school – the individual sportsman who moved outside the social circles of the team-sport players, the jocks and the cheerleaders.

Floyd Landis made an interesting observation of Armstrong. While the Texan is capable of great personal charm, and is an engaging, dynamic presence, the difficulty he had making friends at school seems to have followed him into adult life. 'I was friends as much as you can be a friend with Lance, but his friendships are limited to a certain distance,' Landis told Paul Kimmage in an interview for the *Sunday Times*. 'You don't get closer than a certain distance with him, because for whatever reason, I can't possibly know why, he just doesn't let people be too close with him.'

Even further back than high school, Armstrong was the only child of a very young, permissive, competitive mother who fostered a spirit of us-against-the-world. The journalist Bryan Appleyard, in an interview in *The Times* with the Labour politician Tristram Hunt, quoted Freud in assessing the effect of a close maternal relationship. 'I ask him if he knows what Freud said about men who, as boys, were favourites of their mothers,' Appleyard wrote. 'Freud said that such men keep for life the feeling of a conqueror, that confidence of success, that often induces real success.'

Armstrong also had, for a significant part of his childhood, a strict, competitive stepfather who tolerated no weakness and used corporal punishment on the young Armstrong. It was no wonder he was so obsessed with fighting and not only winning but psychologically dominating his opponents. Between his mother and stepfather, he'd been taught little else from an early age.

Tyler Hamilton tells the story in his book *The Secret Race* of a six-hour training ride he'd gone on with Armstrong. 'This small car comes tearing up the hill behind us at top speed, nearly hitting us, and the driver yells something as he goes past,' wrote Hamilton. 'I'm mad, so I yell back at him. But Lance doesn't say anything, he just takes off, full speed, chasing the car.' Armstrong knew the area, and correctly guessing where the driver was headed, took a shortcut to head him off at a traffic light. 'By the time I got there Lance had pulled the guy out of his car and was pummelling him, and the guy was cowering and crying,' continued Hamilton. 'I watched for a minute, not quite believing what I was seeing. Lance's face was beet red; he was in a full rage, really letting the guy have it. Finally it was over. Lance pushed the guy to the ground and left him.'

It took a long time for Armstrong to crack the Tour de France. Before his cancer, he'd started four Tours, finished one, taken two stage wins and not looked at all like a general classification contender. The one time he did finish, he was 36th, in 1995 (this officially remains his best finish in the race – his race results having been stripped from 1998 onwards).

Once he did crack it, thanks to a combination of organized doping and hard work, his performances were extraordinary, even when the doping was taken into account. Somehow, he avoided crashes, punctures and ill-health for seven straight years, although he did hit the ground during the close-run 2003 race. The level of control he exercised on the race was unprecedented, even compared to Merckx and Indurain. Consequently, the years 1999 to 2005 weren't as exciting as previous eras had been. Armstrong's dominance, along with the strength and tactics of his team, plus the fact that the sprinters were allowing fewer opportunities to slip through their fingers, seemed to strip out the unpredictability that made the Tours of the 1980s, for example, so entertaining.

In 1999, Armstrong was the best time triallist and the best climber in the race, against a comparatively weak field. He won the long time trial in Metz, then took the first mountain-top finish at Sestrière two days later. But he'd already put himself well beyond some of his rivals when a crash split the field into four pieces, separated by minutes, on the second stage to Saint-Nazaire. A large number of riders crashed on the slippery Passage du Gois, a road on the west coast of France which is submerged by the sea during high tide, and Armstrong put his team to work on the front of the first group. The eventual runner-up, Alex Zülle, was one of those caught out, and Armstrong put six minutes into him on this stage. Armstrong was the luckiest and strongest rider – no wonder his eventual margin of victory was almost eight minutes.

In 2000 he had stronger rivals, with Ullrich and Pantani, both previous winners, on the start line. But it was still relatively straightforward, and he repeated the tactic he'd used in 1999 – attack hard on the first mountain stage, build up an unassailable lead and establish total psychological dominance. On Hautacam, the first summit finish, he was second on the stage, but Ullrich was three minutes behind and Pantani five minutes down. In Paris, his lead over second-placed Ullrich was six minutes.

In 2001, Armstrong hit his physical peak. In his habitual first summit finish attack, he put two minutes into Ullrich on Alpe d'Huez, then another minute the next day in the mountain time trial at Chamrousse. It was another win by six minutes. The following year, Armstrong's US Postal team, already the strongest in the race by 2001, had been boosted to such an extent that Armstrong's final mountain *domestique*, Roberto Heras, was coming in the top three of the summit finishes. Armstrong beat runner-up Joseba Beloki by seven minutes in 2002.

In 2004 and 2005, Armstrong's dominance had become

nonchalant. In both cases, again, he had victory wrapped up by the first summit finish of the race. It was only in 2003, when he seemed slightly off-form and came up against Ullrich, who'd managed to find his best form for the Tour for the first and only time since he'd won it in 1997, that he wobbled. Armstrong didn't dominate on the first summit finish at Alpe d'Huez, and Ullrich put significant time into him during the long, hilly time trial at Cap'Découverte. Armstrong was forced to reverse his usual tactic and save the best for the final summit finish at Luz Ardiden, where he won the stage and put just enough time into Ullrich that the yellow jersey was assured.

Armstrong's growing legion of roadside fans loved those seven years. The wins came with monotonous regularity, but while journalists grumbled about the lack of suspense, and a few were trying to chip away at the myth which they were certain was a cover-up for his doping, the money was flowing in, which dissuaded the cycling establishment to look too hard at Armstrong's methods. A lot of the money was flowing in Armstrong's direction – he was building a fortune estimated at being well north of 100 million dollars, while even a high-quality and important *domestique* like Landis was on 250,000 dollars a year at US Postal; a lot of money, but not in comparison to his leader, and not enough to retire on.

Armstrong reinforced his own myth by constantly referring to the hard work he put into training for the Tour. This is also an important part of his self-perception now as the rightful winner of those seven Tours – Armstrong more or less claimed that he trained harder than his rivals, and that's what made the difference. Not, he insists, the sophisticated doping methods. Is it easier to justify the sense of entitlement with the assertion that success is down to nothing more complicated than hard work, rather than a win in the genetic lottery which gave Armstrong the jackpot of strong legs and an efficient cardiovascular system, plus being a good responder to blood doping and EPO?

Armstrong could have left it at seven Tours. For a while, he did. But the same personality traits which made him such an effective winner of the Tour made it impossible for him to sit on the sofa and watch those he considered lesser riders take the yellow jersey in Paris. Coincident with this, the perception was that the sport was starting to clean up – how could the Armstrong years look anything but bad in comparison? He couldn't resist it – in 2008 he announced he would be making a comeback. And in doing so, he turned a minor midlife crisis into a real crisis.

The peak of Lance Armstrong's popularity, and even more importantly to him, his currency as a celebrity, came around the time he was announcing his comeback. At the time, his detractors were vastly outnumbered by his fans, and it was assumed that the fairytale finish would be an eighth Tour de France win.

I was the deputy editor of *Cycle Sport* magazine when Armstrong made his announcement, and the excitement at the comeback didn't spread to our office. We'd been blacklisted in the summer of 2002, when the magazine had carried a story by Armstrong's journalistic nemesis David Walsh titled, 'I'll Take Greg', which compared the two American cyclists. I'd never interviewed Armstrong before as a consequence of this, so when he told *Vanity Fair* in September 2008 that the comeback would also include a new policy of *Glasnost* with journalists, I got in touch with his agent.

The interesting thing about our interview, which took place at his house in Austin, Texas, was not the content, so much as a slow-burning realization on Armstrong's part that cycling wasn't universally happy to have him back. I'd asked him about doping, tripped him up slightly about his history of Therapeutic

Use Exemptions (he'd denied ever having had any, until I reminded him that's what he'd used to get himself off the hook for a positive test for corticosteroids in 1999) and we'd had a debate about ethics and rehabilitation versus responsibility. It had all been quite good-natured, because Armstrong, in person, is a charming, engaging individual. But less than a week later, he called me at home, late in the evening, and chewed my ear off about journalistic negativity. It wasn't long after this that he started blacklisting journalists again. By the Giro d'Italia in May, he was barely speaking to journalists at all, instead communicating directly to his fans through homemade videos uploaded to his website.

Armstrong made a telling admission to journalist Juliet Macur when she interviewed him for her account of his fall, *Cycle of Lies*. He'd wanted to stop the comeback, but he didn't have the courage, he said. The comeback was a disaster for Armstrong on every level. He was sucked into a losing battle with Alberto Contador for leadership of the Astana team for which he was racing. He came third in the 2009 Tour, but was stripped of the result after the United States Anti-Doping Agency concluded that he had doped in order to achieve it (a charge Armstrong still denies), but he'd not looked convincing all season. It wasn't just a case of his results being less impressive, and the top-end speed a little less sharp. He looked laboured on the bike, riding with none of the fluency that most professionals have. The peloton refer to this fluency as *souplesse* (suppleness), and the inference is that riding efficiency and energy-saving are important factors for professional cyclists. Armstrong had no *souplesse* – he was muscling the pedals around, and huffing and puffing his way up the climbs.

Macur also reported that Armstrong's coach in his final season in 2010, Allen Lim, who'd also worked with Landis in 2006, was under the strong impression that Armstrong rode the 2010 Tour clean. Unfortunately for Armstrong, one of the other conclusions that Lim drew from their work together was that Armstrong was a vastly inferior athlete to Landis, in terms of natural potential. Armstrong's result in that final Tour was 23rd overall. Clean or not, they stripped him of that one too.

Dan Coyle, the author of *Lance Armstrong: Tour de Force* and co-writer of Hamilton's book, once told me that anybody who thought Armstrong was a nice guy was missing the point. 'The biggest misconception of Lance is that he's a nice guy,' he said. 'He's black or white, friend or foe. The one word he doesn't like to hear is "maybe". He's funny, charismatic, bright. Those things are nice to be around. He's famous. That's nice to be around. But he is not a cuddly guy. His mind works in a binary way and niceness is not a factor.'

Armstrong is also a product of his culture on a more general level, too. Born in 1971, he was a child of the 1980s, unusually obsessed with money and share prices from an early age. Ex-teammates reported that he would retire early from team dinners to go and check on his stocks' performances. Kent Gordis, Greg LeMond's childhood friend, made an interesting comparison between the two American cyclists in the course of my interview with him about LeMond. 'Lance and Greg are very much products of their generations,' he said. 'Greg was part of that last generation of Americans to have the naïve optimism and belief that good would triumph. We think of Armstrong as a doping scandal focused in Europe. But really, at its root, what the Lance scandal is about is using the same kind of ruthless tactics that are used in American high finance. Not coincidentally, Lance's first patron and boss was Thom Weisel, who worked in high finance. It was that culture of win at all costs: nothing matters except winning.' Weisel got the wins he wanted, even if the edifice would come crashing down. He denied any knowledge of Armstrong's doping and was dropped from the government case against him.

Now that the extent of Armstrong's cheating is out in the open, there are far fewer fans who are under the mistaken impression that he's one of the good guys. He was actually voted the second-worst liar of all time in a poll by the *New York Post*, just behind Bernie Madoff, but ahead of Richard Nixon and Pinocchio. But what's still true is that people either love him or hate him, the same as ever, and there is no middle ground. Armstrong is probably fine with that; after all, it's the fight, and the criticism, which keep him alive. The day before the 2004 Tour de France started in Liège, one of the local newspapers led with the headline 'Everybody Against Him'. You get the impression that would have suited him just fine.

14

Óscar Pereiro
2006

Walkowiak might have taken advantage of internal rivalries among the national teams, but knowing how to exploit that was a good tactic. Little 'Walko' ended up beating the big boys, therefore he was one of the big boys himself. He might have been the winner of a Tour without great stars, but he was the winner of a great Tour, which, in our eyes, is even better.

Jacques Marchand, *L'Équipe*, 29 July 1956

You could rerun the 2006 Tour one thousand times and still not get the same result. The circumstances that led to Spanish rider Óscar Pereiro winning the yellow jersey were so convoluted and unlikely that compared to almost every Tour since even before the Second World War, the result looks like an aberration. The Tour has often turned on tactical decisions, good decision-making or a bit of luck, but in general these things tend to make the difference between two or more riders who are among the strongest handful in the race. Tour winners are thoroughbreds, not plodders, and there are very few exceptions.

Pereiro was a good rider, a solid mountain *domestique*. Up until 2006, he was best known for riding off the road for a televisual excursion into an Alpine meadow on the descent of the Col de la Madeleine during the 2005 Tour. He'd come 10th and 10th in the two Tours he'd ridden before 2006; he finished 10th the year after, too, which might help you draw conclusions about what his natural high-water mark was in the race.

However, it's more complicated than that. In 2006, he was the beneficiary of some very strange tactics by the race favourites – he'd lost close to 30 minutes in the Pyrenees, but then took it all back in a break on a rolling stage through the Languedoc to Montélimar. Whatever had been wrong with his legs in the Pyrenees didn't affect him in the Alps, and his rivals had to prise his fingers one by one from the race lead he'd been gifted, and only an extraordinary performance in the Alps by Floyd Landis allowed the American rider to ride into Paris wearing the yellow jersey, with Pereiro in second. It turned out that Landis's performance was a little too extraordinary – he tested positive for testosterone, and after a drawn-out and unedifying legal battle was stripped of his victory. Pereiro was presented with his yellow jersey – not on a hot summer's day in front of the cheering throngs of the Champs-Élysées but under the strip lights and square polystyrene ceiling tiles of a Madrid boardroom in October 2007, once all Landis's appeals had failed.

Pereiro was seen as a surprise winner, notwithstanding the circumstances of him getting promoted from second to first, but there were still warning signs for his rivals in the way he'd ridden the year before. He was an opportunist, the kind of rider who slips into breaks but isn't quite considered dangerous enough to chase down. 'I think I was a very clever rider,' he said in an interview with *Procycling* magazine. 'A rider who knew exactly where to be at the right time.'

It's easy to fall into the trap of thinking that the final top 10 or 20 of the Tour are ordered according to a logical hierarchy of strength: strongest rider wins, second-strongest rider comes second, seventh-strongest rider comes seventh, 11th-strongest rider comes 11th and so on. But it's a little more subtle than that. Public attention during the Tour de France is generally focused on the battle for the yellow jersey, and by association, the battle for the podium. But behind the top three there are riders either striving to move up, or doggedly defending their position in the top 10. Riders in the top 15 might be doing much the same, some looking up the general classification and coveting a higher placing, some looking behind. For the riders wanting to move up, there is the choice of doing it through brawn (this only works if the rider is stronger than those ahead of him on general classification), brains or raw luck. Pereiro used a combination of the latter two.

2005 was the last of Lance Armstrong's seven wins. By this point, Armstrong had smothered the tactical enterprise of his rivals so effectively that, from the first mountaintop finish onwards, there was no doubt who was going to win the race. There were sideshows, such as the Danish rider Michael Rasmussen gaining enough time on a break through the Vosges that he held second place into the Pyrenees (he would lose almost eight minutes in a farcical final time trial and slip to seventh overall) and a ding-dong battle for fifth place between Kazakh Alexandre Vinokourov and the USA's Levi Leipheimer, in which Vinokourov would prevail after a last-ditch attack to win the Champs-Élysées stage, along with a time bonus.

Meanwhile, Pereiro had dropped off the pace in the Alps – with two stronger team leaders in his Phonak team, Landis and Santiago Botero, he'd been working mainly for them, and after the first Pyrenean stage to Ax 3 Domaines, he was 24th overall, a distant 24 minutes behind Armstrong, and 16 minutes from 10th place.

His primary motivation had become stage wins, but the by-product of getting into breaks that contest stage wins is time gains. The next day, the hardest Pyrenean stage to Pla d'Adet, Pereiro got into the break. He was outsprinted for the stage win by Armstrong's teammate George Hincapie (since stripped of the result for his admission of doping), but they'd been left to get on with it by the main contenders – Armstrong and Ivan Basso were five minutes behind and Jan Ullrich six and a half minutes back. Pereiro was up to 17th.

Two days later, in the final Pyrenean stage, and still hunting a stage win, Pereiro got into the break again. This time Cadel Evans, who was in 11th place and engineering his own assault on the top 10, was also in the break, so the escapees got less leeway. Pereiro got his stage win, plus another three and a half minutes, moving him to 15th. Then, on a rolling stage through the southern Massif Central to Le Puy-en-Velay, just two days before Paris, Pereiro made the break again. Giuseppe Guerini won the stage, but the Spanish rider had stolen another four and a half minutes. In those three stages, he'd furtively taken 13 minutes back and moved up to his final position of 10th. He also unsurprisingly won the Combativity Award for that Tour, giving him his first appearance on the Champs-Élysées podium.

The misconception people have about Pereiro, thanks to his Tour win and those 10th-place finishes, is that he was a general classification rider. But he wasn't, really. He was a chancer, too inconsistent to be reliable, but one who got into the right break so often that it couldn't just have been pure luck. When the race was straightforward, Pereiro wasn't generally good enough to climb with the very best, but that's why he was so under-estimated in 2006.

The 2006 Tour began and ended in disgrace. The Landis disqualification was the sorry postscript to a race that was already struggling for credibility. Several of the biggest names in the peloton, including former winner Ullrich and favourite Ivan Basso, were withdrawn from the Tour just before it started in Strasbourg, as the *Operación Puerto* investigation blew up. *Operación Puerto* was, of course, the police investigation into the blood-doping network centered on a Madrid gynaecologist, Eufemiano Fuentes. Knowing what we now know about the Armstrong years, which themselves came on the back of the Festina scandal and the EPO abuse that was rife in the 1990s, *Puerto* and the start of the 2006 Tour look like the tipping point for public opinion about cycling. Although cleaning up has been a long and unnecessarily drawn-out process which continues a decade later, the turning point came at the 2006 Tour. That's not to say that the race was any cleaner than previous years – the Landis disqualification is partial proof of that. Perhaps a better way of looking at it is to consider 2006 as rock bottom for cycling.

The 2006 race was the last Tour in which Jean-Marie Leblanc was in full charge as director of the race. Leblanc worked at the Tour in many different capacities – he'd been a rider, a journalist, then race director; he was a bruiser as a cyclist, before thousands of working lunches changed his broad-shouldered racing physique into a benign portliness. His first Tour had been the revolutionary 1989 event, which finished with a time trial and resulted in the closest ever finish (Leblanc doesn't take credit for that race – he inherited the *parcours* from his predecessors at the Tour organization). But by the end of his stint as Tour boss, the Tour had settled over the Indurain and Armstrong years into an almost fixed template – a flat first week to 10 days with a long time trial, followed by the first mountain range and some transition stages, then the second mountain range before another long time trial. 2006 was no exception – the novelty came not from the route but from the retired Armstrong's absence, along with many of the favourites being pulled out. It was an open race, exciting and unpredictable on the surface, but tainted for ever by the associations with doping.

Pereiro, who'd changed teams from Phonak to Caisse d'Epargne, didn't figure until the race was coming towards the end of its second week. If his team leader Alejandro Valverde hadn't crashed out of the race, he might never have got his opportunity. The sprinters' teams kept the race in a vice-like grip through the first 10 days, with the monotony broken only by an uphill finish on the Cauberg climb in Valkenburg, without significant time gaps, and the long time trial in Rennes, which was won by Sergei Gonchar with Landis in second. Pereiro was 23rd. Worse was to come for the Spaniard in the main Pyrenean stage, which finished at Pla de Beret in his home country, where he lost 26 minutes. Denis Menchov won a three-man sprint ahead of Landis and Leipheimer, with Evans and Carlos Sastre just 17 seconds behind. Nobody else was within a minute, which enabled Tour followers to conclude that Landis, now in the yellow jersey, and Menchov were the favourites – Leipheimer had suffered from a disaster in the first long time trial, while Landis and Menchov were both climbing and time-trialling well. Evans and Sastre, along with German rider Andreas Klöden, were all within three minutes of Landis's lead. Pereiro, for his part, looked like he was completely out of the running, 28 and a half minutes behind in 47th place.

Had the American in the yellow jersey been Lance Armstrong, and not Floyd Landis, what happened next would never have been imaginable. Armstrong was not above letting riders who were no threat on the general classification off to gain time – in 2001, a break of 14 riders was allowed to gain 35 minutes on stage eight, while French rider Thomas Voeckler owed his 10 days in the yellow jersey in 2004 to getting into a long break during the first week. But he wouldn't have allowed a rider who'd finished in the top 10 the year before to gain significant time on him. Part of the reason for this was that Armstrong liked to be in charge of the race, but the other part was that his team was strong enough to control things, from the first week to the last if necessary. The US Postal, then Discovery Channel teams, helped by a very organized doping strategy, were capable of spending all day, every day, on the front of the peloton.

Landis was less confident in his Phonak team. Taking the yellow jersey so early in the race was a risk for him – if Phonak had had to work to defend his lead right through to Paris, he might have been vulnerable in the Alps. Although it's not set in stone, peloton convention dictates that the team holding the yellow jersey contributes to controlling even the flat stages, for the first half of the day at least – having to do this would have eaten into resources Phonak might not have had.

Giving away the yellow jersey temporarily is a calculated risk, although it doesn't happen that often. Cyrille Guimard and Lucien Van Impe did it in 1976, allowing Raymond Martin to lead the race through the Pyrenees; while Armstrong and his manager Johan Bruyneel decided to give Voeckler his opportunity in 2004, just to take the pressure off US Postal for a week or so. In each of these cases, the beneficiary was not too far off the yellow jersey in the first place. Pereiro, on the other hand, was about to be ushered into the race lead from 30 minutes back.

Stage 13 of the 2006 Tour, to Montélimar, was the longest of the race, at 231 kilometres. In Béziers, where the stage started, temperatures were already into the 30s, and with the long flat opening phase of the Tour and the Pyrenees in the riders' legs – and well over a week to the finish – it was the kind of day in which the break is likely to go all the way to the finish. A truce for the sprinters and general classification riders, but a day full of possibilities for the *baroudeurs* – the escape artists and stage hunters.

Those stage hunters knew it. There were a lot of riders attacking in the first 30 minutes of racing, but the composition of the break was never quite right, until a sextet of riders – Pereiro, German Jens Voigt, French riders and Cofidis teammates Sylvain Chavanel and Arnaud Coyot, Italian Manuel Quinziato and Ukraine's Andriy Grivko – attacked after 23 kilometres. Two Cofidis riders might have been too many for their rivals' liking, and the Française des Jeux team chased hard. Coyot dropped back to the peloton while the remaining five were now in a team-pursuit race against Française des Jeux, under the beating Languedoc sun. Slowly, the lead inched out, over the next 12 kilometres, to over a minute, and suddenly Française des Jeux relented. Phonak went to the front to impose a more reasonable pace for the peloton, while Pereiro and company set about building a more solid lead.

After 50 kilometres, the lead was six minutes. After 80 kilometres, with 150 still to ride, it had doubled to 12 minutes. The lead breached 15 minutes with 130 kilometres to go and hit 20 minutes with 85 kilometres to go. And as the kilometres ticked over, Pereiro's Tour aims slowly reverted to plan A. 'At first I thought I should simply go for the stage win, but as the time rose higher and higher my plans changed. Lord knows we were away long enough for me to do all the sums in my head,' Pereiro said later.

The huge lead guaranteed that the five leaders would contest the stage win. But instead of starting to at least maintain the gap, Phonak slowed the bunch even further. With 66 kilometres to go, the gap was 25 minutes, and it seemed to then steady at 27 minutes, not quite enough for Pereiro to take the yellow jersey. Grivko was dropped from the lead group after puncturing, while Voigt and Pereiro went away from Chavanel and Quinziato. The spoils were shared in the traditional way – Voigt took the stage, while Pereiro profited from the time gain. With Phonak all but riding into Montélimar with their brakes on, they managed to engineer a final 29-57 deficit for themselves. Pereiro was the new race leader. Initially, it suited both parties – Landis and Phonak had got themselves out of a few days' hard work, while their ex-teammate Pereiro was enjoying the most unlikely few days of good publicity.

Perhaps it was the lack of a *patron* in the Tour that made the race such an unpredictable one. Armstrong wouldn't have let a rider like Pereiro 30 minutes up the road, even if he had ridden badly in the Pyrenees, and Armstrong would also never allow what happened to Landis in the subsequent Alpine stages to happen to him.

At Alpe d'Huez, three days after Montélimar, it looked like business as usual. Landis put enough time into Pereiro to take back the yellow jersey by 10 seconds. Pereiro's dream looked to be over, and the podium was not guaranteed, especially with the dangerous-looking trio of Menchov, Sastre and Klöden all within two and a half minutes of him. But the next day, at the summit finish of La Toussuire, the roles were reversed. Pereiro finished third on the stage, while Landis cracked terribly on the final climb. The Spanish rider was back in the yellow jersey, Sastre and Klöden were two minutes behind, while Landis had lost eight minutes and slipped to 11th.

In an interview with Paul Kimmage of the *Sunday Times* in late 2010, Floyd Landis talked about Lance Armstrong's retirement speech on the Champs-Élysées at the end of the 2005 Tour. Armstrong had said, 'There are no secrets – this is a hard sporting event and hard work wins it.' Landis explained to Kimmage that he had his own interpretation of Armstrong's words. 'What he meant is, there is a parallel world where the fans see what's put in front of them and appreciate it for what they believe it to be, and beside it is the peloton who know the real story. Therefore there are no secrets within the peloton,' he said.

The La Toussuire stage, and the stage to Morzine the next day, straddle those parallel worlds. What fans saw and what we know now about Landis's positive test are two versions of the truth, but the real truth is very difficult to tease out between multiple layers of lies, conflicting accounts and denials. Landis eventually admitted that he'd undergone two blood transfusions during the 2006 Tour, one before the Pyrenees and one on the eve of the Alpe d'Huez stage. But his positive test came from the Morzine stage, three days later. Even now, he says he hadn't used testosterone for the 2006 Tour, although, ironically, he'd used it throughout 2005 without testing positive.

Morzine, on the surface, was the most exhilarating Tour-winning attack in modern history. Landis went away early, and stayed away over multiple climbs in the northern Alps, gaining enough time to put him within striking distance of the yellow jersey, with a long time trial to come. That's why the subsequent positive test caused such a sensation. But if the other general classification contenders' teams hadn't made such poor tactical decisions, he'd never have built the five-minutes-plus lead he held to the finish. Pereiro's Caisse d'Epargne team didn't have the strength in depth to chase all day, while CSC and T-Mobile, for Sastre and Klöden, inexplicably left it to the valley road before the final climb, the Col de Joux Plane.

Pereiro lost the Tour de France one more time before he won it. He was fourth in the final time trial, one place behind Landis, and so rode into Paris in second place. It was still a freak result, as freakish in its way as Landis's comeback to Morzine had been.

Pereiro, for whatever reason, was reluctant to criticize Landis too much. 'All it is is a positive dope test,' said Pereiro. 'He's not committed a crime. He'll get a sanction and that's all there is to it.'

Fans expecting the inheritor of Landis's yellow jersey to use the opportunity to strike a blow for anti-doping rhetoric would have been disappointed. In the end, perhaps Pereiro's reaction was appropriate for a race which teetered precariously between farce and scandal.

15

Alberto Contador
2007, 2009

Alberto Contador, a quiet, thin Spanish racer who had joined the team just before camp started, walked into the room for his meeting, sat down, and said, 'I wish for my first race to be Paris–Nice.' 'That's good, Alberto,' I said. 'We already have it scheduled for you.' Contador nodded and, as if it were the most natural thing in the world for us to hear from a near-rookie at his first training camp with the world's best team, said, 'As well, I will win it.'

Johan Bruyneel, *We Might as Well Win*

Alberto Contador is chasing Grand Tour records. At the time of writing, he lies sixth in the all-time list of overall victors, with six winners' jerseys – two yellow, one pink, two red and one gold (the Vuelta a España, which Contador has won three times, used to give the winner a gold – actually dark yellow – jersey, before changing to red in 2010). One more title will put him joint fourth with Miguel Indurain and Fausto Coppi. Two more would put him equal third with Jacques Anquetil. It's unlikely he'll ever match Bernard Hinault's 10 or Eddy Merckx's 11 titles, but at least he's over halfway there.

However, he's second in another, less prestigious, league table. Contador has been stripped of more overall titles than anybody except Lance Armstrong – the Spanish rider was disqualified from victory in the 2010 Tour de France after he tested positive for clenbuterol, then had his 2011 Giro d'Italia win taken from him when his ban was finally confirmed and retrospectively applied to the results he'd achieved in the interim.

There will always be a 'but' when speaking of the career of Alberto Contador, an asterisk appended to his name in the results sheets. Yes, there are the six/eight Grand Tour wins, along with three Tour of the Basque Country titles, two Paris–Nice wins and the Tirreno–Adriatico. But there is also the positive test, the extraordinary climbing speeds he managed in 2007 and 2009, and the fact that his team managers have been Manolo Saiz, Johan Bruyneel and Bjarne Riis, arguably three of the most toxic names in cycling thanks to their involvement with organized doping. The name of Alberto Contador seems to cause cognitive dissonance among cycling fans. Do they celebrate the aggressive, attacking riding and climbing talent, or does the evidence against Contador, circumstantial and real, taint his name, like molecules of clenbuterol in a steak?

Scandal has followed Contador's career from the beginning, and he's been unable to shake it off with the same effectiveness with which he drops his opponents in the mountains. In a sport which likes to divide its protagonists into heroes and villains, black and white, good and bad, Contador seems to lie somewhere in the middle. He's the nice guy with the nice smile, the boy who stood on the balcony of his family's home after school and whistled to the doves which would fly down and congregate on the railings while he fed them. But that's not to say he's a soft touch. He was the first rider to face down Lance Armstrong at the Tour. He was the man who refused to give a DNA sample to definitively remove his name from the *Operación Puerto* files, using the logic that he was innocent, therefore he shouldn't have to. (On a wider level, a reasonable position to take – presumed dopers have civil liberties too.)

The trouble begins when you try to define Contador. He's a chameleon, whose colour changes according to the context and situation, but the main thing you need to know about him is that just because he looks like a nice guy, doesn't mean that he is a nice guy.

My favourite image of Contador is the front cover of *L'Équipe* the day after the 'dropped chain' incident that affected Andy Schleck during the 2010 Tour de France – we'll come to that again in his chapter. Schleck had a mechanical just after attacking on the Port de Balès climb, and Contador carried through the counterattack, which netted him a time gain that turned out to be exactly the same as his eventual overall margin of victory – 39 seconds. The social-media backlash against Contador cornered him into two unwise decisions: first, to bend the truth to the press and initially say that he hadn't been aware of Schleck's problem, then, later in the evening, to issue an apology by YouTube. He tried initially to appear innocent, then apologetic, when there was no need to be either.

But the truth was there for all to see on the front of *L'Équipe* the next day. The headline: '*Contador sans pitié*' (Ruthless Contador), and the photo showed his face, with a wide smile, and a wink. They couldn't have found a more devious image. You could imagine the same expression on his face after dropping Lance Armstrong, or refusing to give a DNA test. Or ingesting clenbuterol, accidentally or otherwise.

Contador's Tour career has coincided with wave after wave of doping scandals and intra-team cycling politics almost from the very beginning. He'd finished the race in 31st place in 2005 on his debut, at the age of 22 – not a bad result, although a fair way behind the achievements of Laurent Fignon and Jan Ullrich, for example, who came first and second on their respective Tour debuts at the same age in 1983 and 1996.

In 2006, Contador was expecting to improve on that – he'd come fifth in the Tour of the Basque Country and second in the Tour of Romandy earlier in the season, and looking at what he went on to achieve, it's easy to imagine that Contador could have finished in the top 10 or 15 riders. Unfortunately for him, the season had also been played out against the percussive background rhythm of doping scandals. His Liberty Seguros team manager Saiz was a central figure in the *Operación Puerto* investigation, which was led by the Spanish police. When Saiz was arrested by police on leaving the premises of Dr Eufemiano Fuentes, the ringleader of a blood-doping operation in Madrid, he was found with a suitcase full of cash. Not a crime in itself, but a difficult thing to explain under the circumstances.

The scandal forced Liberty Seguros, an insurance company, to pull out of their sponsorship deal, only to be hastily replaced by Astana, a consortium of Kazakh companies who were coming to the rescue of team leader Alexandre Vinokourov. When the Tour's organization tried to prevent Astana from starting the race, they were overruled by the Court of Arbitration for Sport. However, on the eve of the Tour, the list of riders' names connected with *Operación Puerto* was published in the Spanish newspaper *El País*, and even as the riders were being presented to the public, the ones on the list were being forced to pull out of the race. Five of Astana's nine riders were initially named in the report: Contador, Allan Davis, Joseba Beloki, Sérgio Paulinho and Isidro Nozal. Given that the team was now down to four riders, they were barred from starting, according to the rules of the event. Ironically, all five riders, including Contador, were later officially cleared of involvement. Even more ironically, of the four who'd been left, Vinokourov, Andrey Kashechkin and Carlos Barredo would later test positive, while only Luis León Sánchez continues to protest his innocence of involvement. Sánchez's current team in 2015? Astana.

Contador left Astana that year, transferring to Discovery Channel, who were looking for a Tour-winning replacement for the recently retired Armstrong. The Spaniard won the yellow jersey for Discovery Channel in 2007, but the sponsors had already decided to withdraw their support at the end of the season, and the team, having won eight of the last nine Tours (retrospectively reduced to one after Armstrong's admission of doping), disbanded, unable to find a suitable replacement.

A lot of the Discovery Channel riders and staff, including Contador and manager Bruyneel, pitched up at Astana for 2008, and scandal and controversy continued to dog the team and Contador. They were not invited to the Giro d'Italia or the Tour de France, although the Giro later relented and invited the team to the race, which Contador won.

At the end of the 2008 season, Armstrong made his shock announcement that he would be making a comeback to professional cycling, and he was belatedly shoehorned into the Astana team roster. The former best Tour rider in the world and the current best Tour rider in the world were forced into an uneasy cohabitation, but while Armstrong unleashed an increasingly bitter psychological war against Contador, the Spaniard remained impervious to the pressure. Contador was head and shoulders above his rivals at the 2009 Tour, and he won the yellow jersey for the second and, at the time of writing, last time.

Contador's positive test for clenbuterol in 2010 led to a drawn-out legal battle over whether he'd deliberately doped or not. The amount of clenbuterol found in his system was extremely small, but the fact it was there needed to be explained, and Contador's excuse was that he'd eaten a contaminated steak during the Tour's rest day. While the Court of Arbitration for Sport deliberated over his case, he signed for Saxo Bank, whose manager's career also wasn't without scandal. Bjarne Riis had confessed to doping for his Tour win in 1996, and it would also emerge in *The Secret Race* that he was aware of his riders doping on his CSC team in the 2000s. Contador won the Giro with Saxo Bank in 2011, then came fifth in the Tour, before the final verdict on his clenbuterol positive in early February 2012 voided these results. He's managed to avoid scandal since his comeback from his doping ban in August 2012, although the deterrent effect of what turned out to be a six-month ban from racing might be open to question. But he's also not managed to find the same form he had before 2010. He's won the Vuelta twice since his ban, but was easily beaten by Chris Froome at the 2013 Tour de France. You wonder whether he preferred the concurrent success and scandal he used to enjoy, or the results that have come with a quiet life.

If there was ever going to be a surprise winner of the Tour, 2007 was going to be the year it would happen. Armstrong had retired, Jan Ullrich and Ivan Basso's links with *Puerto* were keeping them out of the race, while Tyler Hamilton and Floyd Landis were having their own problems with the anti-doping authorities. And then during the Tour, yellow jersey Michael Rasmussen and Contador's former and future teammate Vinokourov would be thrown off the race, Rasmussen for his whereabouts issues (although his utter and uncharacteristic dominance of the race also rang warning bells), and Vinokourov for a positive test. The final yellow jersey would be fought out between Contador, the best young rider in the race, grizzled veteran Levi Leipheimer (just a few years away from his own doping ban) and Australia's Cadel Evans.

Through the Alps, Rasmussen had virtually ridden away with

the race – he'd attacked early on the stage to Tignes, and his rivals let him go, mainly because in previous years he'd only shown interest in the King of the Mountains classification. But when the dust settled after the Alps, Rasmussen was almost three minutes clear of Alejandro Valverde and Evans, his most likely challengers. Contador was 3-10 down.

Rasmussen then defended his lead in the Albi time trial, conceding a minute and a half to Evans and 37 seconds to Contador. The top three going into the Pyrenees were Rasmussen, Evans a minute behind and Contador 2-31 in arrears. With three tough stages in the Pyrenees, it was hard to imagine the order changing. But Rasmussen and Contador found a new level in the Pyrenees. They dropped everyone with astonishing speed on the summit finish at Plateau de Beille, leaving Evans almost two minutes behind. Contador couldn't drop Rasmussen, but nobody else could match him.

The same happened on the final climb of the Col de Peyresourde the next day, with Contador and Rasmussen attacking each other with mighty surges, and putting another minute into Evans. Finally, Rasmussen won again at the summit finish on the Col d'Aubisque, with Leipheimer second, Contador third and Evans fourth. The yellow jersey was Rasmussen's with Contador safe in second at 3-10, Evans third at 5-03 and Leipheimer fourth at 5-59. The final podium looked like it was set in stone.

But that was before the rumours about Rasmussen's whereabouts problems finally forced his Rabobank team to withdraw him from the race. He'd told the UCI that he was training in Mexico, but had been spotted riding in Italy by an Italian journalist, Davide Cassani. The realization that Rasmussen had lied to the anti-doping authorities came on the back of Vinokourov's positive in the Pyrenees, and suddenly the race found itself with a new yellow jersey, and only a time trial to go.

Contador defended his newfound lead in the time trial, although not by much – Evans closed to within 23 seconds, and Leipheimer to 31 seconds. But the whole competition had been so distorted and falsified by Rasmussen's presence that it was rendered almost meaningless. Evans could rightly complain that while he'd finished the race 23 seconds down, Contador would have benefited from riding with Rasmussen during the three Pyrenean stages – even though Rasmussen was ejected from the race, it affected the overall standings. However, over the next two seasons, Contador emerged as the strongest Grand Tour rider in the world, with wins in the Giro d'Italia and Vuelta a España in 2008. Then came the high-water mark of his physical abilities: 2009.

There wasn't really much competition on a sporting level at the 2009 Tour. Contador was clearly the strongest rider, Andy Schleck was clearly the second-strongest rider, and only the battle for third place, between Lance Armstrong, Bradley Wiggins, Fränk Schleck, Andreas Klöden and Vincenzo Nibali provided any sporting intrigue. The route also turned out to be a bit of a dud. It started in Monaco and headed west, then into Spain, up into the Pyrenees and then across France for a long schlep to the Alps via the centre of the country. The only summit finish in the Pyrenees, Arcalís, was neutralized by the wind and negative tactics, so, effectively, race followers had to wait two weeks for significant general classification action, which would come at Verbier in the Alps. However, the ongoing soap opera of the rivalry between Contador and Armstrong more than made up for it.

The two had skirted around each other all season. When Contador made a silly error at Paris–Nice and lost his leader's jersey, Armstrong's not-at-all-well-meaning tweet of support – 'Amazing talent, but still a lot to learn' – caused anticipation to rise. Armstrong went to the Giro and finished 11th, while

Contador looked in better form – he was first at the Tour of the Basque Country and third at the Critérium du Dauphiné Libéré.

At the Tour, although the Astana team did an effective job of covering up the worst of it, the two were at loggerheads. Contador was winning the physical battle – his second place in the opening Monaco time trial put him 22 seconds ahead of Armstrong. But the psychological battle was closer. On stage three to La Grande-Motte, the Columbia team forced the race to split in the crosswinds of the Camargue, and 27 riders finished 41 seconds ahead of the next group. Armstrong, along with Astana teammates Yaroslav Popovych and Haimar Zubeldia, had made the front group while Contador was left behind. The rumour in the race entourage was that Columbia rider George Hincapie, who'd been Armstrong's teammate during every one of his seven Tour wins, had tipped off Armstrong to make sure he was well positioned before it split. Furthermore, Armstrong had marshalled Popovych and Zubeldia to ride on the front to help prevent the next group, which contained Contador and most of the other favourites, chasing them down.

The next day, Astana won the team time trial and came within 0.22 seconds of putting Armstrong into the yellow jersey, which would have changed the dynamic of the entire race. Certainly Contador's attack in the final two kilometres of the Arcalís stage would have had an entirely different complexion had Armstrong been in the yellow jersey – as it was, Contador held second place, two seconds ahead of Armstrong, while the Ag2r team's Italian rider Rinaldo Nocentini wore the yellow jersey through to the Alps.

Contador killed the race as a sporting competition on Verbier – he made an unanswerable attack on the Alpine climb, putting 43 seconds into Andy Schleck and a minute and a half into Armstrong in just six kilometres. He co-operated with the

Schleck brothers on the hardest stage of the race, to Le Grand-Bornand, bartering the stage win, for Fränk Schleck, for help in increasing the gap to Nibali and Armstrong, the next two riders home, to over two minutes. When Contador put a further minute and a half into Armstrong in the Annecy time trial, the race was over, and Contador the easy winner.

However, rumours of discord behind the scenes at Astana were starting to spill out. In a press conference on his return to Spain, Contador let rip on his American teammate. 'My relationship with him is zero,' said Contador. 'He has won seven Tours and he's played a great role in this Tour. But at a personal level it's different. I have never had a great admiration for him, nor will I.'

It emerged that Contador had allegedly been left without a car to travel to the start line of the Annecy time trial, after Armstrong had commandeered the last team car available to pick up his family and some friends from the airport. The *Diario Sur* newspaper in Spain carried an article headlined, CONTADOR'S PRIVATE PARTY, in which some of the extent of Armstrong's harrying and bullying behaviour was revealed. 'Contador's toughest climb was not recorded in images. It was fought in the hotel and the bus. During one stage, Armstrong sat his guests at the very back of the bus, right in Contador's usual seat. He kept his mouth shut, listening to Armstrong's jabs: "It doesn't take a Nobel prize to figure out what happens with side winds." Contador didn't reply in the hotel. He did so on the road. He was the first cyclist to stand up to Armstrong. And he did it in silence,' wrote Jesús Gómez Peña.

After Contador's press conference, Armstrong confirmed the irrevocable breakdown in relations. He tweeted, 'Hey, *pistolero*, there is no "I" in team. What did I say in March? "Lots to learn." Restated.'

Don't be taken in by the nice smile. Alberto Contador is a

hard case, stubborn and impervious to pressure, and he beat Armstrong both physically and psychologically, which is not something many riders can say they have done.

Since 2009, his performance levels have dropped off at the Tour. Before he was stripped of the yellow jersey in 2010, he'd only beaten Andy Schleck by 39 seconds, while he was beaten fairly in 2011 by Evans and by Froome in 2013. He remains largely popular with the Spanish public, but even considering the results that still stand, it's surprising he's not reached anything like the level of public adulation given to Miguel Indurain, for example. This is partly Contador's fault – he's been surrounded with questionable managers, and has been accused of climbing at speeds which were perceived to have become impossible with the development of cycling's blood-passport system. To call Contador the best Grand Tour rider of his era is a statement about Contador. But it's also a statement about the era he's ridden in.

16

Carlos Sastre

2008

The computer needs to understand me. I don't need to under-stand it.

Carlos Sastre, *Overcoming*

Carlos Sastre sometimes gets a bad rap as a Tour winner. It's partly Lance Armstrong's fault – around the time he announced his comeback, on the eve of the 2009 season, the Texan remarked to a journalist that he considered the 2008 edition of the race, won by Sastre, to be 'a bit of a joke'. (Statements like this, of course, say far more about Lance Armstrong than they do about Carlos Sastre, and Armstrong later apologized for his comments, but you couldn't help suspecting that he still thought them to be true.)

Sastre is sometimes considered to be fortunate with his timing – his one Tour win came when Alberto Contador, the winner in 2007 and 2009, was unable to race after his Astana team were barred from the start for their terrible record on doping. There's also the feeling, apparently especially within the team itself, that CSC carried him to victory, and that both Fränk and Andy Schleck were stronger riders. Furthermore, the

Spanish rider was not as showy as his predecessors in the yellow jersey club – you would probably have to go back to at least the 1960s to find a less celebrated Tour winner. Sad-eyed, understated Sastre just seemed to lack star quality.

Sastre's career was a classic slow burn. With the exception of the 2005 Tour, where he finished a disappointing 21st, his result improved every season from his 2001 debut to his victory in 2008. He came 20th, 10th, ninth then eighth in his first four races. Then, in 2006, he improved to third, third again in 2007 (following Levi Leipheimer's retrospective disqualification) and finally first in 2008. While some riders look and ride like they were born to win the Tour, Sastre looked like he'd had to work extremely hard for it. His Grand Tour results were actually very underrated. Gérard Vroomen, who owned the Cervélo company which provided bikes for CSC then sponsored Sastre's team in 2009, once described him as the best general classification rider of his generation, and when you look at the results you can see his point. Sastre achieved 15 top 10s in Grand Tours, which is the same number as Eddy Merckx, more than Joop Zoetemelk and Lucien Van Impe managed, and only three fewer than Pedro Delgado, who holds the record. He was twice second in the Vuelta, third, fourth, sixth, seventh and eighth. There was no one riding at the same time who could match that consistency.

It would be easy to fall into the trap of thinking that Sastre was a climber who won the Tour. It's natural to classify Tour winners, and we tend to organize them into two types: climbers and time triallists. In reality, it's more of a Venn diagram, with significant overlap between the two fields, but it's an effective way of systemizing and understanding how the race has been won. Ullrich: time triallist. Pantani: climber. Armstrong: bit of both. Pereiro: climber. Contador: bit of both. Sastre: climber. (It might be useful to add a third field, titled 'drugs' for Ullrich, Pantani and Armstrong, at least.)

But I think that while Sastre was a good and very consistent climber, his primary asset was that he was a superb and bold tactician, the first real tactician to win the Tour since Stephen Roche in 1987.

Mainly, however, Carlos Sastre was enigmatic, and very few people in cycling understood him. His old teammates alternately describe a quiet, shy, softly spoken individual who was nevertheless stubborn, argumentative and obstinate. He often found himself at loggerheads with his team manager, Bjarne Riis. Karsten Kroon, who rode on CSC with him, said the arguments between Sastre and Riis were more a clash of wills than real opinions. 'Sometimes Carlos was this really quiet, shy boy. And then, out of the blue, he could be impossible, especially when he had discussions with Bjarne,' he says. 'They were both stubborn. To me, it was not worth the energy, it was more like a struggle between two alpha males. Carlos was very sure of himself.'

Riis himself wrote in his autobiography *Stages of Light and Dark* that Sastre was particularly headstrong. 'He could argue for hours about the smallest things, and it was almost impossible to change his mind and convince him that there were alternative choices when it came to equipment, training routes or race tactics,' he said.

'Carlos wasn't the skinniest all the time and it drove Bjarne nuts,' recalls Bobby Julich, another CSC teammate. 'Carlos would say, "We're training, we're not at the race. I know where I'm at." But he was the only one who had that relationship with Bjarne, where they could fight and argue and disagree. They had a very close bond.'

According to both Kroon and Julich, Sastre was also very relaxed about things, too relaxed for their liking. 'He'd say, "No stress, Bobby. No stress",' recalls Julich. 'I'd say, "Dammit, Carlos, sometimes you've got to show some emotion." He used to drive me and Jens Voigt up the wall – he was our leader and needed to be motivating us, and all he was saying was, "No stress." It was tough to deal with.'

Kroon describes riding for Sastre on the stage of the 2008 Vuelta, which finished on the steep climb of L'Angliru. 'It was raining, and my job was to stay with him and position him,' says Kroon. 'It was windy and raining and I said, "Please, Carlos, move up." I was trying to motivate him to move up because the climb was starting in a few kilometres. I started moving up, looked round after about five minutes, but he wasn't there. He was still sat at the back of the peloton. I could never follow the logic because it cost him energy, but he was totally different to other riders.'

There's one more thing about Sastre. His nickname was *Don Limpio*, or Mr Clean. When he won the Tour after the race had suffered from years of ongoing doping scandals, Riis said to the Tour organizer Christian Prudhomme, 'There's your clean winner.'

Sastre rode during a dirty era. He spent four years with ONCE, whose manager was Manolo Saiz, the same Manolo Saiz who was heavily involved in *Operación Puerto*, and seven at CSC with Riis. It would be easy to find Sastre guilty by association (as with Contador in the previous chapter). On the other hand, Sastre's results improved as the sport started slowly cleaning itself up after 2006, and his reputation was good. Sastre does himself a disservice by refusing to discuss the issue in specific terms, although that's not unusual – he's much given to gnomic utterances and bland philosophizing. In the end, he has the benefit of the doubt in a way that Riis never did.

I'd first noticed Sastre in the 2002 Tour, when he attacked the Lance Armstrong group on the Alpine summit finish at La Plagne. While he'd left it too late to close down the stage winner Michael Boogerd, not many riders in those years could ride away from Armstrong, and the American saw to it that he bridged up to Sastre, possibly to keep a closer eye on his potential as a threat. The following year, Sastre won a Tour stage at Plateau de Bonascre, this time attacking from further out. But he really came of age over the 2006 and 2007 seasons. In 2006, notwithstanding Floyd Landis's antics, Sastre was probably the strongest climber in the Alps – it was his attack on the stage to La Toussuire that detonated the front group and sent Landis backwards, and Sastre was also clearly the best of the rest behind Landis on the stage to Morzine.

Sastre was in fifth overall going into these two stages, following the stage to Alpe d'Huez. Landis was in yellow, Óscar Pereiro second at 10 seconds, Cyril Dessel, a remnant from a long escape earlier in the Tour, in third at 2-02, then Denis Menchov at 2-12 and Sastre at 2-17. When you look at the riders ahead, Landis was destined to test positive, Pereiro wouldn't normally have been there except he'd been gifted 30 minutes in a long break, and Dessel was in a similar situation. Menchov, who would also test positive much later, was only five seconds clear. Even before La Toussuire and Morzine, Sastre wasn't far at all from being the best rider in the Tour. Second place at La Toussuire (and first of the general classification contenders) moved Sastre to second overall.

On the Col de Joux Plane, the final climb before Morzine, Sastre destroyed his general classification rivals, save the flying Landis, who was six minutes up the road. He attacked fluently up the climb, spinning a low gear, and putting one and a half minutes into Pereiro and Andreas Klöden. Going into the final time trial, Sastre was second, 12 seconds behind Pereiro, 18 seconds ahead of Landis and 2-17 ahead of Klöden. Unfortunately for Sastre, he rode poorly in the time trial and dropped to fourth overall, then finally settled in third when Landis was disqualified.

Sastre was reportedly angry with his team for allowing the Pereiro break to Montélimar to gain so much time, especially as CSC rider Jens Voigt was also up the road, and was working in the break. Sastre wanted Voigt to sit in and concentrate on winning the stage (which he did anyway) and for CSC to help bring the break back under control – he could see the danger from Pereiro.

In 2007, Sastre didn't quite have the legs to match his performance at La Toussuire and on the Joux Plane – he'd gone into the final Pyrenean stage in fifth place overall, over six minutes behind. It was a very tough day, crossing into Spain over the *hors-catégorie* Port de Larrau and crossing the high plateau of Navarra before going back into France over the Col de la Pierre Saint-Martin, before two more climbs, the Col de Marie-Blanque and a summit finish on the Col d'Aubisque. Instead of defending sixth place, or maybe waiting for the final climb to see if he could squeeze up to fourth, Sastre decided to risk everything with a well-placed attack at the foot of the Larrau, very early on. His aim would be to bridge to the break over the top, and work with them on the long flat section to La Pierre Saint-Martin, then reassess. He was accompanied by Mauricio Soler, riding for the mountains classification, and Iban Mayo – the trio managed to catch the leaders, and while the general classification contenders chased, Sastre's group maintained a lead of four minutes. The pursuit began in earnest over the Marie-Blanque, and the lead was halved by the summit. Then Sastre was pulled back on the final climb, although he was still strong enough to finish eighth and held on to his fifth place, which would improve to fourth when Michael Rasmussen was pulled out of the race and then third when Leipheimer's result was later nullified.

But the point was that in 2006 Sastre had tried to climb his way towards overall victory, and in 2007 he'd tried to think his way towards overall victory. Neither strategy had quite worked, but they were excellent practice runs for 2008.

There was one final tactical masterpiece for Sastre in 2007, towards the end of the Vuelta a España. Going into stage 18, which finished in his home city of Ávila, Sastre and CSC improvised an excellent strategy off the back of an attack by the Caisse d'Epargne team. Caisse d'Epargne had Vladimir Efimkin in second overall, and Vladimir Karpets in eighth. The Spanish team decided to send Karpets on the attack early in the stage to Ávila, to force Efimkin's rivals to chase and perhaps give him the opportunity for a counterattack. Karpets' mistake was to take three strong CSC climbers with him – Chris Sørensen, Volodymir Gustov and Christian Vande Velde.

It might have looked as if CSC were after a stage win, but then Sastre suddenly attacked from the peloton to the group, swiftly followed by race leader Denis Menchov and a handful of other contenders, but not Efimkin. Sastre linked up with his teammates at the front, and the CSC riders drove the break two and a half minutes clear. Sastre's clever tactics had moved him from fourth to third overall, while Caisse d'Epargne's attack had blown up in their face and Efimkin dropped to fifth. The attack didn't win Sastre the Vuelta – Menchov was too strong in the end – but Sastre's final position was second, as much thanks to tactics as climbing speed.

There was little doubt CSC were the strongest team in the 2008 Tour – for the general classification they had Sastre and the Schleck brothers, and Fabian Cancellara and Voigt heading a strong roster of *domestiques*. But they weren't united. The Schleck brothers, who were popular within the team and held a lot of sway, felt that Fränk Schleck should be the leader. Sastre felt that Riis and the Schlecks were trying to marginalize him. In his book, Riis describes the discussions and process of training in the mountains with Sastre before the race: 'The Schleck brothers and Carlos had been at odds with each other on multiple occasions. Small power games, jibes and disagreements, which, if left unresolved, could grow into something bigger and more damaging to the team. They needed to understand that they needed each other if they wanted to get the best out of the race.'

A team insider, with knowledge of the situation, told me in the course of researching this book that Riis's mountain training camp itself might have been an attempt to marginalize Sastre. 'The week before the Tour Sastre was forced to go on crazy training rides in the mountains and prove he was fit enough for the Tour, because Riis didn't want to select him, and the Schlecks didn't want him there,' said my source. 'It actually turned out to be brilliant preparation.' The team carried the schism into the race. 'There was a Schleck camp, which included Jens Voigt, and a few riders who tried to stay away from it all, like Cancellara. The Schleck camp was bigger than the Sastre camp.'

In the Pyrenees, Fränk Schleck attacked and gained time on the stage to Hautacam, which was a mixed day for CSC. They'd put Cancellara into the break, and he was able to help drive the general classification group, including the Schlecks and Sastre, clear of their rival Alejandro Valverde, who had faltered on the Col du Tourmalet. But Andy Schleck had suffered from a hunger flat and he fell out of the running. In a finely balanced Tour, Cadel Evans led by a second from Fränk Schleck. Sastre was in sixth, 1-28 behind.

According to Riis, relations were getting worse and worse between his riders. 'The conflict . . . began to boil over. Things were tense between them, and none of them knew where they stood with each other,' he said. 'Carlos had the feeling that the brothers were only riding for each other and not to help him win. The brothers told him that he was imagining it. Carlos sent a few taunts their way, but was then touchy when the two boys from Luxembourg gave as good as they got.'

At Prato Nevoso, the first Alpine summit finish, Sastre finished ahead of the other general classification contenders, putting Evans out of the yellow jersey, but Fränk Schleck into it. The top order was incredibly tight, which is why 2008 was one of the best Tours of the last two decades – only 49 seconds separated Schleck from Sastre in sixth place. Two of the top six, Vande Velde and Menchov, lost time over the Col de la Bonette two days later, and then the Tour came down to a straight shootout on Alpe d'Huez.

CSC held the yellow jersey with Fränk Schleck, but with Evans only eight seconds behind and a time trial to come, the lead wasn't secure at all. Either Schleck or Sastre would have to put time into Evans – the advantage was that with two of them, they could gang up on the Australian, so long as at least one of them gained sufficient time on him. Riis pressed them at the morning meeting to find out who should attack on the Alpe. '[Frank's] reply was defensive both in attitude and tactically,' said Riis. ' "What about you, Carlos? What should we do today?" I asked. "Win the stage on Alpe d'Huez," he said, without hesitation. It was that kind of willingness to take a risk that I wanted to see from him.'

Sastre attacked just a kilometre into the climb of Alpe d'Huez, and he gained over two minutes on Evans, while the Schleck brothers duly marked Evans and their other rivals all the way up. But the story was more complex than that. There were rumours that one of the reasons the Schlecks were so diligent in marking their rivals' attacks on the Alpe was that they were hoping somebody was going to be able to take Fränk Schleck back up to Sastre, so he could launch a counterattack. They were allegedly particularly keen to encourage Valverde to chase Sastre, explaining to him what the benefits could be, but Valverde reportedly refused to chase a fellow Spanish rider down. In the end, it was left to Evans to chase, but all he could do was limit Sastre's gains, not eradicate them. Sastre's attack had put his rivals into a box but, more importantly, it had done the same to his two teammates.

Riis recalls in his book that Sastre's attack had fairly settled matters, and that he was looking forward to peace being re-established in the team. Then the rumours began to swirl of Sastre leaving for the new Cervélo TestTeam which was being set up for 2009. That was the thing about Carlos Sastre. When he'd made up his mind about something, he was as stubborn as a mule.

17

Andy Schleck
2010

The future ain't what it used to be.

Yogi Berra

I couldn't take my eyes off Andy Schleck during the Alpe d'Huez stage of the 2008 Tour de France. His ride to the summit might not have been the most newsworthy of the day – his CSC team-mate Carlos Sastre was up the road, riding his way into the yellow jersey; his brother Fränk was *in* the yellow jersey; and he was the lowest placed overall of the eight-man group which fought up the climb in the backwash of Sastre's attack – but there was no doubt who the dominant personality in that group was. Schleck, riding his first Tour, defined the boundaries within which his companions were allowed to behave. Attacks were smothered, the pace varied according to his wishes, and Schleck's mere presence seemed to dissuade anybody from mounting a coherent pursuit of Sastre.

Here are a few of the things which happened on the climb. With 12 kilometres to go, Vladimir Efimkin attacked. Schleck chased him, sitting down. When he caught Efimkin, Schleck rode beside him, easily, then turned around and looked back to check on the rest of the group, pedalling along for a good 10 metres while looking behind him. Next, Bernhard Kohl attacked, and Schleck shut him down. Efimkin jumped again, then Christian Vande Velde, both chased by Schleck. When the group was together again, Schleck sought out his brother Fränk and rode next to him, talking.

Nine and a half kilometres to go, and Alejandro Valverde attacked. Chased down by Schleck. When it slowed down again, Schleck felt around in his back pocket for something, riding along with no hands on the bars. A kilometre later, Stéphane Goubert went, and Schleck rode up to him, passed him, then pedalled along, looking back. Efimkin had another go, and it was Schleck who chased, then looked back again, riding with one hand on the bars. The next attack was Vande Velde. Schleck chased.

At five kilometres to go, Efimkin made his last attack, chased initially by Valverde. But the gap wasn't closing fast enough so Schleck rode past to close down the Russian. Four to go, Cadel Evans made his move, followed by Schleck. With two kilometres to go, Samuel Sánchez attacked and finally got a gap on the group. Schleck let him go, then ripped clear, catching Sánchez. Perfect teamwork? On the surface of it, yes, although there's more to the story than that, as you saw in the last chapter.

The expression on Schleck's face as he put the hex on his rivals was curiously neutral – he made racing up Alpe d'Huez look far easier than it should have been. Every now and again he grimaced, but from a distance it was difficult to tell – it could have been a smile. All I could think was that at some point soon, Andy Schleck was going to start winning Tours, and given that he was barely 23 that day on Alpe d'Huez, he was going to win a lot of them.

Six seasons later, I spent quite a bit of time watching Schleck at the 2014 Paris–Nice. They say that the great champions have an aura. My experience is that some do, and some don't. But Andy Schleck, whether he's a great champion or not, doesn't. At the starts, he didn't stand out at all from all the other faceless racers, invariably rolling up with brother Fränk and sometimes fellow Luxembourger Bob Jungels, and more or less blending in with the riders around him. At the finishes, he was rarely in the front group. Nor were the fans and press paying much attention to him.

I asked the Trek team PR if I could interview Schleck, and a couple of days later, as the race got to the Riviera, I got the OK. There was just one condition, I was told. Andy didn't want to speak about the past.

In the end, Schleck won one Tour, and Liège–Bastogne–Liège. He also collected a lot of second places. Then, for the last three seasons of his career, he withered visibly – poor form through spring 2012, a crash and broken sacrum which, apart from a late-season DNF at the Tour of Beijing, kept him out of racing until 2013, more poor form through 2013 and 2014, another crash, and that was it. In the end, the physical problems caused by the crashes put a stop to his career when he was only 29. That's what Schleck said at his retirement press conference, and it's what he told me when we spoke over the telephone before I wrote this chapter.

But there's more to it than that. Schleck stopped looking happy on the bike after the 2011 Tour de France. It was as if his injuries were just the physical manifestation of a crisis of morale which was terminal.

Cycling seemed to come so easily to Schleck throughout most of his life. Everybody's got their favourite prodigious Andy Schleck story. The Finnish rider Jussi Veikkanen, who rode with Schleck at the VC Roubaix team in 2004, told *Procycling* magazine in 2007 that Schleck showed up to their first race together with 2,000 kilometres in his legs. That's fewer than most fourth-category amateurs might do before their first winter handicap of the season. 'He said he'd been doing exams at school. He just laughed and said he'd be fine. In fact, he rode really well,' Veikkanen said.

Karsten Kroon, an ex-teammate at CSC, remembers their first training camp together. 'When I saw him, I thought, "And this kid is going to be a bike rider?" It seemed like he was constantly fooling around. Then we rode and I thought, "Fuck, this kid is strong. He was just playing."'

Denis Bastien, a journalist with the Luxembourgeois newspaper *Le Quotidien*, followed Schleck's career from an early age. He met him for the first time in 2002, when Schleck was just 16. Bastien had been briefed to interview Schleck's father Johny, who'd ridden for former Tour winners Jan Janssen and Luis Ocaña, in advance of Luxembourg hosting the *Grand Départ* of the Tour that year: 'I went to Johny's house to do the interview and Andy was correcting his dad's stories. He really knew his stuff. Later I saw him when he was a junior, and I knew he was capable of winning the Tour. He was naturally such a good climber and above all had character. I thought he was terrific on a bike, a great pedaller for his age, and he was always ahead of his peers, even on a lot less training. He won the Flèche du Sud in May 2004 with 5,000 kilometres' training. Everybody else would probably have done 10 or 12,000 by then.'

Bobby Julich, his former teammate, says, 'Andy's an artist at riding his bike. Jens Voigt and I used to joke that he could take his bike out of his garage, put it in his living room and just look at it, and get more fit than Jens and I would by training for two months.'

Which brings us back to his last three seasons. Schleck was a born cyclist, and he was good at cycling when it was easy, but maybe in relying on his natural class, he missed out on the knockbacks, challenges and adversity which might have made him good at cycling when it was hard. Robbie McEwen told me that he'd been small and less developed than a lot of his rivals through his teenage years as a BMX racer. He had to beat his rivals by outthinking them rather than outriding them, meaning that he'd learned extra skills which then benefited him once he'd caught up physically. His biggest rival had relied purely on precocious and brute strength, which meant he had less to fall back on when the playing field had levelled, and he disappeared from the sport. Similarly, Andy Schleck was good at being the best. He wasn't so good at being mediocre. A lot of riders seem to be able to start average then, through hard work and repeated knockbacks, beat themselves into elite cyclists. Riders who start at the top and get knocked down, for whatever reason, seem to sometimes find it harder to make the return journey to the top.

Of course, cycling fans aren't blind. There are plenty more hypotheses for why Andy Schleck, runner-up in the Giro d'Italia at the age of 21, three times winner of the white jersey at the Tour de France and winner of the race in 2010, when he was 25, somehow became mediocre from 2012 onwards. One of the reasons I went to Paris–Nice in 2014 was to try to find out exactly why Andy Schleck wasn't as good as he used to be, but he'd given me the same explanation as always: the broken sacrum, the months of lost condition, trying to rush his comeback, bad luck. He was the same person, he had the same engine, he told me.

I spoke to another ex-teammate of Schleck, who went further than most in actually acknowledging that there was an issue, but without saying what it was: 'I know what's been bothering him the last few years and I think he had a tough time. In the end he just didn't like to ride his bike any more.'

There's one other thing about Andy Schleck which is important, and that is the way people react to him. People can't help infantilizing him a little – a lot of people I've spoken to about Schleck talk extremely highly of him, but in a very paternal way. Julich tells me, 'He was a really cool and mellow kid.' Kroon's first words to me about Andy Schleck were, 'He was the sweetest kid.'

They're absolutely right. I like Andy Schleck, too – he's very good-natured, full of gangly energy – and the stories that leaked out, of him having the messiest suitcase in the team, of leaving his cycling shoes at the hotel, made him seem more human, more like the rest of us, than the serious, focused supermen he was up against. His form was either amazing or terrible, because, the rumours went, he could only focus for a short while. He was thrown off the 2010 Vuelta by his own team manager, Bjarne Riis, for going out drinking with his teammate Stuart O'Grady. It's as if he were an ordinary guy, trapped in the body of the best cyclist in the world. How else would you explain what happened at the Tour of Georgia in 2005?

Georgia was one of Schleck's first races as a professional rider. He was still only 19, but seemed to be determined to make an impression. Julich recalls the first stage: 'We were coming on to a finishing circuit, which we had to ride three times. I was riding next to Lance and I saw Andy attack with just over a lap to go. I was thinking, "Wow, he's really giving it 100 per cent." He was looking back, looking up at the finish line, and all of a sudden Lance looked over at me and said, "He knows we have one more lap to go, right?" I looked at Andy and thought, "Andy, don't do it!" He came across the line, threw his hands up in every victory salute you can think of. Lance was laughing his ass off, we came flying past, and then he realized. He didn't like that; he didn't like us jibing him about it.'

The hardest stage of the race, which finished at the summit of the Brasstown Bald climb, came four days later. Julich, who'd already won Paris–Nice and the Critérium International in the spring, was riding just ahead of the main group of favourites on the penultimate climb when his chain snapped. 'I'd put a 28 [sprocket] on, to have a bailout gear if I needed it,' he says. 'Turns out it was too extreme a gear to have and the chain wasn't long enough.'

Schleck, who wasn't far behind, gave Julich his bike, and waited for the team car to get Julich's spare. Matters were complicated by the fact that Julich rode oval chainrings, while Schleck had regular ones. Schleck had to ride from behind the third group, where the team car was, all the way up through the second group, and back to the first. Both riders were on the wrong bike, but didn't have the time or energy to swap. 'Next thing I know, he's back next to me, on my spare, with the Osymetric rings, and he says, "I've got this," and went in front of me to pull me back. I was absolutely on the limit,' says Julich.

When Schleck pulled Julich back up to the lead group, which was down to Armstrong, Levi Leipheimer, Floyd Landis and eventual winner Tom Danielson, Armstrong reportedly turned around to Schleck and said, 'What the fuck are you doing here?'

Schleck was finally dropped on Brasstown Bald, but not before he'd irritated Armstrong by leaving a gap in the line of riders for him to close. 'I left a gap behind Floyd because I needed to talk to the car to ask what to do,' says Schleck. 'I wasn't used to the bike – with the chainrings, pedalling was like rowing a boat and I felt terrible. Lance rode past and called me a "fucking pussy". I was really upset about that.'

Armstrong said sorry the next day after Julich had a word, which struck Julich as unusual because 'these were the days Lance didn't apologize to anyone'. Schleck points out to me that when the Texan made his comeback four years later, he stood on the second step of the podium of the Tour de France, while Armstrong was on the third.

'Were you tempted to lean across and call him a fucking pussy?' I joke.

'No,' says Schleck, horrified. 'I was never mean to other riders.'

Cyrille Guimard, Schleck's manager at VC Roubaix, still thinks he turned professional one year too early. 'Physically, he might have been ready, but he was not ready. He was not an adult,' Guimard tells me.

Schleck admits that he struggled in his first couple of professional seasons, but a stronger ride at the 2006 Tour of Germany, where he was 16th overall, indicated that he was improving. Riis told him to focus on getting into good condition for the 2007 Giro.

'Everything changed with that race,' says Schleck. 'I was no longer Fränk's little brother. I was Andy Schleck.'

Schleck, who was still only 21, rode astonishingly well and consistently in a mountainous race and came second overall, 1-55 behind the winner, Danilo Di Luca.

The top order of the 2007 Giro doesn't bear too much scrutiny: Di Luca was later suspended for doping; third-placed Eddy Mazzoleni, a six-foot bruiser riding for the Astana team who'd previously only occasionally made an appearance in the top 20 of Grand Tours, was suspended for his involvement in the Italian Oil for Drugs scandal in 2008. Schleck's initial disappointment at the race came from the CSC manager Alain Gallopin preferring him to ride a conservative race, rather than attacking. But he's a bit more outspoken about the result now. 'I won that Giro, in my head,' Schleck tells me. 'You can't tell me that Di Luca was clean that year. I'm not naïve and I'm not stupid, but if he was doping after that Giro then he was doing something during it and before.'

Schleck followed up his result with 11th place in the 2008 Tour, where he'd ridden in support of Sastre. He'd lost nine minutes of his eventual 11-32 deficit on one single day in the Pyrenees, when he'd suffered from a self-inflicted hunger knock. 'You know, sometimes I can be a stupid character,' he admits. 'We ate breakfast and I was eating white bread with Nutella and Bjarne came down and said I shouldn't be eating that. I was annoyed and went to get my suitcase ready. That was a mistake – I didn't eat properly before the stage.'

The stage crossed the Col du Tourmalet before the finish at Hautacam. On the Tourmalet, Alejandro Valverde was in trouble, so the whole CSC team worked to get rid of him. 'We dropped Valverde, but at the bottom of Hautacam I was feeling dizzy and hungry. It was too late. Three kilometres from the finish, Valverde came back past me, tapped me on the shoulder and gave me an energy gel. He'd lost time because of our plan, but he's a gentleman and said to sit in his wheel. But I was going left to right and lost another five minutes in the last three kilometres.'

Add those nine minutes at Hautacam to the two minutes he sacrificed by working for Sastre on Alpe d'Huez, and it becomes clear that Schleck was physically ready to win the Tour.

The following year, Schleck came second at the Tour, but was outridden by Alberto Contador – he lost a minute in the opening time trial, another 40 seconds in the team time trial, 20 seconds at Andorra, 43 seconds at Verbier, and another minute and three-quarters in the Annecy time trial. With the time losses coming so regularly, Schleck was criticized in the last two mountain stages for seeming to be more concerned with trying to lift Fränk into a podium spot than with trying to win time back from Contador. In fairness, Schleck couldn't drop Contador, and he was fairly safe in second place, so you can understand his tactics. Given the choice between second place by four minutes and possibly having his brother on the podium, or second place by three minutes and not having his brother on the podium, he went for the former.

I remember my perceptions of Schleck changing slowly over this period. The 2007 Giro and 2008 Tour made me think he was a Tour winner-in-waiting, but 2009 made me think he was going to have to work hard not to settle into a groove of second places. It was hard to see where he was going to find four minutes on Alberto Contador, who was only two and a half years older.

Hindsight makes my assessment seem a bit harsh on Schleck. Firstly, Contador was never as strong again as he was in 2009. Secondly, Schleck tweaked his training for 2010. 'I just needed to adapt my riding skills to beat him,' he says. 'I couldn't accelerate on the climbs like he could and we realized quickly that if I was to beat him next year I'd have to train on a really high threshold, attacking and continuing on the threshold. I did that all the time in training camps, and it paid off.'

Schleck was initially second again in 2010, but this is an era in which Grand Tours are won and lost in time trials, on the climbs, and in the courtrooms. When Contador tested positive, Schleck finally gained entry to the yellow jersey club.

It took a long time, however. The final verdict on Contador's clenbuterol positive came 566 days after the final day of the race – perversely, the Luxembourger had already achieved another second place in the Tour by then. And even after he was finally confirmed as the winner, it took a long time for him to rationalize it. He told cyclingnews.com in December 2012 that he didn't really feel like the Tour winner. When I spoke to him at Paris–Nice in 2014, I asked if he saw himself as a Tour winner, and there was a long pause, before he started talking about Contador attacking him on the Port de Balès climb in the Pyrenees when his chain jammed. As with the 2007 Giro he has become more outspoken on the matter now: 'I'm proud to say I've won it,' he says. 'Contador did something that was not allowed and because of that I have the title. I regret not standing on top of the podium on the Champs-Élysées but I now realize that was my Tour.'

Then he adds, oddly, 'It was quite difficult. I think I was too nice of a guy to win the Tour.'

Apart from Contador's positive test, the 2010 Tour rested on an exquisite accident of timing, tactics and contentious ethics: that 'dropped chain' episode on the Port de Balès in the Pyrenees. Schleck, wearing yellow, attacked a few kilometres from the top, but he crunched his gears and came juddering to a halt. Contador had countered, and swept straight past Schleck, with Denis Menchov and Samuel Sánchez, third and fourth overall, in tow. Contador, with a little help from Sánchez, carried his counterattack through, leaving Schleck behind.

It's been overlooked in the noise of debate over the rights and wrongs of Contador's attack, but I think the next few minutes of the Tour showed Schleck at his physical finest. Schleck was in full cry as he rode in pursuit of Contador – watching him carve through the groups of riders who'd passed him with a power born of anger, adrenalin and fear showed what he could have been capable of. Other champions have the kind of personalities where they can access and channel that depth of motivation whenever they want – I should add that this might even be a psychological defect in terms of everyday life. Schleck, on the other hand, usually couldn't, except on this one occasion. A full 30 seconds passed before Schleck got going again, plus acceleration time, and he'd closed to about 18 seconds by the summit of the climb. But Schleck was renowned as being a less confident descender than many of his rivals, and the run-in down the mountain to the finish favoured Contador and his companions. The gap went out again to 39 seconds by the finish line. Contador's final winning margin in Paris: 39 seconds. It could only happen to Andy Schleck.

Contador received quite a lot of critical blowback for not waiting for Schleck, and Schleck believes the Spaniard should have relented, but the race was on by this point. The Tour was not just about Contador versus Schleck – Menchov and Sánchez rode too, and why shouldn't they have, with their closest rival for the podium, Jurgen Van den Broeck, distanced? Contador was perhaps a bit more visible on the front than Schleck's fans would have liked, but you don't train your whole life to not gain a bit of necessary advantage when the opportunity presents itself, and Contador's instinct was to prioritize the positive outcome of the situation (time in the bank) over the negative (a bit of potential criticism about an ethical grey area). Canada's Ryder Hesjedal summed it up after the stage: 'If you draw your sword and drop it, you die.'

Of course, there was more to the 2010 Tour than this one event, even notwithstanding Contador's disqualification. The closer the race, the more tantalizing the what-ifs. What if Fränk Schleck hadn't crashed out on stage three? What if there hadn't been a race-wide neutralization orchestrated by Schleck's teammate Fabian Cancellara following a series of crashes on stage two, which heavily favoured Schleck?

But there's one what-if which sums up Schleck's difficulty moving from second to first place in the Tour more than any other: what if he'd attacked earlier in the Alpine stages? He went for it on Avoriaz, the first high mountain summit finish of the race, but only with less than a kilometre to go, gaining 10 seconds. There's a pattern over Schleck's career of waiting too long to attack. If you can't time-trial, as is the case with Schleck, it's not the right tactic. In 2007, he followed his rivals in the Giro, rather than attack (although he was following team orders). In the 2009 Tour he followed Contador's attacks but didn't make any significant ones of his own until the final two mountain stages, to Le Grand-Bornand and Mont Ventoux. In

2010 he was more aggressive, but the late attack to Avoriaz was insignificant, he fluffed the Port de Balès attack and preferred an anticlimactic series of surges on the final summit finish on the Col du Tourmalet to two or three all-out jumps, meaning that he couldn't drop Contador.

Schleck likes to be in his comfort zone and likes to be surrounded by his people. His home in Luxembourg is 200 metres up the road from brother Fränk, his parents are 300 metres away. The Schlecks hang out together, going fishing on their days off, or gathering round their parents' kitchen table for a shared dinner. When he and Fränk helped form the Leopard–Trek team at the end of 2010, all their buddies from Saxo Bank – Voigt, O'Grady, Cancellara – came with them. Did this desire for normality and familiar surroundings translate into risk-averse tactics on the bike? Whether it did or didn't, Schleck had the very human and normal tendency to postpone difficult decisions in a bike race.

A similar situation happened in the 2011 Tour. The Schlecks spent the Pyrenees, which came before the Alps, sitting back. Fränk took 20 seconds by attacking three kilometres from the summit finish of Luz Ardiden. Then Andy left it until 500 metres to go two stages later at the very hard Plateau de Beille finish, gaining a paltry two seconds. It was less an attack than a finishing sprint. It looked like they were basing their race around staying ahead of Alberto Contador, who'd lost time in the opening week and had already ridden the Giro that year. Meanwhile their real rival, eventual winner Cadel Evans, happily sat in their slipstreams, knowing that 20 seconds or so conceded here and there wasn't going to stop him winning the Tour, with a long time trial to finish the race. The Schlecks' decision was clearly to wait until the Alps, with two very hard summit finishes at the Col du Galibier and Alpe d'Huez, but they hadn't factored in their vulnerability on the descents which finished off the first two days in the Alps. By the morning of the Col du Galibier stage, both Schlecks trailed Evans, Fränk by a few seconds, Andy by over a minute.

'We should have done more before,' Schleck admits. 'I really wanted to win at Plateau de Beille but there was so much head-wind. I waited for the last kilometre and launched a sprint which took three seconds, which showed how strong I was. We should have kept on trying – at one point one of us could have got away. Waiting there was a mistake.'

The fact that the Tour was all but lost seemed to liberate Andy Schleck. Released from the fear of risking victory, since it had already gone anyway, Schleck was free to embark on his career-defining victory, on the Col du Galibier. With his Leopard team, he plotted an ambush on the rest of the race that would not only distance his rivals in the general classification but also, just as importantly, put space between himself and the perception that he was tactically too meek to win the Tour de France.

The stage crossed the Col d'Agnel and Col d'Izoard before climbing the Col du Lautaret, turning right at the top and climbing straight up the Galibier. Leopard put Joost Posthuma and Maxime Monfort into the early break. The plan was for Schleck to attack well before the top of the Col d'Izoard, with 60 kilometres to go. If he was chased down, Fränk would counter-attack; if not, Andy could link up with Monfort and Posthuma up over the Izoard, down the other side and up the long, shallow climb of the Lautaret.

It's a sobering thought that if the wind had been blowing in the opposite direction on 21 July 2011, Andy Schleck would probably have gone down in history by now as a two-time Tour winner. Posthuma paced him up the Izoard, as far as he could, then Schleck caught Monfort just over the top, and the pair worked on building their lead, with the remnants of the break.

All the way up the Lautaret, Monfort, with a little assistance from rival rider Dries Devenyns, paced Schleck, into a strong headwind. Despite this, their lead inched out to almost four and a half minutes at the top of the climb. Enough time for Schleck to win the Tour.

But the effort had taken its toll and a determined chase by Evans brought the gap back to just over two minutes. It probably wasn't enough for Schleck to win the Tour, but it was the first time in many years that such a serious contender for overall victory had attacked so far from a stage finish.

And, in the way that only Andy Schleck could, he blew it the very next day. One day you attack early and fans celebrate the exploit of the cycling decade. The next, you attack early, and it's the worst tactical decision of your life. 'My biggest mistake was to follow Contador's attack on the Alpe d'Huez stage,' Schleck says ruefully. 'I felt good, so I followed him, but it was meaningless.'

Contador had attacked as the race passed back over the Galibier in a short stage to the Alpe. Schleck followed, initially with Evans and Thomas Voeckler, but Evans developed a mechanical that was either lucky or contrived and dropped back to the peloton, while Voeckler simply couldn't follow the pace. Schleck's tactics were flawed because the same headwind that hampered his progress up one side of the Lautaret the day before now slowed his progress down the other side. Schleck and Contador were safely chased down, and the Luxembourger had already spent the energy he might have used trying to gain more time on Evans on the climb to Alpe d'Huez. Instead, he could barely stay with the Australian.

'Why did I follow him?' laments Schleck again. But that was Andy – always chaotic, always second.

During my conversation with Karsten Kroon, I asked him if it wasn't frustrating to watch one of the most talented athletes in the peloton stumbling through his career. Imagine how many wins he would have had, I say, if he'd had the organizational skills to match his physical talents.

'But he didn't,' says Kroon. 'If he was organized then you might have a more equal level through his career, and he would probably still be riding now. But the strength of Andy was that he was always fooling and playing around. I think he'd even get sick of himself, kick himself in the butt and say, "OK, now that's enough and it's time to go." And then he'd be at 100 per cent. Andy could only focus on one big goal, like the Tour, or Liège–Bastogne–Liège, and then he'd be at the top of his game. Sometimes you'd feel sorry for him, how badly he was going, and then all of a sudden he was there.'

Denis Bastien, the *Quotidien* journalist, says that fans in Luxembourg see Schleck as a champion, but one who could have won more than one Tour. 'He did not have a normal career,' he says. 'I think he had natural class, but he couldn't be like the others. It's true that if he'd been more serious he could have got better results, but then he wouldn't be Andy Schleck.'

That's the point about Andy Schleck. He liked being a racing cyclist, but he liked not having too stressful a life just as much, and that combination of preferences gave him one Tour de France, one Liège–Bastogne–Liège and a lot of high placings in stage races, but no more. At Paris–Nice, in his last season, I asked him if he found the life of a professional cyclist stressful, and he broke down the daily life into all the things he had to do to maintain his fitness: 'You've got to eat the right breakfast. You've got to do five hours with intervals. You get back from training and you are tired. You drink a protein shake, lie down for a bit, eat dinner. The cycling is stressful because you go out, and after two hours you have to do 20 or 30 minutes three times, then you are kaput and you still have to do two and a half more hours and another interval.'

He missed being a racing cyclist initially, but less so the increasingly strict routine that came with it. 'It was my life from when I was 15 or 16,' he says now. 'Once the press conference was behind me to say I had retired I felt a lot better. Now I wake up at 7 in the morning, I look out and it's raining, and I say, "Well, I'd like to ride my bike, but not in these conditions." I don't have to do that any more. I'll wait for decent weather.'

But don't be fooled by the lingering impression that Schleck was too lazy to be a successful cyclist. At the end of our conversation, Karsten Kroon interrupts me, winding up the call to make sure that I understand what he thinks about Schleck. 'I want to say one more thing about Andy,' he says. 'He has something inside of him that is really special, like a killer instinct. He could push himself to the point where he forgot everything around him. I saw the same in the eyes and expression of Armstrong in his top years. Andy came past me towards the end of Liège–Bastogne–Liège one year and he was not on this planet, he was somewhere else. He could hurt himself so bad you cannot imagine. I hope he remembers the special days, when he won Liège–Bastogne–Liège and was the best bike rider on the planet.'

18

Cadel Evans

2011

Panache is good for television, but it doesn't win you the Tour.
Cadel Evans

Cadel Evans left it late to win the 2011 Tour, in more than one way. His main move on the yellow jersey came in the time trial on the penultimate day – he'd spent the whole race in the top four, but wore the yellow jersey on only one day, the final stage into Paris. But victory was also late in that it came three years after many thought his best chance to win had come and gone. He was 34 when he joined the yellow jersey club, the second-oldest winner in the Tour's history.

Evans was a grafter, who wore his suffering on his sleeve and his stress on his face. There was little to love about his riding style, both aesthetically and tactically, although the latter was from necessity, not choice. He was extraordinarily gifted physically, with superb stamina, but what the Lord giveth in terms of endurance, the Lord taketh away in acceleration. Evans's attacks resembled a swan taking off from water: a great beating of wings before a slow-motion winding-up of speed and, finally, lift-off. He ground his way up the mountains of the Tour, front wheel weaving, elbows bent and face locked into what seemed like an agonizing grimace (then you'd see him off the bike, and realize that he often carried that same pained expression back into the real world with him).

He was a very good time triallist, and tenacious in the mountains – he only really had one climbing speed, but it was asphyxiatingly fast. He could also tolerate a high level of pain. George Hincapie once said that Evans could suffer more than any other bike racer. These physical attributes meant that Evans had to use negative tactics in order to win races: doughty defence in the mountains, and big gains over the climbers in the time trials. When this led to defeat, it was easy to criticize, but it also gave Evans a yellow jersey. He's certainly not the first Tour winner to race defensively. Miguel Indurain, Greg LeMond and Bradley Wiggins all did so to a lesser or greater extent – the aim was to win the yellow jersey, not necessarily the hearts of racing fans with their methods.

Evans spent much of his career not quite looking like a Tour winner. He led the Giro d'Italia with just four days to go in 2002, his first full season as a road professional, but blew horribly, losing 17 minutes in a single day in the mountains. Two frustrating years at Telekom followed, before he came eighth in his Tour debut in 2005 with the Davitamon-Lotto team. He rose to fourth in 2006, then second in both 2007 and 2008, each time by less than a minute. But from 2009 onwards, bad luck got in the way, and it seemed like he was destined to finish his career as the only rider in history to have twice finished within a minute of the yellow jersey without actually having won it.

Rupert Guinness, an Australian journalist who covers cycling for the *Sydney Morning Herald*, told me that he'd never been sure if Evans could win the Tour. 'My dream when I first went to Europe in 1987 was to report on an Australian winning the Tour,' says Guinness. 'Evans was eighth in 2005 and I thought he could get close. After he was fourth, I thought he was in the frame. But even after that, it wasn't until he won it that I thought he could win.'

Guinness also describes Evans as a 'square peg in a round hole'. He was referring to his two years at Telekom, but it could apply on a more general level. Evans is a prickly, defensive individual. His background in cycling is in the world of mountain biking. You'd expect him to be easy-going and relaxed – the stereotypical mountain biker is laid-back, the stereotypical Aussie is laid-back. Evans, on the contrary, is highly strung and extremely complex.

When Evans rode his last professional event, the eponymous Cadel Evans Great Ocean Road Race, in February 2015, the *Guardian* ran a short story, pulled from the newswires, to mark the occasion. It was a perfunctory seven paragraphs, mentioning the winner, Gianni Meersman, then Evans, who'd come fifth; a couple of hundred functional words about how the race unfolded; then a couple of quotes from Evans. Below the line, some pseudonymous correspondents had chipped in with their comments. The first from 'IlbungaCreekBlowfly': 'Thanks for the memories, you have been a credit to your sport.' And next, from 'BarryKowalski': 'And an unbearable little twerp.'

Mendrisio is the southernmost district of the Ticino canton in Switzerland, a square packet of land surrounded on three sides by the Italian border. The main town, also called Mendrisio, has a population of about 15,000 and is just a few kilometres up the road from Stabio, where Cadel Evans made his European home. It's also where the 2009 World Road Race Championships were held.

Evans's win in the worlds is the result which I think defines his career, more so even than victory in the Tour de France. Before he won the rainbow jersey in 2009, he was seen as a rider who could achieve good results, but one who lacked race-winning spark. Of course, Evans had won races before then, including the Tour of Austria in 2001 (as a first-year professional) and 2004, and the Tour of Romandy in 2006, as well as stages in various races. Tellingly, he'd also won the ProTour, the UCI's season-long points ranking competition, in 2007. The ProTour is a competition which favours riders who can achieve consistent good results, rather than a single peak. As a cross-country mountain biker in the 1990s, Evans had often fallen short at world championships and Olympic Games, but he twice won the season-long World Cup competition. It was clear that he was a stayer.

The Mendrisio circuit was just under 14 kilometres long and featured two climbs, each a couple of kilometres in length. Neither climb was anything like as hard as a Tour mountain, but with 19 laps to cover, and therefore 38 climbs, the cumulative fatigue would have a similar effect on the peloton.

On the final lap, a group of nine, including Evans, had forced its way clear of the rest of the race. Local favourite Fabian Cancellara was there and was providing most of the attacking impetus from the group (it was his attack which had drawn the others clear). Three Spanish riders – Alejandro Valverde, Joaquim Rodríguez and Samuel Sánchez – also made the selection. Belgium's Philippe Gilbert, Denmark's Matti Breschel, Italy's Damiano Cunego and Russia's Alexandr Kolobnev made up the nine.

Cancellara was the strongest rider there, but he did such a poor job of making any secret out of it that every time he moved, he was chased down. Yet every time somebody else attacked, the others looked to Cancellara to chase. The Spanish team had strength in numbers, but wanted the race to come to a sprint, in which Valverde would be the favourite – every time one of their riders joined a move, they refused to contribute, nullifying the attack.

The prelude to the race-winning attack came under a railway bridge – Evans, Kolobnev and Rodríguez drifted off the front, almost accidentally, while one of the other Spanish riders let the gap open. Evans and Kolobnev saw the space between themselves and the others, and accelerated. A 20-metre gap widened to 50, then 100, as individuals tried to chase but then relented. There was no coherence in the group behind: the two Spanish riders left there wouldn't chase, for obvious reasons; the others refused to lead Cancellara up, while Cancellara reciprocated. Then Evans attacked, while Kolobnev and Rodríguez looked at each other. The Australian, perhaps not expecting to have made much of a gap, turned, realized he was away, and went for it.

They never saw him again. But Evans hadn't just put distance between himself and his eight main rivals for the gold medal – in the five-kilometre stretch of racing that remained, he'd also effectively dropped the stereotype and perhaps the self-perception as the follower, the negative rider and the runner-up.

As Evans crossed the line, he made just a low-key wave, once to the left and once to the right. His victory celebrations have often been noticed as being odd, or understated, but not in a modest way, more in a very self-conscious way. I've often thought that Evans exhibits extreme uneasiness when he's aware people are watching him, and the heightened emotions of winning don't mitigate this. In Mendrisio, he looked overwhelmed – stunned – standing astride his bike a short distance after the finish line, kissing his wedding ring again and again. Evans had done the two things his detractors said he never did – he'd attacked, and he'd won.

'So what's Cadel like?' I ask Robbie McEwen, his compatriot and ex-teammate from Lotto, who won the Tour's green jersey three times.

'Simple question. Difficult answer,' says McEwen. 'Cadel is a nice guy. He's a good person.' McEwen pauses, briefly. 'But he's a bit awkward.'

Evans wouldn't be a very good poker player. Emotions roll across his face like shadows cast on the landscape by cumulus clouds. In public, especially when the microphones and Dictaphones of the press point his way, he looks alternately petrified, angry, emotional, self-conscious and stressed. Sometimes he looks like he's on the verge of tears.

Stories about Evans's weird interactions with the press are common. I've even got one of my own. I was angling for a pre-Tour de France assessment of form and morale during the Critérium du Dauphiné Libéré in 2007, and I doorstepped him in the lobby of the hotel we both happened to be staying in. 'Just a quick couple of questions, Cadel,' I said, and he reluctantly agreed. When he sat down at the table opposite me, he turned his chair so he was more or less facing away from me – the lack of eye contact was uncomfortable.

There are far worse examples on YouTube. In one, from the 2008 Tour, he's placid one moment as he is interviewed after taking the yellow jersey, then he snaps, slapping away a journalist who's tried to get his attention by touching Evans's arm. In fact, it's more than just brushing the journalist off – in that one second Evans really loses control, almost screaming at the journalist not to touch him, then he quickly regains his composure. Later in the same Tour, he responded to one request for a television interview by lowering his head and butting the camera with his helmet. Another clip from 2011 shows him trying to squirt his water bottle at a race official who he felt had barged him out of the way at a stage finish. The official moved just when Evans squirted his bottle, and the jet of water hit Mark Cavendish in the face.

I've always thought Evans would be a lot less stressed if he hadn't turned out to be one of the best cyclists in the world. A rider like Lance Armstrong loved the pressure, and thrived off it. Evans is the opposite. Rupert Guinness told me that the fewer people there are around, the happier Evans seems. 'I reckon he would love to ride the Tour if there were no fans, no media and no television, just 200 blokes riding around,' he said. 'Away from cycling, he's quite a placid sort of person. He's not outgoing and he doesn't have a lot of friends. He had people who lived nearby who he rode with, but as far as mates you'd go down the pub with, I don't think he has a lot of those. That's his nature. When he was a kid he was fine in his own company. He was best mates with himself.'

McEwen was on the 2008 Tour with Evans, and experienced Evans's growing stress through the race first-hand. 'When there's a bit of pressure on him he tends to back himself into a corner,' says McEwen. 'He just gets defensive. You can see the stress building up, and he'll be questioned at the stage finishes, being asked why this, why that. "Why did you get dropped? Why didn't you attack?" And he feels like he's being attacked, and he can lash out, or be really prickly at what are fairly normal questions. In private, he's looser. He's civil, and he's still Cadel, but he's less guarded. It's unfair to judge someone during a Tour when they are under pressure. You are not yourself – I wasn't either.'

That's the public Cadel Evans, and it's the only one most of us will ever see, although it remains to be seen if he mellows in retirement. But the private Cadel Evans, while equally complex, is a little different. 'As strange as he can come across, he also likes to do nice things for people and not have it publicized,' says McEwen. 'He went to Nepal to work with underprivileged kids, and adopted with his wife. He can be really compassionate to others, to fans, and to the underprivileged. And then,' McEwen jokes, 'he'll turn around and say how shit his teammates were.'

*

Cadel Evans grew up a cyclist, but he wasn't a cycling fan. 'I love riding my bike. I enjoy racing. But television generally bores me. The only time I watch cycling is if I've just finished a big training ride and there's a race being shown and I can't be bothered doing anything else,' he said in his book *Close to Flying*. 'Even then I don't pay a lot of attention,' he added. (It might be apt that the book itself suffers from a kind of identity crisis – it's presented as an autobiography, but written in the third person by his ghostwriter Rob Arnold.)

Cycling was first a way of exploring the world for Evans, then an outlet for his competitive drive, but it also allowed him to indulge a streak of perfectionism which struck even his fellow professionals as unusual.

He was born in Katherine, in the Northern Territory, and grew up in Barunga, a small settlement 80 kilometres east of Katherine. He was an only child, his mother was just 19 when she had him, and with no siblings to play with, Evans was left to his own devices. That included riding around on his bike. His father, Paul, recalled that he didn't really teach Evans how to ride. 'He just rode away. There'd be times when he'd be gone so long it was dark and we had to go out and look for him,' he said.

When Evans's parents separated, his mother and the young Cadel eventually ended up in Victoria, which is where he started mountain biking. He was a prodigy – too good for the other juniors, so they moved him up to the elites when he was still only 17. As a second-year junior he competed in the elite race at the Australian round of the World Cup, and came fifth. He became one of the world's best mountain bikers, taking multiple medals at world level, along with the two World Cup titles.

But once he'd started road racing – first to train for mountain biking, and then as an end in itself – he seemed to have found his calling. Interestingly, he's said that the team ethos of road racing is why he prefers it to mountain biking. 'Being in a road team suits me much better,' he said in an interview with *Cycle Sport* magazine in 2003. 'The team aspect of road racing is pivotal. A teammate in a mountain bike race just happens to wear the same coloured jersey. Within the team you are competing against your teammates.'

The irony, of course, is that Evans's prickly self-sufficiency, developed over an isolated childhood, might have been much better suited to the individualistic sport of mountain-bike racing than team-based road racing.

McEwen certainly found him difficult to work with when they were both at the Lotto team. 'He was so caught up in his own bubble, he didn't realize how much people were doing for him behind the scenes and all around him. He could be extremely self-absorbed,' McEwen says. McEwen once accused Evans of being 'incredibly un-Australian' by not paying enough attention to the work his team had been doing for him during the 2008 Tour.

Allan Peiper, who was a team manager at both Lotto and BMC when Evans was riding for them, has mixed memories of Evans as a team member. While he rates his compatriot's cycling ability, he didn't find him easy to work with. 'Cadel is a very, very complicated person, and he doesn't trust many people,' he says. 'He can be really short and rude with people, so much so that he can alienate himself in the team. For a lot of us at BMC it was a countdown to when we could move on to another chapter and start working unencumbered by this tiptoeing around.'

As BMC moved up to the WorldTour division of cycling, the team took on more riders and staff, and Peiper's role was to make sure the team was functioning and getting results as it grew. This, according to some team observers, meant getting rid of some of the older riders, who'd been well paid but weren't achieving the results to justify their pay packets. 'Cadel likes things just as they are and doesn't like change. He saw me as a person who changed the environment, and that was difficult for him.'

What everybody seems to agree on concerning Evans is that he is a perfectionist – and the real world, with all its compromises and imperfections, isn't always the easiest place for a perfectionist. His former teammate Dario Cioni felt Evans was years ahead of his time. 'He was really focused. Now everybody is completely professional and very dedicated in their lifestyle, but he was already doing this at the beginning,' he says.

Robbie McEwen also noticed the attention to detail. Evans is often talked about as a genetic freak, his lab test results demonstrating a vanishingly rare physical talent, but McEwen thinks his analytical attitude was as important to his success: 'There are a lot of physically talented guys. But he is so meticulous about everything he does. I don't reckon he ever goes out for a ride not knowing what he's going to do.'

BMC teammate George Hincapie said that Evans was 'consumed' by bike racing, and that's why he was so often misinterpreted. 'He studies course maps for hours,' said Hincapie. 'He analyses the width of roads, looks at the elevations of all the big climbs and even researches potential wind directions. He's one of those guys who needs to know every detail of every race they ride. And that intense focus is often mistaken for unfriendliness or even rudeness. It couldn't be further from the truth.'

The combination of being obviously very emotional, yet analytical and obsessive about detail is an unusual one. It raises the obvious, but perhaps misleading question: is he happy? Now that he's retired, can he liberate himself from the need to analyze the details?

'I think he's busy,' says Guinness. 'But that doesn't mean you're happy. He's always been quite demanding of himself. I'd like to see him lighten up a bit, kick back and enjoy things, maybe not take everything in life so seriously.'

McEwen thinks Evans will be different now he's not competing as a professional cyclist. 'He can finally relax and look back on his career, and say he did what he set out to do,' he says. 'I've seen him mellow in the last couple of years, comparing 2008 with the man he is now. He's mellowed a lot. But he's still not cool as a cucumber.'

Ironically, given Evans's emotional volatility, his Tour win was a masterpiece of tactical calm and control. Maybe he realized it was probably his last chance.

In 2007, of course, Evans had lost the Tour by 23 seconds to Alberto Contador. That was the year race leader Michael Rasmussen withdrew in the third week after it emerged that he'd lied about his whereabouts to the doping authorities. Rasmussen had been dominant in the mountains, with only Contador able to match him on some climbs. Ifs and buts don't win yellow jerseys, but Contador had been drawn clear of his rivals by Rasmussen's attacking, and it's easy to conclude that if Rasmussen hadn't been in the race, Evans might well have won.

The following year, Evans was the favourite, but despite holding the yellow jersey through the Pyrenees and into the Alps, he was carrying injuries from a crash at the end of the first week. The build-up of physical fatigue and stress left him short in the final time trial, where he couldn't take enough time back from Carlos Sastre to win the race. His most impressive ride of the Tour was on Alpe d'Huez, where he was left to chase Sastre almost single-handedly, with no co-operation from his rivals. Evans, white-faced with fatigue, led the chase group for the final five kilometres in a desperate bid to keep his race alive. It wasn't enough, and it looked like second would be the best he could ever do.

But something changed in 2011. Rupert Guinness noticed it, both in Evans's tactics and in his attitude to the racing. 'He finally threw his inhibitions out,' the writer says. 'He gained a few seconds on stage one, on the uphill finish, then he won the stage at Mûr-de-Bretagne. That was the moment I thought, "He really wants this." All he needed was a Tour where he could get the best out of himself. No disasters, have a bit of luck and go into it healthy and strong. I thought in 2011 he wasn't afraid, he was almost enjoying it. It was the first time I'd seen that, and I think it made a difference. He became more amenable, without panicking or getting frustrated. In previous years, something would go wrong and he'd have a hissy fit at the finish line, but he was really calm through it all.'

The structure of the 2011 race – which started with a road stage with an uphill finish, a team time trial, a sprint, then another uphill finish – favoured organized and vigilant riders. The uphill finishes weren't that hard, and the team time trial was only 23 kilometres long, and it would have been easy to conclude that not much time could be lost. But Evans saw the opportunity to gain time.

The most effective tactic that Evans and his BMC team used in 2011 was to ride at the front, deep into the final few kilometres even on the flat stages, knocking shoulders with the sprinters' teams. It kept Evans right at the front, and out of trouble. The race favourite Contador lost over a minute getting caught behind a crash on stage one, whereas Evans was second, three seconds clear of the group containing most of his rivals. Three seconds doesn't sound like much, but his 23-second defeat in 2007 had consisted of a 20-second time bonus Contador had gained winning the stage at Plateau de Beille. Three seconds gained on stage one were now three seconds his rivals had to take back from him.

BMC were second in the team time trial, a discipline in which

Evans had lost minutes in previous Tours with Lotto, then Evans won the stage on the steep climb above the Breton village of Mûr-de-Bretagne. After four stages, he was second overall, and while most of his rivals were within a handful of seconds, the more important thing was that he was riding assertively and already gaining time.

Then he switched to defensive mode, correctly reasoning that his main rivals, the Schleck brothers and Contador, needed to gain significant time on him before the long time trial on the penultimate day. Through the Massif Central and the flat stages of the first 10 days, Evans waited, and the attacks never came. Even in the three Pyrenean stages, his rivals seemed to be reluctant to attack. At Luz Ardiden he conceded 20 seconds to a late attack by Fränk Schleck, then Andy Schleck gained a measly two seconds on him at Plateau de Beille.

Evans was helped by the fact that Thomas Voeckler had gone into the yellow jersey by escaping in the second Massif Central stage – all the media attention was on the popular Frenchman. Meanwhile, as the race left the Pyrenees, with only a week to go, he was third overall, 2-06 behind Voeckler. Fränk Schleck was ahead of him by 17 seconds, and Andy Schleck behind him by nine seconds. Contador was already two minutes behind Evans.

The race looked like it would be decided between the two Alpine summit finishes at the Col du Galibier and Alpe d'Huez, and the time trial. The Schleck brothers were expected to attack in the Alps, but Evans pre-empted them on the medium-mountain stage to Gap. Evans followed a series of attacks by Contador on the climb of the Col de Manse, above Gap, but it was on the descent that large gaps began to develop. Evans, a good descender, finished three seconds ahead of Contador and Samuel Sánchez, but his other rivals had conceded significant time: Fränk Schleck was 20 seconds back, Andy Schleck had lost over a minute. Evans's strategy of staying at the front had put him back into second overall, a few seconds clear of Fränk Schleck, but he was now well over a minute clear of Andy Schleck.

The attacks finally came in the Alps. Andy Schleck attacked over the Col d'Izoard *en route* to the summit finish on the Col du Galibier, building a lead of nearly four minutes on Evans and the others. While Contador contributed a little to the chase, he didn't have the legs, and just like on Alpe d'Huez three years before, it was left entirely to Evans to close the gap. What followed was Evans's greatest ride in the Tour de France.

'Nobody was going to help him,' says Guinness. 'He had nine kilometres to whittle that lead down. All the work he'd done, the idyllic race he'd had so far, this was the window of opportunity where he had to save his Tour. He said all his experiences, both good and bad, came into that moment of holding on to his chance of winning the Tour.'

Evans led an infernal pursuit of Schleck, with only a few riders – Fränk Schleck, Voeckler, Ivan Basso and Pierre Rolland – able to hang on. Even Contador cracked. The gap came down painfully slowly, but Evans's efforts reduced it to two minutes. He was still a minute behind Andy Schleck overall, but he could still be confident of taking that back in the time trial.

Evans was either the luckiest or smartest rider the next day on the short stage back over the Galibier to Alpe d'Huez. Contador felt he had a point to prove, and he attacked early in the stage, drawing Andy Schleck, Voeckler and Evans clear. Contador's pace had destroyed the peloton, and it looked as if the leading quartet was riding away from the race, but something seemed to go wrong with Evans's bike and he stopped to fiddle with it. He later said that he felt his brake was rubbing against the wheel. Voeckler was then dropped, leaving Contador and Schleck ahead.

The momentum, formerly with the leaders, was now with the chasers, and it was lucky Evans had had his mechanical, because he could sit in the group, a significant advantage on the long, shallow descent to the foot of Alpe d'Huez. Andy Schleck had looked like the boldest rider the day before on the Col du Galibier, but his boldness on the Alpe d'Huez stage probably lost him the Tour. Evans and the others caught him before the final climb, and the Luxembourger had used up the resources that he could have saved for an attack on the Alpe. Evans was able to contain him on the climb, and he went into the time trial with less than a minute's deficit.

In the end, Evans won the Tour by a minute and a half, which was just under the amount of time he'd squeezed back from Andy Schleck on the Col du Galibier. You could pinpoint the descent of the Col de Manse, where he gained a minute, or the comeback on the Galibier, where he gained two minutes, or the opening few days, where he gained a handful of seconds – but Evans had won his Tour by riding with control and organization over the entire three weeks.

The 2011 Tour de France had been a real slow burner. There was the long, steady build-up of not much happening; extended periods of monotony and unresolved tension; and the feeling that an indefinable spark was missing. With the long opening phase and the first mountains out of the way, I'd wondered if anything was going to happen at all. Then it came alive in the last quarter. It was a microcosm of Cadel Evans's entire career.

19

Bradley Wiggins

2012

Time is on loan – only ours to borrow.
What I can't be today – I can be tomorrow.
And the more I see – the more I know.
The more I know – the less I understand.

Paul Weller, 'The Changingman'

The first time I saw Bradley Wiggins riding – I mean *really* riding – was in the prologue of the 2007 Tour de France. I was standing on the grass at the bottom corner of Green Park, just up the Mall from the Queen Victoria Memorial, right at the start of the finishing straight.

Through the crowd of heads and shoulders, I could only see Wiggins's top half as he followed a perfect horizontal trajectory from right to left across my field of vision. His back, when he rides a time-trial bike, is flat and almost motionless. There's no perceptible vertical movement, none of the nodding-dog bobbing from the hips which happens when most people ride a bike. Filmed from behind, Wiggins does have a small amount of lateral movement, although less than just about any other professional cyclist – his shoulders rock with the symmetry and regularity of a pendulum. With a lot of riders, even elite ones, you get a sense of legs taking it in turn to press down on the pedals – Wiggins's action is more circular.

As he went past, he must have been pedalling his bike at about 60 kilometres per hour, yet all I could see was his perfect, motionless upper body flickering between the heads of the crowd. It was lovely to watch – beautiful, even though cycling is no beauty contest. The experience of watching Bradley Wiggins on a time-trial bike is similar to that of watching Roger Federer play tennis, or Ed Moses hurdling – the winning is interesting, and is the point, but it looks like a by-product of the effortless-looking style. 'Aesthetically, Wiggins is pretty stunning,' international cyclist and writer Michael Hutchinson told me when I emailed to make sure it wasn't just me.

What's happening when Wiggins is time-trialling? Not much, on the surface of it. Head, arms, body: locked still. Legs: rotating. Result: speed.

But there's a lot more to it than that. Inside his head, Wiggins's motor cortex, acting on information from all over the brain, is sending signals via the motor neurons in the spinal cord to the leg muscles to tell them to contract. The contraction is caused by a chemical reaction within the muscle cells, which breaks down molecules of adenosine triphosphate (ATP). The chemical reaction demands oxygen, which is absorbed into the bloodstream through the lungs. The heart is pumping oxygenated blood from the lungs through the arteries to the muscles. The breakdown of ATP results in waste products, primarily carbon dioxide, which is transported back into the blood, through the veins and to the lungs to be expelled. Inside Wiggins's body there is a highly complicated feedback loop of biochemistry, electric impulses, chemical reactions, fuelling, waste production and recycling going on. His heart is pumping at around 180 beats per minute, his lungs pulling in litres of oxygen to fuel the tiny explosions that are happening on a cellular level in his legs. There's a considerable amount of pain involved with maintaining the level of effort and with holding the upper body in an aerodynamic tuck.

It may all look very smooth on the outside, but there's a lot going on inside. That's Bradley Wiggins.

Wiggins won his Tour de France in 2012, and never went back. In 2013, injuries to his knee and morale kept him away from the race. He might have nursed the physical problems through (albeit not in race-winning form), but the crisis of a well-publicized falling-out with teammate Chris Froome was more serious. A passive-aggressive struggle between the two riders over the Sky team leadership was not properly resolved, even if in the short term the knee injury meant that the team's management could evade the issue. The following year, the management lanced the boil, left a very fit Wiggins on the sidelines and patted themselves on the back over a decisive and focused piece of man management. They were then able to repent at leisure after Froome crashed out in the first week of the Tour.

Wiggins is atypical among elite athletes. These days, most cyclists specialize, in order to maximize their success. Sprinter Mark Cavendish, for example, could train himself to climb better, but he might consequently only win five races a year instead of 15. Wiggins is capable of the same focus, but there's an aspect of his personality which is very important when we look at his career and results: he's an obsessive collector.

At various points in his life, Wiggins has collected guitars, boxing memorabilia, vinyl and Belgian beers. He's also collected major cycling achievements. He became the best individual pursuiter in the world between 2003 and 2008, winning multiple world and Olympic gold medals. He's also the part-owner of world and Olympic titles at the team pursuit, plus a Madison at the world championships. The breadth of cycling ability needed to excel in these three events is already rare.

After the Beijing Olympics, Wiggins reinvented himself as a road rider. He'd been competing on the road for his whole career, but he had treated it as the means to an end. He shed upper-body muscle and worked his way up to a Tour de France win, coming fourth in the race in 2009 and second in the 2011 Vuelta a España, in between collecting a series of shorter but prestigious stage-race wins: the Critérium du Dauphiné (twice), Paris–Nice and the Tour of Romandy.

Following his Tour win in 2012, he also won world and Olympic time-trial titles, and given his track and time-trialling pedigree his planned assault on the World Hour Record in 2015 stands an extremely good chance of success. For Wiggins, the collection of these different race wins has been as meaningful as the collection of Tour wins has been for multiple winners of the race.

I think Bradley Wiggins is the greatest cyclist in British history, ahead of Beryl Burton, Nicole Cooke, Chris Hoy and Mark Cavendish, in that order. I also think he's one of the greatest all-round cyclists ever. Lance Armstrong was mainly good at riding the Tour de France, and that's without taking the drugs into account. Miguel Indurain spread himself a bit more widely, but only ventured into a velodrome to break the Hour record. Greg LeMond, Bernard Hinault and Laurent Fignon won Tours and major one-day races, but had no significant track pedigree. Even Eddy Merckx, who dabbled in Six Day riding, never won a world track championships medal. The only other rider in history to win a world track gold and a Tour de France is Fausto Coppi, while Francesco Moser won a world pursuit title and a Giro d'Italia. Cadel Evans won a Tour de France and two mountain bike World Cups. Where exactly

Wiggins fits into the list depends on subjectivity and prejudice, but the physical and mental ability to be the best at the range of events that he has been is vanishingly rare.

There is a caveat to my assertion. Wiggins has not been a prolific winner of road events, and there are three main reasons for that. The first is that sooner or later, the pressure will get to him. The question with Bradley Wiggins is not *if* his head falls off, but *when*. One of the bargains he has made with his talent is that he will nurture it and exploit it to its fullest extent then, in return, he gets to have his life back for a while. These days, getting his life back means spending a more healthy amount of time with his family, but in the past it has meant spending time exercising an extraordinary capacity for drinking beer or drifting through his training.

The second reason is more conjectural, but it is significant: the first half of Wiggins's road career was spent competing in an era when there was a lot of cheating happening. Wiggins was lucky here. While most athletes faced a stark choice – dope or fail – he had a third choice: stick to the track. It's not that track cycling has been completely clean, but it has been more for-giving as a discipline to athletes who didn't dope.

The third reason is that while he's physically gifted and has a very good understanding of that capacity in terms of power output and endurance, he's rarely shown a huge aptitude for the dark arts of road-racing tactics. Partly, he's not needed to. His main tactic has been to be the strongest rider, and also to have a very strong team. It's an effective strategy, but the differ-ence between a good tactician and an ordinary one is the ability to win and shape races when one is not the strongest rider, and Wiggins is less good at that. There are exceptions – Wiggins did get his hands dirty in winning Paris–Nice in 2012, finessing his way into the front group of only 21 riders on the windblown first stage. But even then, with the week-long race finishing with an uphill time trial, he was still able to rely on being the strongest rider, just to make sure.

Wiggins is a test case of how the British public like their heroes, and it took people a long time to warm to him. In 2008, in spite of having won his second and third Olympic gold medals, he was a distant ninth in the BBC Sports Personality of the Year award, which was won by another cyclist, Chris Hoy – Hoy got 50 times more votes than Wiggins. Nicole Cooke also beat him pretty comfortably. Blond, good-looking, muscular, well-adjusted, polite, middle-class Hoy is universally liked and admired. Wiggins, initially, was harder to like – more quirky, inaccessible and spiky, his John Entwistle sideburns and haircut in stark contrast to Hoy's sensible short back and sides.

But four years later, the British public got Wiggins. Wiggins is a natural co-pilot of the zeitgeist – his ascendancy coincided with the rise of hipster culture, and the public were only too willing, by 2012, to embrace him as their sporting hero, as much for the sideburns, London accent, swearing, tattoos, working-class mannerisms, sharp clothes, equally sharp tongue and swagger as for his yellow jersey and gold medal. Everybody loved Wiggo. Tabloid newspapers printed cut-out-and-wear sideburns, and when he stood on the Tour podium and told the crowds he was going to pull the winning numbers in the raffle it cemented his position as working-class hero made good.

Even now, Wiggins appears an unlikely hero. There's the crooked, Dickensian nose, the hint of an overbite, the piss-taking grin. In real life, he's a gangly, elongated, angular string bean – his legs may be the main components of one of the most perfect bike-riding units ever seen, but off the bike it looks like walking doesn't happen as easily, although his long limbs make him a very good clothes horse. When he talks, he gestures a lot with his hands, which are absolutely enormous – I bet he could play an 11-note span on a piano.

Wiggins has the charisma of both class clown and rock-music frontman. His one-liners are straight from the pool halls, turf accountants and dog tracks of his Kilburn youth, while the insouciant confidence he wears like a protective coat reflects the cultural backdrop to his teenage years: Britpop and Cool Britannia, *The Word* and *TFI Friday*. Wiggins was 14 when Oasis, one of his favourite bands, released *Definitely Maybe*, and 15 when *(What's the Story) Morning Glory?* and Paul Weller's *Stanley Road* came out. There's a bit of chameleon about Wiggins – he walks a little like Liam Gallagher, and he often affects the studied diffidence of Paul Weller when he is being interviewed. Wiggins the national hero is a product of his upbringing – the cycling, music and fashion-obsessed kid who grew up into a cycling, music and fashion-obsessed adult.

He was born in Ghent to a young mother and a father whose talent for bike racing only partially and temporarily covered up the fact that, as a human being, he was a dead loss. Gary Wiggins's life took him from Australia to London to Belgium and ultimately back to Australia, and he left a trail of beaten opponents, occasional black eyes, broken relationships, fatherless children and emotional carnage in his wake. Gary was a boozing, brawling braggart who made a bit of cash on the side selling whizz to his fellow cyclists – he once smuggled drugs into Belgium, in Bradley's nappy.

Wiggins's mother Linda had fallen in love with Gary in London, then gone with him to Belgium, where he briefly tasted success in track competition. When Linda went back to London for a holiday with Bradley, when he was two, Gary phoned her up and told her not to come back to Ghent because he'd found somebody else. And that, save for a trip to the zoo when Wiggins was three, and some belated and half-arsed attempts at reconciliation when Wiggins was in his twenties, was that. The bleak postscript to the non-existent relationship between father and son was that Gary died in 2008, apparently having been beaten up pretty badly.

Bradley Wiggins's reaction to having had an absent father was different to that of, say, Lance Armstrong. While Armstrong's experience with his genetic father and stepfather instilled in him a deep and textbook suspicion of male authority figures, Wiggins found surrogates – his granddad George and, later, his coach and mentor at British Cycling, Shane Sutton, although in his first autobiography, *In Pursuit Of Glory*, Wiggins describes his granddad as much as a mate as a father. George's London was that of the British Legion, pubs and bookies. The young Bradley played darts, pool and cards, and watched the greyhound races at Wimbledon dog track. Wiggins acquired his mannerisms from George, and his dress sense from working-class London and the terraces of White Hart Lane. And then he discovered cycling, after being captivated by watching Chris Boardman winning the 1992 Olympic Games individual pursuit. Somewhere along the way, he also gained a sense of emotional self-sufficiency and a tendency to bottle up problems, or ignore them. 'Cath [Wiggins's wife] sometimes describes me as emotionally retarded but what she means is that I really struggle to express my emotions and I bury my head in the sand over a lot of stuff,' he wrote in his second autobiography, *My Time*.

The wounds caused by Wiggins's father and his abandonment of his son have healed, although they've left scar tissue. And who knows how Bradley Wiggins would have turned out if Gary had been a better father?

'The word I'd use to describe Brad is "complex",' says Shane Sutton.

If you had to write down Sutton's job description as Wiggins's former coach, the primary role would be that of the guy who tells Wiggins to pull himself together. Sutton knew Gary from his own racing days, and he has the kind of working-man's authority and the stereotypical Aussie straight-talking that Wiggins (Junior) seems to respond to. Ask Sutton about Bradley, and he'll tell you about the 2002 Munich Six Day race. A Six Day is a track meeting, held over six evenings, involving a series of races, but focusing around the two-man Madison event. The Madison, and Six Day races, were also Gary Wiggins's speciality.

'Bradley was riding with Marty Nothstein, the Olympic sprint champion,' Sutton tells me. 'The first chase of a Six Day is always a very difficult one, and they were down a lap, but they were making a hell of a chase, and Bradley was flying.'

At Munich, the track is a tight one, and the riders' pits are right up against the track. Sutton squeezed himself into the space between the pits and the track and watched the 22-year-old going up against the stars of the Six Day circuit. 'He came to a stop after the race, hooked his leg over the handlebars of his bike, and I can remember him undoing his mitts and saying to me, "I was born to do this." Same as Messi was born to play football. Brad's a clever bloke. People don't always see his intelligence, but he's an intelligent guy. He's a historian of his business, he is in the business of bike racing and making money from that – that's his business and nobody does it better. You can train and train and train, but ultimately you've got to be clever in how you do things. Brad understands all these things about cycling. He understands the demands of the event better than everybody else, and that's why he's been able to win in so many different disciplines. He does his homework better than anybody else. Numbers-wise there's probably nobody out there better.'

That's the good news. The bad is that Wiggins is difficult to manage.

In 2010, things went wrong for Wiggins, really for the first time in his career. He'd had a blip after winning the Athens Olympic individual pursuit in 2004, investing the energies he'd previously put into training in an off-season-long bender, and it took him the best part of a year to refocus. But then, he'd been underachieving on the road before 2004, so when he equally underachieved in 2005, nobody really held it against him. 2010 was different.

In 2009, Wiggins had come fourth in the Tour de France, riding for the Garmin team. He'd signed for Garmin for 2010 as well, but the prospect of joining the newly launched Sky team at the end of 2009 became too tempting to turn down. Sky might have been happy to wait until 2011 to sign Wiggins, but while they'd been building their squad, he'd changed from a part-time, non-committal road racer into a genuine Tour hope, and Sky had a vacancy for a genuine British Tour hope. For Wiggins, it meant an off-season of protracted contractual negotiations and bickering, followed by the realization that suddenly he was under a lot of pressure. Wiggins is very good at dealing with pressure in the context of a bike race, but he's terrible at dealing with it off the bike. In this scenario, he did what he always does when the pressure mounts: he told everybody what they wanted to hear, and went and buried his head in the sand. That meant not training with the same focus and motivation as 2009, and consequently fluffing the Tour. (He actually came 24th – later promoted to 23rd after Alberto Contador's disqualification – which at the time was still the 13th-best result by a British rider in the history of the race, but it was well short of his ambition.)

'Brad hates confrontation,' says Sutton. 'He's a guy who can win massive battles on the bike, but off the bike he gets nervous, he doesn't want to get a bollocking, so he tends to go into a hole. He's a terrible communicator. He's not a multi-tasker, but he's very good at being single-minded. He's very hard on himself when it matters.' Sutton stops, then adds: 'It's hard to explain him, because nobody else lives in the mind of Bradley Wiggins.'

Bradley Wiggins's Tour win was, depending on your outlook on life, either a masterpiece or a dud; an answer to the question of whether winning ugly has any less value or meaning than winning pretty.

In cycling, there is a tendency among fans and press for mythology and nostalgia – matched perhaps only by boxing. It's no coincidence that written coverage of these two sports has often erred towards the literary and heroic. For the first 50 years of its existence, cycling reporting was almost exclusively the preserve of the written press, and the history of cycling is built on exaggerated, romanticized reports of heroic exploits. This has left a legacy of glorification of aggressive, attacking riding – Fausto Coppi is remembered for the mountain attacks that won him the 1952 Tour de France, Eddy Merckx for putting 10 minutes into the entire peloton in one Pyrenean stage in 1969, and Bernard Hinault for the panache with which he rode his final Tours. Wiggins? He was paced up the mountains by a rolling maul of *domestiques* and won a couple of time trials by an anticlimactically large margin.

For romantics, the 2012 Tour was a long three weeks. Wiggins and Sky rode defensively, sitting on the front of the bunch through the mountain stages and imposing a pace that asphyxiated the chances of their rivals. It was the cycling equivalent of putting 11 men behind the ball and sitting on a 1–0 lead, a three-week demonstration of *catenaccio*. Wiggins didn't attack. His rivals, cowed, were unable to find any way through his defence, and they more or less stopped trying for the last week of the race. (That's not to say the Tour was boring that year – while the race for the general classification was bereft of fireworks, the daily races for stage wins were absorbing, exciting and unpredictable, to my mind the most entertaining in 20 years.)

On the other hand, it was as classically perfect a Tour as it is possible to ride. Wiggins was never lower than second overall, none of his rivals put any time into him in the mountains, and he was by far the strongest time triallist in the race. He finished in the top 22 in 17 of the 21 stages (three of the others were sprint stages, where the peloton would all be credited with the same time as the winner so it didn't matter where he finished, while the other, in Boulogne, saw Wiggins held up by a crash on the finishing climb). Any ambitions his rivals might have had to ambush him tactically were snuffed out by the smothering strength of Sky. Even the time he spent in second place, the first week, was tactically advantageous – he was ahead of all his serious rivals, but the responsibility of controlling the race fell to the team of the yellow jersey, Fabian Cancellara.

The irony is that Wiggins is a lifelong cycling fan, who went to sleep at night as a youngster with posters of Johan Museeuw and Miguel Indurain on his wall. He might be a romantic about the history of the sport, but he's a classicist in his method of racing. His choice of heroes is interesting, however. Indurain won his five Tours in the same defensive style when Wiggins was an impressionable teenager.

Wiggins came as close as anybody has to making winning the Tour look easy, although his method was a physically and mentally expensive one – to prevent rivals from attacking, Sky and Wiggins had to hold a searing pace in the mountains, over long periods. It didn't look spectacular.

His *modus operandi* was exactly the same as the one British

Cycling used to win gold medals on the track over the last four Olympic Games: identify the challenge, strip it down to quantifiable aims and minimize the uncontrollables. The narrative of the Tour de France, previously told in embellished, florid prose, was being rewritten in the language of science: equations, logic and academic rigour. While previous Tour winners talked mysteriously of 'form', a capricious quality which came and went unpredictably, Wiggins's confidence came from his trust in the 'numbers'.

The 'numbers' happen after having done the 'work'. Look at the picture of Wiggins crossing the finish line of the final time trial of the 2012 Tour in Chartres, wearing a yellow skinsuit, on the day of one of his finest ever performances. He's just won the Tour de France – his right fist is punching the air, his face is fixed in a yelling rictus of triumph and relief. But look down at his left hand. Even at the very pinnacle of his life as a competitive cyclist, as he achieves victory in the biggest bike race in the world, he's pressing the stop button on his power meter.

Of course, Wiggins was not the first rider to win the Tour by gaining time in the time trials and doggedly defending in the mountains, but the exactness with which Sky rode in the mountains was a new development. Wiggins, in his winner's press conference, said as much. 'There's a lot of romance in the sport, and a lot of people want to see attacks. But cycling's changed. The Tour is more human now. If people want to see those incredible 220-kilometre lone breaks in the mountains, maybe that's not realistic any more, as wonderful and as magical as they were to watch. We would be riding on the front at 450 watts, or whatever, someone would attack and Mick [Rogers] would say, just leave him, he can't sustain that. Someone is going to have to sustain 500 watts on a 20-minute climb to stay away, which is not possible any more. That's the reality of it.'

As far as Sky's rivals were concerned, there were three key

days in the Tour: stage seven, finishing on the steep and middle-length climb to La Planche des Belles Filles in the Vosges; stage nine, the time trial in Besançon; and stage 11 to La Toussuire, the first major Alpine stage and the hardest day of the race. On the first of these, Wiggins and Sky effectively eliminated all but two rivals from the general classification: Vincenzo Nibali and Cadel Evans. In the time trial, Wiggins essentially won the Tour, putting two minutes into Nibali and Evans. And on the stage to La Toussuire, he snuffed out the last remaining hope for his rivals – Evans went for a long-range attack on the mid-stage Col du Glandon, hoping to link up with two teammates who were up the road in a break, and it was this attack which Wiggins was referring to in his final press conference. Sky weren't even looking at Evans – the readouts on their power meters were all they were watching as they slowly pulled him back. And that was that. The Tour was barely at its halfway point, and it seemed to be over. Then Chris Froome attacked.

Wiggins's teammate had won the stage to La Planche des Belles Filles. He'd been second in the Besançon time trial. Behind Wiggins, he looked like the strongest rider in the race. The motives and wisdom of Froome's attack with five kilometres to go at La Toussuire will be covered in his chapter, but Wiggins took it extremely badly.

On the bike, Wiggins was a model of self-control and focus. Off it, things looked chaotic. Four days previously, he'd turned the air in the post-stage press conference as blue as the stripe on his Sky kit, railing profanely against pseudonymous accusations of doping on Twitter.

You never know who you are going to bump into at the Tour de France. I had skipped the yellow jersey press conference that day, and was standing in the *zone technique*, which had been erected in a field just outside Porrentruy. The *zone technique* is a temporary village of lorries, makeshift television studios, trailers and gazebos, all linked and connected by a central nervous system of miles and miles of cables. I was waiting to interview the FDJ team manager Marc Madiot, whose rider Thibaut Pinot had won the stage. Madiot was just finishing with French television. Behind me, a door banged open, as Wiggins emerged from the press-conference trailer. 'Fucking wankers,' he said, punctuating his words by slamming the door shut behind him and making his way down the metal steps. He slumped into a chair outside the anti-doping-control trailer. To me, he looked tired and unhappy, as if the Tour was already stripping away the layers. That's what the Tour does to a rider – the pressure and fatigue affect not just the body, but the mind. As the race goes on, tempers fray, focus drifts and small things suddenly seem more important than they are.

When Froome attacked at La Toussuire, Wiggins cracked. He texted his team manager Sean Yates that evening: 'I think it would be better for everyone if I went home.'

It was an overreaction and, of course, Wiggins was not going to go home. As an attention-seeking strategy it worked very well – Yates called Froome to heel (after Dave Brailsford had ducked out of the confrontation, as Yates revealed in his autobiography *It's All About the Bike*), and with only two more really difficult mountain stages to go, plus a time trial which Wiggins would win, mutiny was averted. But it was primary evidence that underneath Wiggins's serene physical progress to the yellow jersey, behind the quantification and logic of Sky's method, human ambition and emotion were still significant drivers of the Tour's narrative.

There was an interview a few years ago with Steve White, who played drums for the Style Council and other Paul Weller bands, in a film about his frontman. 'Paul,' said White, 'is a lovely bunch of people.' It was an ambiguous compliment, with an unspoken subtext: not all of the people might be hugely likeable. The attributes that make Weller such an interesting human being don't necessarily make him easy to live with.

And it's not just because Weller happens to be one of Wiggins's favourite musicians that this statement reminds me of Wiggins as well. It calls to mind something Cath Wiggins said of her husband in the documentary *A Year in Yellow*, which was released in late 2012. Cath differentiated quite easily and naturally between Bradley the husband and father, and Bradley the cyclist: 'My husband is brilliant. He's proper good, considerate, patient, kind, brilliant with the kids, really appreciative of me and the family.'

There was a pause. Then, Cath continued, there was the cyclist. She asked if she was allowed to swear. 'He's a bit of a twat.'

What's Bradley Wiggins really like? I don't know, because as soon as I decide, I realize that the opposite is equally true. He's pretty friendly – he'll sit down for a chat, he's a good and open interviewee – but then another day he'll walk right by you without even acknowledging your presence. He'll contradict himself from one interview to the next, not because he's lying in either case, but because he's got a tendency to say whatever's on his mind right at that moment. It used to bother me, but then I realized he's just not particularly dogmatic.

He's a real comedian, a born performer. There was a press conference during his Tour of Romandy win in 2012 when he sent up the francophone press – in French – and signed off, saying, 'Try to think of some better questions tomorrow.' He's still the class clown from St Augustine's school in Kilburn. Yet at the same time, he can be stroppy and curt. He's a natural celebrity – for a short while in the summer of 2012, he was possibly the most popular man in the UK, but he hates the consequence, of paparazzi camping out at the end of his road, or endless interview requests. At the same time, he has a photographer, embedded with Sky, who specializes in moody black-and-white portraits. The iconography says a lot about how Wiggins might like people to see him – much in the same way as he sees the rock-star heroes of his teenage years.

You could say Wiggins has been lucky with the timing of his life. He just happened to be a very impressionable 12-year-old when Chris Boardman won in Barcelona (British cyclists hadn't won an Olympic gold for 72 years before that). When British Cycling set up the World Class Performance Plan in 1998, which ultimately led to all those Olympic medals in 2008 and 2012, Wiggins was the first athlete on their books. He changed his focus to road racing just as the sport started to make a few tangible inroads into eradicating the doping problem. At the same time, Team Sky was started up. He was at his absolute peak just as the Olympic Games took place in his home town. He's been in the right place at the right time for a lot of the key moments of his career.

Sometimes, I think all Wiggins wants is an easy life – to be left alone, and to spend his days lounging on the sofa, absorbing information about whatever his latest obsession is, getting up to kick a football around with his kids and not answering his mobile phone. That's a conclusion I drew from several encounters with him, and conversations with people who know him. Yet this is the same person who worked himself with unimaginable single-mindedness into an athlete capable of winning the Tour de France.

At the end, you have to differentiate between Wiggins the man and Wiggo the public persona. There's significant overlap, but sometimes people's expectations are confounded, when they are hoping for Wiggins and get Wiggo, or the other way around.

He told me once, 'I'm not easy to work with. But if someone

has the patience to work with me, the machine is fantastic if they can get it running. The offset of the athlete who could do [what I did in 2012] was that he's going to be a fucking pain in the arse at times.'

20

Chris Froome

2013

Men rise from one ambition to another: first, they seek to secure themselves against attack, and then they attack others.
Niccolò Machiavelli, *The Prince*

Chris Froome gazes out from the cover of his autobiography *The Climb*, a clean-cut boy-next-door with sandy hair, sharp cheekbones, pale-green eyes, boy-band smooth skin and not the slightest hint of stubble nor trouble. Cycling hasn't left much of a mark on Froome's face. An erosive combination of wind, sun and grimacing usually sculpts the faces of professional cyclists into wrinkled, leathery contours – a cowboy complexion – but Froome's unlined face belies the fact that he's one of the strongest endurance athletes in the world. From a distance, his face is neutral and unthreatening – everything about the portrait seems initially to project the impression that Froome might not be gritty, combative, intimidating, profound or mysterious, in the way that sports-book publishers like their subjects to appear, but he's certainly *nice*.

I've often thought that while Bradley Wiggins is the Tour winner you'd want to go down to the pub with, Froome is the

Tour winner you'd want to date your daughter. (That said, Wiggins made a point of taking a very long time to pay Froome his share of the 2012 Tour winnings after they fell out during the race – Wiggins might be a good laugh in the pub, but you'd have to keep an eye on him to make sure he bought his round.) Froome exudes sensibleness – his two brothers became accountants, Froome was midway through an economics degree before he dropped out to pursue his sporting ambitions, and you can imagine that if he hadn't been the kind of physical freak who becomes a professional cyclist, he'd be working as a bean counter in an office somewhere, putting 20 per cent of his income into a pension and driving a Mondeo. He always says 'please', and he always says 'thank you'.

You actually have to get much closer to the picture on *The Climb*, and look quite hard, to spot the details, which are almost invisible. The left side of his mouth is ever so slightly above the horizontal, the vanishing hint of a smile framed by a lightly inscribed nasolabial fold, which is the wrinkle that curves from nose to chin around the mouth. Likewise, the skin around his left eye is pulled a little more tightly than on the other side. He's not exactly smiling, but there's a barely discernible tension in his facial muscles which makes the unthreatening boy-next-door look a little more steely.

Or is it smugness? Or maybe he's just self-conscious with the camera pointing at him. It's difficult to tell, because in life, as with the photograph on the cover of his book, there's something unreadable about Chris Froome, a Teflon-like quality.

In Noh theatre, masks are worn by actors to represent certain characters, either general or specific, which means the actors can't convey emotion through changing their own facial expressions. The masks are rigid, but they are also three-dimensional and designed in a way that the expression subtly changes according to lighting, or the angle of the head. A skilled

Noh actor will be able to communicate a wide range of expressions, emotions and feelings through the most minute, exact and subtle of movements. But you have to watch carefully, or you'll miss the significance.

A lot of commentators have remarked upon the central contradiction of Chris Froome, which is that he is polite, well adjusted and affable, but that it is impossible to see behind the polished exterior. The question is, is he hiding his emotions very well? Or is he not feeling them at all? Froome seems to exhibit a specifically British middle-classness in his unfailing politeness that an upbringing in Kenya and South Africa did nothing to roughen or dilute. The unflappability might be a function of an education at a private boarding school for boys in Johannesburg. Or it could just be that once you've been chased up a tree by an angry hippo while out fishing, it's easier to keep the minor irritations of life in perspective.

Just as you have to get really close to the photograph on the cover of *The Climb* to see that the Noh mask has actually got a much more interesting and variable expression than you initially think, in order to understand Chris Froome better, you have to get closer. But he won't let many people get close to him. And so we stand back and look at the career and life of Chris Froome, and think we both know, and don't know, who he is.

Did Chris Froome attack his Sky team leader Bradley Wiggins on the climb to La Toussuire in the 2012 Tour, or not? The answer is buried beneath layers of PR polish, crisis management, ego and ambition.

Froome was part of a very small group of riders left on La Toussuire, the summit finish of the hardest stage of the 2012 Tour and the first real day in the high mountains. Ahead, Pierre Rolland was winning the stage, but the general classification contenders had been whittled down by Team Sky's relentless pressure. Midway up the climb, Vincenzo Nibali had attacked with Jurgen Van den Broeck, Thibaut Pinot and Janez Brajkovič, gaining 100 metres on Froome and Wiggins, who in turn had just dropped Fränk Schleck, and BMC teammates Cadel Evans, the defending champion, and Tejay van Garderen. Going into the stage, Wiggins was in the yellow jersey, Evans was second, just under two minutes behind, Froome third at 2-07 and Nibali fourth at 2-23. The margins were still quite tight and Froome was very keen on gaining time overall to move into second place.

As they reached five kilometres to go, Froome pulled Wiggins back up to Nibali's group, and as soon as the junction was made, he accelerated. Pinot followed, then Nibali and Van den Broeck. Wiggins only followed insofar as he was riding in the same direction – he was definitively and easily distanced by Froome's move. The next shot showed Froome speaking into his radio, sitting up and looking back, while Wiggins painfully inched his way back up. Normal service was resumed, with Froome pacing Wiggins all the way to the finish line, although Froome's very strong finishing sprint gave him a couple of seconds on his leader on the finish line.

It could have looked like a simple mistake. If you're the kind of person who refuses to believe the worst in anyone, you might have thought that Froome hadn't realized Wiggins was in trouble and, as soon as he did, he waited for him. With all the noise, heat and fatigue, it would be quite easy to make a mistake like that.

The French television commentary team, however, knew something was up. As the cameras cut to Froome, just after his initial jump, the tone of their voices changed, getting more excited with each sentence. 'Accélération de Froome,' said the commentator. 'Hup, hup, hup. Accélération de Froome.' And again: 'Accélération de Froome, he hasn't got Wiggins with him.'

Then the camera cut to Wiggins. 'Wiggins has stalled! Wiggins has stalled! The yellow jersey has stalled! *Ooh là là*, what is going on here?'

From a purely tactical and objective viewpoint, Froome's attack was risky. He was followed by Pinot, Nibali and Van den Broeck, and while he would have moved up the general classification, he would also have pulled Wiggins's rivals closer to him, which would have meant Sky had a smaller, less safe lead. It would also have given Wiggins's rivals confidence and momentum. And Froome was going to move up to second anyway, since Evans had been dropped. (Ironically, Evans was being paced up the mountain by his younger teammate van Garderen, who was in better shape than his leader, in a direct echo of the situation at Team Sky.)

Sean Yates, the Sky manager in the team car, told the story of Froome's attack in his book *It's All About the Bike*. '"What the fuck?" I said, followed by something like, "Froomey, what the fucking hell are you playing at?"' wrote Yates. 'I made it pretty clear on the radio that this was NOT the plan and he had better wait.' More information emerged when David Walsh published his book *Inside Team Sky*, written after spending the 2013 season embedded with the team. According to Walsh, Froome had asked if he could attack with three kilometres to go at the team meeting on the morning of the stage, but he was told that Wiggins's lead needed to be preserved. 'Nothing would be allowed to damage the team's pursuit of the Tour's yellow jersey,' wrote Walsh. 'An attack that far out? It's unlikely, Froome was told, but maybe in the last 500 metres.'

Froome went into a bit more detail in *The Climb*, which came out following his Tour win in 2013. 'The stage was made for me,' he recalled. 'I suggested that it might be possible for me to attack towards the end of the stage.' He persisted with his requests. Froome felt that Evans and Nibali could be eliminated (which turned out to be half-true – Evans was indeed dropped, but Nibali was climbing more strongly than Wiggins), and that he could perhaps win the stage. The point Froome wanted to make to the Team Sky management was that attacking 500 metres from the end of the stage wasn't going to gain him any significant time, so he asked what the difference was if he attacked from further out, so long as Wiggins was safe. Yates and general manager Dave Brailsford argued that if Wiggins had a puncture while Froome pulled his rivals clear, Sky risked losing the yellow jersey.

Froome wasn't convinced. He summed up his assessment of the situation as he pulled Wiggins back up to Nibali's group with five kilometres to go: 'Me – feeling good. Nibali – spent. Pinot – spent. Van den Broeck – spent. Brad – spent but with a teammate to pull him along.' So he attacked.

At the team hotel, the inquest began. Wiggins was threatening to go home, while the media, who'd had little in the way of excitement in the general classification battle so far, sensed a cracker of a story. And even as Sky tried to manage their crisis internally, Wiggins's wife Cath and Froome's girlfriend (now wife) Michelle Cound took to Twitter. Cath Wiggins tweeted her appreciation of Sky's teamwork: 'See Mick Rogers and Richie Porte for examples of genuine, selfless effort and true professionalism.' You get the impression that it wasn't only the 140-character limit that prevented her from including Froome's name in her list of Sky's *superdomestiques*. Cound's response was, 'Beyond disappointed.' Then: 'If you want loyalty, get a Froome dog . . . A quality I value . . . although being taken advantage of by others!' While Sky spent the rest of the Tour trying to smooth over the incident, and even Wiggins and Froome toed the party line in their public statements, the real emotion and frustration of the situation was being given an outlet through the proxy of their partners.

The roots of Froome's frustration lay in two different occasions. His breakthrough race was the 2011 Vuelta a España, where Wiggins had gone into the race as team leader and Froome as an underachieving *domestique* whose results in the two years he'd been at Sky had been so mediocre that he was likely going to be let go at the end of the year, or at least take a hefty pay cut. However, Froome rode so strongly for Wiggins that in the final few days he emerged as Sky's leader and came second overall, just 13 seconds behind Spain's Juan José Cobo, with Wiggins in third. If Froome hadn't spent much of the race riding on the front for Wiggins, there's little doubt he would have won. At the time, he was pleased with finally having got a good result, but the experience of sacrificing himself while Wiggins took the glory was starting to wear thin by the 2012 Tour.

Secondly, Froome was seething about losing a minute and 25 seconds on the very first road stage of the 2012 Tour, after he'd punctured with 10 kilometres to go. If Wiggins, Sky's leader, or Mark Cavendish, their sprinter, had punctured, the team would have waited and worked to get them back to the front, but Froome didn't have that privilege. Porte waited for him, but with the bunch speeding towards the first sprint of the Tour and crosswinds blowing across the race route, Froome, along with Porte, didn't stand a chance of getting back on. When he later talked about the La Toussuire attack, Froome specifically mentioned trying to get his 1-25 back, as if it were more important than defending Wiggins's lead.

Did Froome attack Wiggins on La Toussuire? Not on purpose, seems to be the party line and the consensus. But Walsh, who also ghostwrote *The Climb*, makes an observation about Froome in *Inside Team Sky*. With Froome, Walsh wrote, 'you soon learn not to confuse politeness with softness'. There was, Walsh added, a 'corner of Froome's soul where you find granite'.

There's one more detail which raises questions about Froome's motivations on La Toussuire. On the morning of the stage, Froome had called Cound to double-check what his contract said about his freedom to ride for the general classification in the Tour. Why would he do that, other than to justify a pre-planned attack? Brailsford, Wiggins and Froome spent the rest-day press conference in Pau denying that there was any friction and that it had all been a misunderstanding. Then Froome did the same thing at Peyragudes, the final summit finish of the Tour, two days later. Maybe it was more than just a corner of his soul which was granite.

Froome might present himself to the world as a kind of inoffensive everyman, a normal guy who just happens to be good at riding bikes fast up hills, but there's nothing normal about his background and cycling history when compared with his peers in the peloton. The affability also masks a vast ambitiousness.

He grew up in Kenya, riding with a ragtag collective of cyclists known as the Safari Simbaz, and was sent to school in South Africa (first to an Afrikaans school, then to St John's College, a private boarding school in Johannesburg). When representing Kenya at the Commonwealth Games and world championships, he was a one-man international cycling team: rider, *soigneur*, manager and mechanic, all rolled into one. He came on to the radar of British Cycling after a strong ride at the Commonwealth Games time trial and, seeing more opportunities with the highly organized British Cycling system than with the chaos of the Kenyan federation, started racing under his British passport in 2008. He rode for the Barloworld team in 2008 and 2009, finishing the Tour in 2008 in 81st, then signed for Sky in 2010. While the British passport has given him racing opportunities he might not otherwise have had, he's made his home in

Monaco, which might be linked to why one of his ex-teammates described him to me off the record as very money-driven.

Stories of his determination are common. When he raced as a teenager, he would occasionally faint from overdoing it. When he felt the Kenyan federation weren't helping his cause, he set up a fake federation email account so he could communicate with race organizers without the endless politicking and ineffectual administration.

But stories of his legendary bad luck and occasional hapless-ness are also common. Froome took part in the world under-23 time trial championships in Salzburg in 2006, and collided with an official in the first 200 metres. That was where he first picked up an unwanted nickname, 'Crash' Froome. More seriously, during one of his trips back to Africa, Froome had also picked up bilharzia, a waterborne parasite which is physically debilitating and persistent, and was his explanation for the mediocre form which dogged him in most of his first season with Sky. The medication he takes for it whenever it flares up, Biltricide, is as debilitating as the disease itself. There are small things, too – he rode the prologue of the 2012 Tour with the Olbas Oil-soaked cotton-wool nose plugs riders use to clear their airways during their warm-ups still in, and wondered why he was having trouble breathing during the race.

According to Team Sky, the Tour-winning potential was always there. Froome's power output was so impressive that his new coach for 2011, Bobby Julich, thought that his power meter had been incorrectly calibrated. How could somebody with such obvious physical talent not be winning races? It somehow took until the 2011 Vuelta to smooth off the rough edges enough so that Froome could compete in high-level races, and even then he endured a difficult start to 2012, only just coming round in time for the Tour. But in 2013, there was a new Chris Froome. This one was invincible, consistent and dominant.

*

Cycling might not have left much of a mark on Chris Froome's face, but it has chiselled his limbs into angular, elongated and scrawny twigs. On the bike, he looks awkward, both in still pho-tographs and on television – elbows poking out, his tight and long sleeves accentuating the angles of his arms, his body slightly off-kilter. He has little of that indefinable cycling attribute – class – which is supposed to mark out champions. There's no fluidity to his movement, none of the hypnotic rotational momentum of a rider like Bradley Wiggins – just a jerky, staccato pedalling action, as if a puppeteer were yanking strings attached to his knees and elbows. The engine is a Ferrari, but the chassis is Chitty Chitty Bang Bang. However, whatever unorthodox biomechanical process Froome is using to convert power into forward momentum, it's incredibly effective. At his best, as he was in 2013, he's the fastest climber in the Tour and all but the best time triallist.

Froome's plan for winning the Tour in 2013 was not dissim-ilar to that of Wiggins the previous year. He would use his team to asphyxiate the challenge of his rivals in the mountains and gain the initiative early on, then defend and pick up more time in the time trials.

It all went to plan on the first mountain stage, to Ax 3 Domaines in the Pyrenees. Sky set a blistering pace over the climbs, chasing down some industrious attacking by the Movistar team, then launched Froome with five kilometres to go. He was actually more dominant than Wiggins the year before – Wiggins gained a few seconds here and there on Nibali in the mountains, but the majority of his gains were made in the time trials. Froome won the Ax 3 Domaines stage by almost a minute, and the superiority of the Sky team was underlined by the fact Porte was second. Froome also made large gains in the first long time trial of the race at Mont Saint-Michel, where he was beaten to the stage win by Tony Martin by 12 seconds, but put at least a minute into most of his rivals – eventual runner-up Nairo Quintana lost over three minutes.

But while Froome's progression to the final yellow jersey was straightforward in terms of his physical superiority, he betrayed far more signs of vulnerability than Wiggins had in 2012. For the first time in two years, Sky were unable to control all the mountain stages. The day after Ax 3 Domaines, to Bagnères-de-Bigorre, they were put under pressure by an ambush early in the stage by Garmin, and then Movistar. While Sky's climbing *domestiques* went backwards – Porte lost 18 minutes and Vasil Kiryienka was eliminated after missing the time cut, having had to work so hard chasing earlier in the day – Froome was isolated in the front group. As Movistar put the pressure on, Froome had to cover the attacks himself, although he was rescued by Movistar's conservatism. The Spanish team had driven the front group so hard that they were effectively doing Sky's work for them. Although Froome was on his own, nobody else was attacking because Movistar's pace was too high.

And on an innocuous-looking mid-race flat stage in central France which finished at Saint-Amand-Montrond, Froome lost time after the race split to pieces in steady but persistent cross-winds. Early in the day, the Belkin and Omega Pharma teams maintained a high pace. They'd noticed that the dominant sprinter of the Tour so far, Marcel Kittel, and general classification contender Alejandro Valverde, had been caught on the wrong side of a split, and they worked hard to keep them there. Froome had made the front group, but then Alberto Contador's Saxo Bank team forced another split towards the end of the stage, which Froome missed. He conceded a minute and had been potentially dangerously isolated, although as the race entered the Alps, he still led overall by two and a half minutes.

Froome hit back strongly on Mont Ventoux. His attack with

seven kilometres to go was the defining moment of his Tour win. Spinning a very low gear which did nothing to improve his elegance, Froome simply rode away from Contador, who'd been the only survivor of a strong surge by Porte. Although Quintana only lost 29 seconds on Ventoux, having attacked earlier on the climb, the other general classification favourites conceded at least a minute and a half. Through the rest of the Alpine stages, Froome defended his lead, although he conceded a little time on Alpe d'Huez after the Sky car broke down and he ran out of energy gels. By the end, he was 4-20 ahead of Quintana, and that included 43 seconds he lost by freewheeling up the Champs-Élysées with his teammates in celebration of their victory.

Froome has never managed to quite control the wayward trajectory of his cycling career. For every good year, there seems to be payback in the form of bad luck, bad form or illness. He was probably the strongest stage racer in the world between late 2011 and 2013, yet in the 2014 Tour he was out in the first week with a broken wrist, having suffered a faltering campaign through the first six months of the year. Chris Froome was a dominant winner of the Tour, but Crash Froome is never too far away.

21

Vincenzo Nibali
2014

When I was a boy, my dad cut up my bike when I got into trouble at school. He only welded it back together when I went on hunger strike.
Vincenzo Nibali, interview in *Cycle Sport*, October 2009

Who is the best Grand Tour rider of the 2010s? Bradley Wiggins? He only won one before his head fell off. Chris Froome? Too inconsistent, too unlucky. Alberto Contador? Tainted by the positive test and subsequent inconsistency. It might well be Vincenzo Nibali, who slowly and quietly developed in the shadow cast by these three riders, then turned himself from 'other' Grand Tour specialist into Tour de France winner with a hugely assertive and confident ride through the race in 2014.

Nibali is a racer's racer. Although he's toned it down a bit since 2014, when he focused his whole season on the Tour de France and was barely visible before or afterwards, he used to try to win everything – from spring Classics like Milan–San Remo and Liège–Bastogne–Liège, through the Grand Tours to the world championships and Tour of Lombardy at the end of the season. He's come close at most of these events – in 2012 he was third at Milan–San Remo and second at Liège–Bastogne–Liège. He was fourth in the world championships in 2013 and fifth in the Tour of Lombardy in 2010. But his main strength is in Grand Tours: he's one of six riders – the others being Eddy Merckx, Bernard Hinault, Jacques Anquetil, Alberto Contador and Felice Gimondi – to have won all three of them.

Nibali grew up in Sicily, although his relaxed temperament is as far from the stereotype of the southern Italian hothead as it is possible to be. His teammates tell of his ability to fall asleep at any time – he's not only better at racing than most of his rivals, he's also better at resting.

Alessandro Vanotti, who has ridden with Nibali since they were both at the Liquigas team in 2007, said Nibali is so good at minimizing distractions that even the next day's racing rarely comes on to his radar. 'Vincenzo goes to sleep at night not even thinking about what he needs to do the next day, let alone worrying about it. You take your eye off him for a couple of minutes on the bus in the morning then look back and he'll be asleep,' Vanotti told *Procycling* magazine during the 2014 Tour de France. 'He starts thinking about the day's stage about five minutes before the start.'

Sometimes, I can't believe stories like this can be true. Bradley Wiggins also often says that he doesn't look ahead to the upcoming stages, preferring to have a glance at the road-book on the morning of the stage. It's an approach that's diametrically opposed to that of Cadel Evans, for example, who pored over maps and weather forecasts to build a detailed picture of the race. When athletes commit their whole lives to working on every last detail of training, nutrition and technology, it seems odd that they would then abandon such a forensic approach in regard to something as important as the route of the race. With Wiggins, it's probably true. With Nibali, the impression is that perhaps through the 2014 Tour he knew a lot more about the structure of the race than he was letting on. That said, it was rumoured that he'd been surprised to find out that the mid-race time trial in the 2012 Tour was an individual test and not a team time trial – that's the kind of oversight which a podium contender shouldn't be making. His relaxed temperament sometimes has the effect of making his approach look a little too laid-back. In the same way, Nibali rides with a languid class, which when he is winning is hypnotic. On the other hand, when he's not winning, it can look like he's not trying.

Although he rode one year for the Fassa Bortolo team in 2005, Nibali spent the formative years of his career, seven seasons in total, with the Liquigas team. Retrospectively, there's an air of destiny about Nibali's progression into a Tour de France champion. He started riding Grand Tours young, but he wasn't a prodigy of the same level as riders like Andy Schleck or Jan Ullrich, who both finished second in their debut Grand Tours.

His first Grand Tour was the Giro d'Italia in 2007, when he was 22. It's doubtful whether anybody except his own team and family, and the most keen-eyed of cycling fans, would have noticed Nibali's 19th place overall – 21-year-old Andy Schleck was ahead, riding into second place, and there it was decided: the future of Grand Tours was Schleck. Although the Luxembourger was younger, the two riders were born only seven months apart, and would be in the same academic year. And the careers of the two riders followed very different paths: Schleck got into a rut of second places before winning the Tour by default, then tailing off terribly in the second half of his comparatively short career; Nibali looks like he has improved with every year he has raced.

In 2008, Nibali rode both the Giro and the Tour, which put possibly too great a workload on his system. He was a consistent but unspectacular 11th in the Giro, but the Tour was harder work. Nibali wore the white jersey of best young rider (before Schleck took it from him in the Alps) and was 12th overall going into the final rest day, but the next two stages, especially the one finishing at Alpe d'Huez, took their toll on him and he slipped back to 20th by the end of the race. He conceded 17 minutes at Alpe d'Huez. 'I probably did a bit too much prior to the Giro,' he said. 'It didn't go too well but the team didn't put me under great pressure. I'm not the sort to lose sleep anyway, and I figured I'd given all I could. It taught me that I needed to be selective about what I rode.'

2009 was when Nibali made the jump from consistent but unspectacular Grand Tour stayer to genuine Tour de France contender. Alberto Contador and Andy Schleck were too good for everybody else, but Nibali was a real factor in the four-way battle for third place, which was eventually won by Lance Armstrong (subsequently stripped of his position). In the final general classification, Nibali had been seven minutes behind yellow jersey Contador, but there were more important bits of information buried in his results. First, he was five minutes clear of the next rider, eighth-placed Christian Vande Velde. Second, he was only two minutes from the podium, if you count Armstrong as finishing third, or only a minute and a half if you count Bradley Wiggins, who was initially fourth. Even more importantly, Nibali had ridden assertively – he didn't just ride round and minimize his losses, on certain stages he actively gained time on his rivals. During the crucial stage to Le Grand-Bornand, where the Schleck brothers and Contador attacked on the Col de Romme, Nibali first stayed with Wiggins and Armstrong, but he put them under pressure on the descents, gaining time both on the Romme descent, and then the final descent of the Col de la Colombière. He dropped Wiggins, and finished with Armstrong, two minutes behind the Schlecks and Contador, but a minute clear of Wiggins.

Nibali's renowned as being about the best descender of the general classification contenders in the Grand Tours, although his willingness to take advantage of this sometimes leads to disaster, as with the Tour of Lombardy in 2012 and world championships in 2013, where he crashed. He tells a story which demonstrates his ease with descending and his confidence: 'In training, I sometimes take a curve tight and with my inside arm, reach down and touch the pavement. I showed this to Richie Porte, who said, "You're crazy!"'

This is what I meant when I said Nibali is a racer's racer. He's never been physically dominant (although by 2014, he was getting closer), so he's had to develop other skills, like descending, and attacking in places other than the summit finishes which impose a more logical order on the standings. Nibali is comfortable when things are a bit more chaotic.

With a strong and consistent finish in the Tour de France under his belt, and his first top 10 in a Grand Tour, he focused on trying to win the Giro, then the Vuelta in 2010. In Italy, he had to play second fiddle to his team leader Ivan Basso, who won overall. But Nibali was probably the second-strongest rider in the race, and came third overall – second-placed David Arroyo had been part of a large group of riders who'd gained 12 minutes on the main contenders on a soaking-wet stage in L'Aquila.

Nibali finally got his first Grand Tour win at the 2010 Vuelta. The opposition was not quite at the level of the Tour de France, but he rode consistently well – his tactic was to climb better than the best time triallists, and time-trial better than the best climbers, and use his all-round strength and consistency to put himself into a position to win. Slovak Peter Velits had won the long time trial in the last week, but the biggest danger came from climber Ezequiel Mosquera, who went into the final summit finish, the steep Bola del Mundo climb, only 50 seconds behind Nibali. Mosquera attacked on Bola del Mundo, and gained 20 seconds with two kilometres to ride. If both had continued at their pace at that point, Mosquera would have won the Vuelta, but Nibali had saved enough for a final surge to the line, and he closed to within 10 seconds of his rival by the finish.

2011 was the first time Nibali's career took a small backward step. Basso's win at the previous year's Giro gave him first dibs on the Tour de France, so Nibali's aims for the year were to try to win the Giro, then defend his Vuelta title. He failed in both – Contador was rampant in the Giro, and though Nibali was promoted from third to second place when Contador's win was stripped as part of the sanction for his clenbuterol positive, he still finished behind veteran rider Michele Scarponi. He'd conceded close to seven minutes to Contador, the same amount as he had two years previously in the Tour, and though there are obvious questions about how Contador achieved his results, it looked like Nibali was stalling slightly in his development. At the Vuelta, he was not on his best form, and he came seventh. It was time to refocus.

Nibali was the only rider to pose anything like a threat to the Team Sky tandem of Wiggins and Froome at the 2012 Tour. It wasn't just that he came third overall – his best result ever at the Tour – but also that he was one of only two general classification contenders, along with Cadel Evans, to attack Sky, both on the climbs and descents, where he felt Wiggins could be put under pressure (wrongly, as it turned out). Though he again lost six minutes by the finish of the race, Nibali could be encouraged by the fact he was four minutes clear of the next rider. There was also encouragement in the fact that if you stripped out the time-trial results from the 2012 general classification, Nibali would have been second overall, 23 seconds behind Wiggins, and a minute clear of Froome (who'd lost that minute with a mechanical on a flat stage). This might have led him to conclude that working on his time trialling would be the logical thing to concentrate on, but Nibali's peak years are, luckily for him, coinciding with a trend in the Grand Tours to reduce time-trialling distance.

The big story of 2013 was that Wiggins would be focusing on the Giro. Nibali, having switched to the Astana team for 2013, was also focusing on the Italian race and, perhaps with a hint of revenge for the 2012 Tour, he took Wiggins apart. The Giro is a lot less controlled than the Tour, with less predictable terrain, and in terrible weather during the first week, Nibali put Wiggins under pressure on the descents, then dropped him on the climbs. Wiggins thrives in controlled conditions, and the formulaic racing at the Tour suited his riding style perfectly in 2012, while the comparative anarchy of the Giro made him very vulnerable. By the time the big mountain stages came around, Wiggins was out of it, and Nibali could then prove that he was the strongest rider in the race by winning the summit finish at Tre Cime di Lavaredo, and taking the overall title, his first pink jersey, by almost five minutes.

Nibali should have won the Vuelta in 2013 as well. Although he wasn't on peak form, his experience and stamina still gave him second overall, behind the surprising Chris Horner, a rider who'd never before come anywhere near winning a Grand Tour, and was just a couple of months shy of turning 42. Ironically, in 2005, Nibali had been in an escape at the Tour of Switzerland as a first-year professional with Horner. The American had allegedly insulted Nibali as they approached the finish, criticizing his refusal to contribute. 'I said many things to him,' Horner had said at the finish. 'When he attacked us, he looked very strong. So when I finally caught him and he wasn't working so much, I said some things to make him work, but he wouldn't, so I attacked him to see if he had something left or not.' Horner won the stage, with Nibali second, and Johan Bruyneel, Lance Armstrong's *directeur sportif*, had been so impressed that he tried to sign Nibali for 2006. (Team Sky also came close to signing Nibali for their first season in 2010, which would have added an extra dimension to the Wiggins–Froome falling-out in 2012.)

By the end of 2013, Nibali had achieved two Grand Tour wins, six podium finishes, eight top 10s and 11 top 20s out of 11 races. Yet as 2014 came around, he was considered only a minor favourite for the Tour de France, behind two-time winner Contador and defending champion Froome. Having seen what Nibali did to race favourite Wiggins in the 2013 Giro, perhaps we shouldn't have been surprised at what happened next.

When he was growing up in Sicily, Nibali's father owned a video shop. The young Nibali's hero might have been Giro and Tour winner Marco Pantani, but his favourite race was neither of these events. His father used to play him old VHS tapes of Francesco Moser winning Paris–Roubaix, and Nibali's dream was to race and win on the cobbles.

If the 2014 Tour had come down to a straight, logical fight, Froome and Contador would probably have been the favourites. They climbed and time-trialled better than anybody bar the specialists. The Tour, especially in its second half, was skewed towards the mountains, with two hard summit finishes in the Alps (Risoul and Chamrousse) and two in the Pyrenees (Pla d'Adet and Hautacam), to add to another Pyrenean stage which crossed the Port de Balès before finishing in Luchon. But before all that, there was a very interesting opening phase, which included an extremely hilly stage finishing in Sheffield, a stage crossing several cobbled sectors from Paris–Roubaix finishing in Arenberg, and some tricky middle-mountain stages in the Vosges. While Froome and Contador saw this opening phase as something to survive, to get out of the way unscathed before the real business began in the mountains, Nibali saw it as an opportunity to win the race and gain unbeatable momentum.

On the hilly stage to Sheffield, Nibali made the lead group, then jumped away to win the stage, taking the yellow jersey and two seconds on his rivals. A small gain, but it was an indication of his form and confidence. However, it was on the cobbles of stage four that he took control of the race, in filthy weather. Nibali rode with incredible poise on the cobbles, piloted by his teammates Jakob Fuglsang and Lieuwe Westra, dropping specialists like Fabian Cancellara and Sep Vanmarcke, and finishing third, 19 seconds behind Lars Boom, but two and a half minutes ahead of Contador. Froome pulled out of the race on this stage – he'd cracked his wrist in a crash the day before, and was physically and psychologically defeated before the cobbles even started. When Contador crashed out of the Tour on the stage to La Planche des Belles Filles in the Vosges, it looked like Nibali was enjoying a lucky Tour, even if by this point he was second overall, two minutes clear of his closest general classification rival, Sky's Richie Porte, and two and a half clear of Contador. On La Planche des Belles Filles, Nibali won the stage, and led Porte by two and a half minutes.

In the four high mountain summit finishes that followed before the final time trial, Nibali's results were: first, second, third and first. He was as dominant in the high mountains as he had been through the more complicated opening 10 days, and even though some observers wondered how vulnerable Nibali would have been in the mountains had Contador and Froome been fit, it's unlikely they would have beaten him, given his form and the head start he'd given himself over the hills and cobbles of the first week. Fourth place in the final time trial, again ahead of all the other general classification riders, secured him overall victory by seven and a half minutes over Jean-Christophe Péraud.

Though it seemed surprising at the time, on closer examination Nibali's Tour win looks like the culmination of a career almost planned to have brought him to 2014 ready to win the race. He's developed steadily all the way since his debut in the 2007 Giro. He tried the Giro first, then the Tour the following year. He then tried to win a Grand Tour, taking the 2010 Vuelta. His next target was winning the Giro in 2011, which he fell just short of, then he went to the Tour in 2012 to be a contender, and came third. He went back to win the Giro in 2013, then, as a double Grand Tour winner, returned to the Tour to win it.

For his trainer Paolo Slongo, Nibali's career progression has been logical. From the moment he first set eyes on him as a junior rider, there was something that set him apart. 'He looked so good on a bike, so natural,' says Slongo. 'He just looked right.'

Before Nibali actually won the Tour, it was uncertain whether he looked like a potential Tour winner or not. Some victors, like Bernard Hinault and Greg LeMond, seem to have their name inscribed on the winner's trophy from birth. Others, like Cadel Evans and Joop Zoetemelk have to work hard for it. Still others, like Stephen Roche and Andy Schleck, shine brightly for one year and, once they've won, never look like doing so again. Still others, like Óscar Pereiro, could be considered a little fortunate to have come first in the Tour.

It's natural to like some members of the yellow jersey club more than others: some are more interesting, or better company than others; some have found success in other walks of life while others never had the same ambition in the real world as on a bike; some are complex, others straightforward. The only real qualification for entry to the club is to have the ability to combine being unusually good at bike racing with being able to seize a moment of destiny when it arrives.

Acknowledgements

Writing the 21 chapters of this book sometimes felt like riding the 21 stages of the Tour de France, only with fewer rest days. I was lucky to have the support of my wife, Ellie, who regularly dug her way through the pile of books, magazines and interview transcripts surrounding my desk to deliver coffee and cake, and of my two children, James and Tommy.

For his patience, advice, support and encouragement, as well as his tolerance of my creative interpretation of the original deadline, I'd like to thank my publisher, Giles Elliott, whose good humour kept me positive through the development of the book.

My agent Kevin Pocklington has been an important influence on *The Yellow Jersey Club*, and helped me keep a steady hand on the tiller while it evolved significantly from the original proposal. My copy editor, Ian Preece, did a fantastic job of weeding out the typos, tidying up the text and helping to turn the raw material into the finished product you hold in your hands.

I was lucky that a number of the yellow jersey club agreed to

talk to me in the course of my research for the book. In chrono-
logical order, they were Bernard Thévenet, Lucien Van Impe,
Joop Zoetemelk, Greg LeMond, Stephen Roche, Pedro Delgado,
Bjarne Riis and Andy Schleck. Each was fascinating to talk to.
Thévenet is a born communicator, and it's no accident that he
is one of the most respected television commentators in cycling.
Lucien Van Impe's infectious enthusiasm for life and for the
Tour was a joy to experience. Joop Zoetemelk is a lot funnier
than he comes across – when he asked how much time I needed
and I pitched conservatively but realistically at 20 minutes, he
expressed mock horror that I would be taking up so much of
his time, then he was still talking 40 minutes later. Greg LeMond
lives his life at 100 kilometres per hour, but once you have him
pinned down, he is a joy to interview – it's literally a case of
switching on the Dictaphone and sitting back while the stories
pour out. I like Roche a lot more than it probably comes across
in the text – he's one of the reasons I got hooked on cycling, and
he's a generous communicator who more than any other of the
men in this book exemplifies the principle that cycling is a sport
where brains can beat brawn. Delgado, with the help of his
English teacher in Segovia, was down-to-earth, and is probably
as close to being a 'normal' person as any member of the yellow
jersey club. I was surprised at how cheerful Bjarne Riis was, in
spite of the fact that when we spoke he was about to lose his job
as manager of the Tinkoff team – he poked fun at his dourness,
but he's still holding a lot back. Andy Schleck sounded a lot
happier than when I interviewed him a year previously.

Many individuals were generous with their time and insight
in talking about the men in the yellow jersey club. In alphabet-
ical order, they were: Kim Andersen, Denis Bastien, Bernard
Bourreau, Dario Cioni, Guy Fransen, Walter Godefroot, Kent
Gordis, Cyrille Guimard, Rupert Guinness, Barry Hoban, Brian
Holm, Michael Hutchinson, Lars Jorgensen, Bobby Julich,

Karsten Kroon, Daniel Mangeas, Robbie McEwen, Allan Peiper, Shane Sutton and Gerard Vroomen.

I am also indebted to many cycling writers and journalists, whose previous work, both in book and magazine form, on many of these riders has been invaluable in my research. I'm thankful to Robert Garbutt and everybody at *Cycling Weekly*, for allowing me access to the magazine's archives. I also mined the back catalogue of *Procycling, Cycle Sport* and *Winning* magazines extensively. In particular, I'd like to thank Lionel Birnie, whose feedback was invaluable, and my friends Mike and Lex Webb for reading an early chapter and suggesting where the tone needed to be adjusted. And thanks also to Sean Ingle, who first dug out the quote from the *Boxing Yearbook* which heads the Marco Pantani chapter.